Signs of the Times

Signs of the Times

Edgar H. Shroyer

Clerc Books
Gallaudet University Press
Washington, D.C.

Clerc Books
An imprint of Gallaudet University Press
Washington, DC 20002

Library of Congress Catalog Card Number 82-81441
ISBN 0-913580-76-7

Gallaudet University is an equal opportunity employer/
educational institution. Programs and services offered
by Gallaudet University receive substantial financial
support from the U.S. Department of Education.

**To my loving parents,
Helen and Virgil**

Contents

Acknowledgments

Considerable time and effort have gone into the production of this book. Suggestions, ideas, and signs came from many sources. I certainly appreciate and wish to thank all those individuals throughout the years who shaped and expanded my knowledge of signs.

Special thanks are due to Charles Floyd, my illustrator, who stuck with a task neither of us thought would be so monumental. Betty McChesney, Jen Haislip, Susan Wells, Kathleen Callaway, Linda Cannon, and Richard Thornberry all contributed to the book in various ways for which I am grateful. Ivey Pittle deserves special recognition for her time, energy, and expertise during the final stages of this book. The encouragement received from other friends and colleagues was also greatly valued.

I am deeply indebted to Susan, my wife, for her many hours as a critic, typist, and proofreader. Her support and companionship brought this book to fruition.

Introduction

Signs of the Times is designed to be used as a classroom text. The purpose of the book is to fill the void that exists between sign language dictionaries and American Sign Language texts. For this reason, *Signs of the Times* offers a unique approach to sign language instruction.

Sign language has become a generic term that refers to all forms of manual communication. Today, most people prefer using the generic term *signing*. However, in past years when the term sign language was used, it generally referred to American Sign Language (ASL)—a signing system that evolved in the early 1800s from a combination of American and French signs. ASL is the native language of approximately 400,000 deaf people in North America and is used among them in their everyday conversations. However, when deaf adults communicate with most hearing adults, they employ a combination of ASL and English. The result is a *pidgin* signing system. (Pidgin is defined as simplified speech [sign] used for communicating between people with different languages.) Consequently, this combined signing system is referred to as Pidgin Sign English (PSE).

Neither ASL nor PSE represents English grammar. Therefore, most educators of the deaf consider neither acceptable as a formal teaching vehicle for deaf children. In an effort to make English visible and, therefore, enhance deaf children's acquisition of the English language, new signing systems have developed in the past twelve years. These signing systems attempt to represent English grammar and are now referred to as Manually Coded English (MCE).

1

The Sign Language Continuum

The different signing systems are perhaps most clearly illustrated on a continuum, a concept first proposed by Woodward (1973).[1]

Nonverbal Communication is used internationally among all people, both hearing and deaf. Body language, facial expression, and/or common gestures, such as a shoulder shrug, are used to communicate information when words are not necessary. A look of gratitude or a baby's smile needs no words for clarification. Nonverbal communication is also used when a common language is not available. It adds emphasis and clarity to the communication process.

In-group Signs, Home Signs, and Childrenese are signs unique to a particular group or family. Generally, these signs are a combination of standard and group-invented signs and are complemented by gestures, pantomime, and facial expression. The signs are generally standardized within the particular group using them but are frequently not intelligible to individuals outside the group.

American Sign Language (ASL) is the native language of a large percentage of the North American deaf population. Unlike English, which is a spoken and written language, ASL is a visual-gestural language. ASL and English are distinct languages. Each has a unique set of grammatical and syntactical rules. However, English is used to describe ASL just as it is used to describe the French and German languages. The examples below demonstrate some of the differences between English and ASL.

English	There is food in the store.
ASL	It store have food.

English	He gave her a trophy.
ASL	Trophy he-present-her.[2]

Considerable research has been done on ASL. Several books describing the rules of ASL (including word order, use of directionality, negative incorporation, pluralization, and facial expression) are available. Students who are interested in learning more about ASL should refer to the Suggested Reading section for texts providing a detailed discussion.

Pidgin Sign English (PSE) combines the standard or traditional signs of American Sign Language and English syntax. The use of fingerspelling is also more predominate in PSE than in ASL. The primary function of PSE is to facilitate communication between deaf and hearing people. Each person brings to the communication process those linguistic structures and vocabulary with which he or she is most familiar. Consequently, PSE takes many forms because it adheres to no specific set of language rules. Variations in PSE sentences depend a great deal on the signer's knowledge of ASL and/or English, as well as with whom the signer is communicating. Pidgin Sign English may be very English oriented, ASL oriented, or an equal combination of the two.

Despite variations in PSE, research indicates some guidelines that are generally followed: (a) standard signs of ASL are used in English word order; (b) the use of various articles and verb tenses is optional; and (c) noun plurality is deleted.[3] The following sentences illustrate some of the differences between English, ASL, and PSE.

English	Last night we went partying with the girls.
PSE	Last night we go party with girl.
ASL	Last night finish we party girl.

Although there is a paucity of PSE research, one study has revealed an interesting aspect about facial expression. The study indicates that facial expression is not utilized to any great degree in PSE by hearing signers, nor is it learned as a part of PSE.[4] This may be due to the fact that sign language students generally are asked to vocalize what is signed in class. They may be relying on speech to convey intonation as opposed to facial expression, which, along with other features, conveys intonation in ASL. Also students must concentrate on several things

---

[1] Woodward, J. "Language Continuum: A Different Point of View." *Sign Language Studies,* no. 2 (1973), pp. 81–83.

[2] Humphries, T.; Padden, C.; and O'Rourke, T. *A Basic Course in American Sign Language.* Silver Spring, Md.: T. J. Publishers, 1980, pp. 122, 160.

[3] Reilly, J., and McIntire, M. "American Sign Language and Pidgin Sign English: What's the Difference?" *Sign Language Studies,* Summer 1980, pp. 151–192.

[4] Ibid.

Sign Language Continuum

	Nonverbal Communication	In-group Signs / Home Signs / Childrenese	American Sign Language (ASL)	Pidgin Sign English (PSE)	Manually Coded English (MCE)	Fingerspelling
Characteristics	Combines pantomime, natural gestures, facial expressions, and body movement	Combines elements of pantomime, natural gestures, facial expression, body movement, invented signs, and some standard signs	Combines standard signs, fingerspelling, and elements of pantomime; has a syntax of its own; is ideographic and idiomatic; follows one sign—one concept rule	Combines standard signs and fingerspelling; contains a lot of English syntax; follows one sign—one concept rule	Combines some standard signs with invented and adapted ASL signs; represents visually the syntax of English, including inflections, suffixes, and prefixes; follows one sign—one word rule	Is a letter-by-letter representation of English
Sign Systems			American Sign Language (ASL), also known as Ameslan	Sign English (Siglish) Signed English Manual English	Seeing Essential English (SEE I) Signing Exact English (SEE II) Linguistics of Visual English (LOVE) Signed English Manual English	Rochester Method Visible English
Relation to English	No representation of English elements	Some representation of English elements	Some representation of English elements	A great many English elements	Complete representation of English elements	Complete representation of English

3

simultaneously while signing; i.e., recalling the appropriate sign, handshape, and movement involved; placing the hands and arms in the correct location; and executing the sign. While thinking of all these aspects, facial expression, which is not the primary conveyor of information in our culture, is often sacrificed. However, the primary objective—communication—is achieved; therefore, facial expression is often not regarded as critical. Frequently, facial expression is incorporated to a far greater degree as sign language skills develop.

Manually Coded English (MCE) is a generic term that includes all of the sign systems devised to represent English grammar. It is generally used in educational settings with deaf children in an attempt to teach the English language. MCE shows plurals, inflections, and articles in sentences signed in English word order.

Some signs have been invented for those English words which had no corresponding sign in traditional sign language. In some cases, traditional signs have been initialized to provide a one-to-one correspondence between English and sign vocabularies. The same movement as the traditional sign is still employed, but the manual alphabet handshape of the first letter of the word is used. For example, the traditional sign for *street* is open *b* handshapes. The sign is initialized with *r* handshapes to indicate *road,* with *p* handshapes to indicate *path,* and with *w* handshapes to indicate *way.* Unfortunately, *s* handshapes are now used to indicate *street,* which results in the traditional sign (open *b* handshapes) being dropped completely.

Several of these initialized signs are introduced in this book, whereas relatively few invented signs are introduced. In both cases, the signs introduced are ones that have found some acceptance among deaf adults. Some of the more commonly signed prefixes and suffixes that are added to the root sign to achieve MCE are shown in the Inflection section.

Traditional signing depends a great deal on conceptual signs—different signs are used to represent different concepts of the same word. In English, the context of the sentence indicates the intended concept or meaning. For example, the word *run* has over fifty different meanings, depending on the context in which it is used. In ASL, these different meanings are conveyed by many different signs. Several of the MCE systems adhere to the principle of letting the context

indicate the concept. Some of the MCE systems refer to this practice as the "two out of three rule." The rule states that if two words meet any two of the three stated criteria, the words use the same sign. The three criteria are

1. the words have to sound alike,
2. the words must be spelled alike, and
3. the words must have the same meaning.

The following sentences illustrate how the criteria are applied. In these sentences, one sign is used for *running* and one sign is used for *right,* regardless of the contextual meanings.

> My nose is *running.*
> Father is *running* the store.
>
> Walk on the *right* side of the road.
> I think you are *right* again.

This particular rule is being cited for informational purposes only. In this book, the students are presented with the traditional one concept–one sign principle in each lesson, in the practice sentences, and also in the Multi-sign Word Appendix, which shows additional usage of traditional signs in different contexts. Most deaf adults use conceptual signs in this manner. For additional practice on conceptual signs, the student should refer to Dicker's book, *Facilitating Manual Communication for Interpreters, Students, and Teachers.* For additional information on specific MCE systems, e.g., SEE I, SEE II, LOVE, and Signed English, see Bornstein's article, "A Description of Some Current Sign Systems Designed to Represent English."

Fingerspelling is a letter-by-letter manual representation of English words. Each of the 26 letters of the alphabet is represented by a specific handshape. Fingerspelling is used in all the systems described on the sign language continuum except nonverbal communication. It is employed in the communication process when an English word needs to be expressed but no sign is available. The most frequently fingerspelled words are generally formal names for people, places, and things.

Objectives

The major objective of this book is to provide hearing students with an understanding of and skill in Pidgin Sign English (PSE) and/or Manually Coded English (MCE). PSE is reportedly the most frequently used system of communication between deaf and hearing people. It has been my observation that very few deaf adults use ASL when signing with hearing people. They generally revert to the more easily understood PSE. Therefore, it seems logical that PSE be taught to hearing students. MCE is primarily used in educational settings, especially preschool and elementary school classes. For this reason, the incorporation of many MCE signs and inflections into this book provides a basic signing vocabulary that teachers can use to represent English grammar to young children.

Both PSE and MCE follow the grammatical structure of English, thus allowing students to give full attention to developing their signing vocabulary. American Sign Language (ASL) is a much more difficult language to learn because students must attend not only to vocabulary, but to a new grammatical structure, as well. Learning PSE and MCE should be a less frustrating and more rewarding experience for beginning signers.

Format

Signs of the Times consists of 41 lessons. An average lesson contains 28 signs. The vocabulary for each lesson, beginning with Lesson 2, was selected from *The Most Common 100,000 Words Used in Conversation,* by K. Berger. The first 1,000 most frequently used words listed in Berger's book were reviewed by sign language instructors, and some revisions in the order of presentation were made to accommodate vocabulary groupings. Signs associated with deafness were arbitrarily selected and added to the appropriate lessons.

The words at the top of each sign illustration represent most of the English word glosses (equivalents) for that particular sign. Space did not allow all the possible English glosses to be listed with each illustration. Therefore, some additional glosses for signs are listed in the Index. Some glosses are followed by a word enclosed in parentheses. The information contained in parentheses clarifies the meaning of the gloss.

Glosses marked with an asterisk (*) are adapted signs. That is, they are standard ASL signs that have been adapted to begin with the manual alphabet handshape for the first letter of the word. If the first gloss is marked with an asterisk, the illustration shows the adapted sign used in

MCE. If the second gloss is enclosed in parentheses, it is the standard ASL sign from which the adapted sign is derived. If the first gloss has no asterisk, it is a standard ASL sign. In cases where the words following the main gloss are marked with asterisks, the signs can be initialized when using MCE. All initialized words can be signed the same way shown in the illustration, if desired. Examples are found in the Special Notes section.

A gloss marked with a dagger (†) is a multi-sign word. It is an English word that can be signed several different ways, depending on the context of the sentence. Contextual sentences using these words are found in the Multi-sign Word Appendix. These sentences provide additional practice in the appropriate use of multi-sign words.

A sentence using the sign in it's proper context appears beneath each illustration. Beginning with Lesson 2, the vocabulary in these sentences is cumulative. That is, each word in the sentence has been introduced before and should be signed for continuous practice. A few of the sentences include words that have either not been introduced or have no sign. These italicized words should be either fingerspelled or omitted, depending on the system (PSE or MCE) that the student is following.

Practice sentences follow each lesson. These sentences use all the vocabulary presented in the lesson, as well as vocabulary from the previous lesson(s). The italicized words represent glosses that have not been introduced; these words should be fingerspelled.

Mind Tickler sections also follow each lesson, beginning with Lesson 2. These sections offer mnemonics to assist the student in remembering how or why a sign is made a particular way. Lesson 1 is unique in that it only contains very specific referents for each sign. It is equivalent to a long Mind Tickler section. The lesson is organized around what the referent does, what is done with it, and so forth.

The Mind Ticklers are a combination of explanations others have shared with me and those which I use to help students remember signs more easily. They are *not* and are not meant to be an explanation of a sign's origin. Such an undertaking of determining the origin of signs would be a monumental task requiring years of research. Students and teachers may think of other mnemonics to assist them in remembering certain signs. Regional signs often have very interesting mnemonics.

A list of all the vocabulary introduced in each lesson follows the Mind Tickler section. These words can be used by the students and teachers for generating sentences, dialogue, narratives, and additional practice.

The final section after each lesson, Additional Signs and Notes, provides a place for the students to put down any additional information that they feel will help them in learning signs.

The design and content of each lesson makes *Signs of the Times* an easy text to use. The unique feature of the signs being repeated in the sentences throughout the book provides excellent practice opportunities for the students. The clear and large illustrations should make the learning process fun and successful. The Mind Tickler sections also provide an exciting way to remember signs.

Notes for the Reader

For the Student

Sign language is similar to anything else you undertake in that the more you use it and the more you practice it, the more proficient you will become. You are encouraged to read all of the sections in the first part of the book to understand better what you are preparing yourself to do and to understand completely the purpose of the book.

It is recommended that you go over the Special Notes section carefully in order to get a good understanding of the movements indicated by the various arrows used in the illustrations. Lesson 1 is designed to show you that many signs have referents that are helpful in vocabulary retention. In learning sign language, think in terms of the referent rather than the English word. When the sign for tree is made, think of a tree, not the word *tree*. The fingerspelling and number section should be used and referred to frequently.

Beginning with Lesson 2, you are encouraged to sign the complete contextual sentence under each illustration, fingerspelling those words that are written in italics. The vocabulary that is included in the contextual sentences and practice sentences following each lesson is cumulative in nature. Again, italicized words should be fingerspelled or omitted, depending on the word and whether you are using PSE or MCE. A self-check system is built into the practice sentences in the Multi-sign Word Appendix to ensure your correct usage of the multi-sign words illustrated in the book.

Be sure to write additional signs and special notes in the Additional Signs and Notes sections. Most importantly, find someone who is also taking sign language with whom you can practice and converse in signs. Also, try your best to associate as much as possible with deaf people. Remember, be actively involved in signing yourself; do not expect to learn how to sign merely by being a spectator.

For the Teacher

It is my strong belief that a teacher of sign language is also an advocate for the deaf community. Students of sign language should not only learn the language, they should also gain knowledge and an understanding of deaf culture. Therefore, it is extremely important that you, the teacher, be knowledgeable about the deaf community and the literature on deafness. The Suggested Reading section provides some excellent readings in this area.

In order for the student to acquire this knowledge outside the classroom, there are several activities that can be assigned for homework. Assigned readings such as Jacob's *A Deaf Adult Speaks Out,* Greenberg's *In this Sign,* Gannon's *Deaf Heritage,* and others listed in the Reading section are excellent resources. Having students read and abstract articles on deafness or sign language, setting up student interviews with deaf families, inviting deaf people to the class to share their experiences, and going to deaf clubs or socials are also excellent activities. These are just a few things that can be done to expand deaf awareness in students.

In using this book, you should share local and regional signs, as well as variations of signs, with students. I have tried to use as few regional signs as possible, although it is sometimes difficult to determine what is and what is not a regional sign. You should also alert your students to the fact that signs are not international; each country has its own sign system. For example, the American sign for France is different from the French sign for France.

You should develop dialogues, narratives, and additional practice sentences for the students while keeping the learning process interesting and entertaining. Similar activities can be assigned to the students. Royster's book on *Games and Activities for Sign Classes* is an excellent resource for teachers.

This book contains 41 lessons. It has been my experience that about one-half of the lessons can be covered in one semester in a three-credit-hour class. You may wish to cover more material, but for mastery, I would suggest doing only the first 20 or 21 lessons. The average of 28 signs per lesson should be more than sufficient to fill a 90-minute class period. This takes into consideration that during each class, time will be spent on reviewing previously learned vocabulary, practicing some fingerspelling and numbers, conversing in small groups, and completing individual exercises. Some classes should be used exclusively for doing review work, testing, and imparting information on deafness. The videotape or film, "Across the Silence Barrier," contains a lot of good information for beginning signers.

It is recommended that you go through the book starting with Lesson 1. The book introduces vocabulary in a cumulative manner. That is, each sign is introduced before it is used in a sentence. Only the italicized words have not been introduced previously. (Italicized words in practice sentences can be fingerspelled.) This affords the student continuous practice and review. At the end of each lesson, you will find a list of practice sentences and a list of vocabulary that you can use in a variety of ways. Feel free to add any additional signs you think would help the students in a particular lesson (e.g., regional signs). These signs should be put in the Additional Signs and Notes section.

You are also encouraged to use the existing Mind Tickler sections and to expand them. These mnemonic devices often help a student remember a particular sign. I am sure that you have some special mnemonics that you can share with your students.

The mechanics of signing, such as hand placement when fingerspelling, speed, clarity, and so forth, should be emphasized throughout the course. Guillory's book on *Expressive and Receptive Fingerspelling for Hearing Adults* is an excellent resource. When you are teaching signs, you should always monitor the handshape, placement, and movement. Although there are specific mechanics related to fingerspelling and signing, signing styles still remain highly individualized. Therefore, this is merely a reminder for you to attend to these mechanics rather than instructions on "how to." I hope that you find this book a helpful and useful guide in your class.

Suggested Reading

"Across the Silence Barrier." An episode of *NOVA.* Boston: WGBH, 1977. (Videotape)

Baker, C., and Padden, C. "Focusing on the Nonmanual Components of American Sign Language." In *Understanding Language through Sign Language Research,* edited by P. Siple. New York: Academic Press, 1978.

Baker, C., and Cokely, D. *American Sign Language: A Teacher's Resource Text on Grammar and Culture.* Silver Spring, Md.: T. J. Publishing Co., 1980.

Bender, R. *The Conquest of Deafness.* Cleveland: Case Western Reserve University, 1970.

Berger, K. *The Most Common 100,000 Words Used in Conversations.* Kent, Ohio: Herald Publishing House, 1977.

Bornstein, H. "A Description of Some Current Sign Systems Designed to Represent English." *American Annals of the Deaf,* June 1973, pp. 454–463.

Bornstein, H.; Saulnier, K. L.; and Hamilton, L.; eds. *The Comprehensive Signed English Dictionary.* Washington, D.C.: Gallaudet University Press, 1983.

Dicker, L. *Facilitating Manual Communication for Interpreters, Students, and Teachers.* Silver Spring, Md.: Registry of Interpreters for the Deaf, Inc., 1981.

Fant, L. *An Introduction to American Sign Language.* Silver Spring, Md.: National Association of the Deaf, 1972.

Fant, L. *Sign Language.* Northridge, Calif.: Joyce Media, 1977.

Frishberg, N. "Arbitrariness and Iconicity: Historical Changes in American Sign Language." *Language* 51 (1975): 696–719.

Furth, H. *Deafness and Learning: A Psychosocial Approach.* Belmont, Calif.: Wadsworth Publishing Co., 1973.

Gannon, J. *Deaf Heritage: A Narrative History of Deaf America.* Silver Spring, Md.: National Association of the Deaf, 1981.

Greenberg, J. *In This Sign.* New York: Holt, Rinehart and Winston, 1970.

Guillory, L. *Expressive and Receptive Fingerspelling for Hearing Adults.* Baton Rouge: Claitor's Publishing Division, 1974.

Gustason, G.; Pfetzing, D.; and Zawolkow, E. *Signing Exact English.* Rossmoor, Calif.: Modern Signs Press, 1980.

Hoemann, H. *Communicating with Deaf People: A Resource Manual for Teachers and Students of American Sign Language.* Baltimore: University Park Press, 1978.

Ingram, R. *Principles and Procedures of Teaching Sign Language.* Carlisle, England: British Deaf Association, 1977.

Jacobs, L. *A Deaf Adult Speaks Out.* 2d ed., rev. Washington, D.C.: Gallaudet University Press, 1980.

Klima, E., and Bellugi, U. *The Signs of Language.* Cambridge, Mass.: Harvard University Press, 1979.

Mindel, E., and Vernon, M. *They Grow in Silence.* Silver Spring, Md.: National Association of the Deaf, 1971.

Moores, D. *Educating the Deaf: Psychology, Principles, and Practices.* 2d ed. Boston: Houghton Mifflin Co., 1982.

Reilly, J., and McIntire, M. "American Sign Language and Pidgin Sign English: What's the Difference?" *Sign Language Studies,* Summer 1980, pp. 151–192.

Royster, M. *Games and Activities for Sign Language Classes.* Silver Spring, Md.: National Association of the Deaf, n.d.

Stokoe, W. *Sign Language Structure.* Silver Spring, Md.: Linstok Press, Inc., 1978.

Tidyman, E. *Dummy.* Boston: Little, Brown and Co., 1974.

Wilbur, R. *American Sign Language and Sign Systems.* Baltimore: University Park Press, 1979.

Woodward, J. "Historical Bases of American Sign Language." In *Understanding Language through Sign Language Research,* edited by P. Siple. New York: Academic Press, 1978.

Woodward, J. "Some Characteristics of Pidgin Sign English." *Sign Language Studies*, Summer 1973, pp. 39–46.

Wright, D. *Deafness.* New York: Stein and Day, 1975.

Fingerspelling and Numbers

Fingerspelling

As described previously, fingerspelling is a letter-by-letter manual representation of English words. Fingerspelling is used when there is not a sign available to express a particular word, e.g., proper names. The use of fingerspelling in ASL is minimal while its use is more prevalent in some of the MCE systems. The student should be introduced to fingerspelling early in order to begin communicating in complete sentences.

Begin fingerspelling with two-letter words, then increase the word length as you become more fluent. Pay particular attention to spelling the syllables in words. When you begin to fingerspell a sentence, pause briefly between words. In words with closed double letters (e.g., moon and meet), the hand opens slightly, moves to the right, and closes again. Other double-lettered words (e.g., mall and tubby) similarly move to the right a little.

The arm should be kept still, and it should be held in a comfortable position with the body as a background. The arm should not be held out to the side of the body. Something to keep in mind is that you should be able to see the back of your own hand when fingerspelling.

Numbers

Numbers are used extensively in signing and should be mastered. They are relatively easy to learn and should be practiced regularly.

The Manual Alphabet

 A

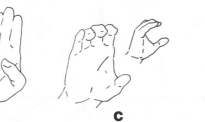 B

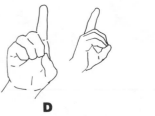 C

D

E

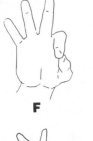 F

G

 H

 I

 J

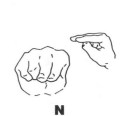 K

L

M

N

 O

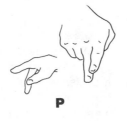 P

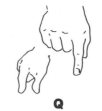 Q

 R

 S

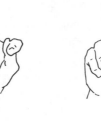 T

 U

V

 W

 X

 Y

 Z

Individual Words

to	jet	told
on	let	mold
so	set	park
me	pet	mark
we	net	bark
as	him	dark
us	vim	hark
he	rim	lark
ha	Tim	shark
be	Jim	stark
do	dim	older
am	Kim	folder
is	wim	bolder
go	mate	holder
or	fate	colder
it	rate	molder
far	date	solder
car	gate	shoulder
bar	hate	waiter
ear	pate	later
jar	late	letter
mar	bold	shelter
par	fold	water
tar	gold	trailer
met	cold	singer
bet	hold	toaster
get	sold	butter

Practice Sentences

Jill is here.
Mother is alone.
Where are the girls?
My date is here.
He hates being late.
Kate is at the gate.
It is cold here.
We gave the waiter a tip.
She is older than Kate.
Let me see it, too.
Fold this for me.
Her pet is wet.
He said, "Ha, ha, ha."
She hates my mate.
He sold the gold.
He parked in the dark.
Let me bet on the Jets.
Set the pet here.
Jim and Kim left.
It is colder here.
That is my mark.
My car is old.
How far is that?
The moon is full.
She made par.
We ate cold meat.
Mom and I will meet Bess at noon.
The vet left.
Tim hates meat.
Say it again.
Kate told Mark to get the milk.
They sold the mold.
The puppy is little.
Go to the store.
The older man is here.
He is bolder now.
Sheep say baaa.
It is colder today.
The lark is alive.
My mate is Jim.
My jar is empty.
Where is mother?
I live in Mississippi.
That is my grandmother.
We live in Pittsburgh.
We like Tennessee.
Where was he going?
There is no more time.
The quick brown fox jumps over the lazy dog.

Numbers

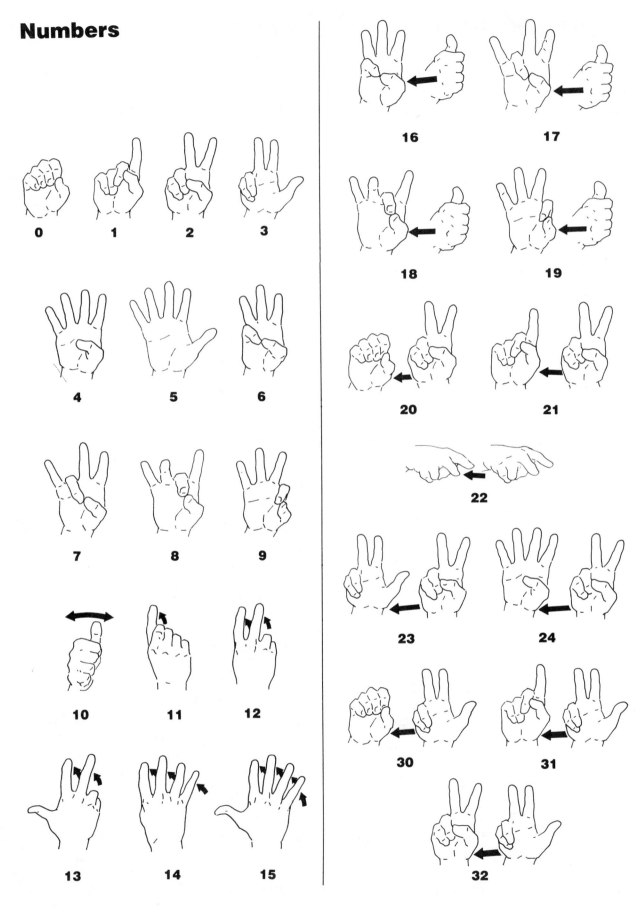

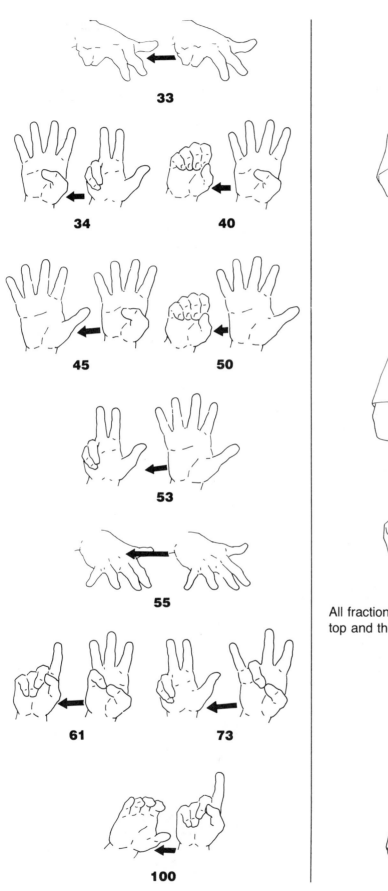

33

34

40

45

50

53

55

61

73

100

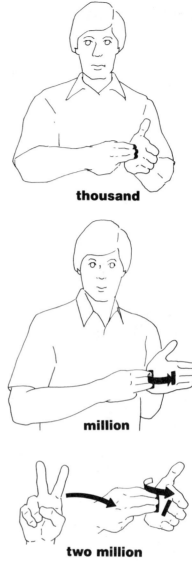

thousand

million

two million

All fractions are signed with the numerator at the top and the denominator at the bottom

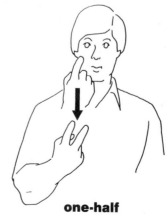

one-half

Number Practice

Years, telephone numbers, and social security numbers are signed like they are spoken.

29	125	4,267	1980	447-7867	268-36-2789
39	267	2,795	1945	657-9980	076-76-2234
19	876	8,933	1982	824-0716	435-76-7765
88	456	1,766	1477	273-9838	323-11-6672
16	921	9,562	1776	379-5934	766-11-4848
43	678	7,985	1787	445-9911	771-43-7868
91	321	7,200	1913	911-3321	435-16-9980
90	492	1,465	2001	818-4439	125-33-1122
59	471	12,875	1216	438-6657	321-43-3214
49	597	56,133	1556	777-8787	477-87-9332
13	711	77,241	1975	546-4546	435-88-3426
78	244	95,111	1966	671-1121	659-44-6591
62	888	54,834			
53	760	33,878			

Special Notes

This section is very important. It provides guidelines and information on how to make all the signs in the book. The guidelines are divided into three sections: an explanation of the arrows used in the illustrations, a description of the sign markers used in MCE, and an explanation of the symbols used to mark adapted signs.

The signs selected to show the intended movement are frequently natural gestures and are easy to do. It is suggested that you do each sign while looking at the illustration and the direction of the arrows. This should give you a feeling for the movement represented by the arrows.

When imitating a sign, remember that the picture on the page is a mirror image. You make the signs while you are looking straight at the person with whom you are communicating. The illustrations showing side views are in this book only for clarity. You are to sign looking forward.

eat

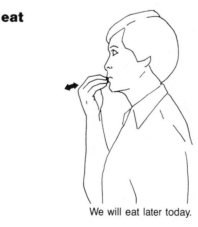

We will eat later today.

17

When an illustration is in a box, it represents the final position of the sign. The illustration not boxed is the initial position of the sign. The hand should move in the direction of the arrow(s).

drink

Do you want a drink of water?

Solid arrows show the direction in which the hand is to move. Unless a side view of the body is shown, this movement is generally parallel to the body.

will, future

When will you go home?

house

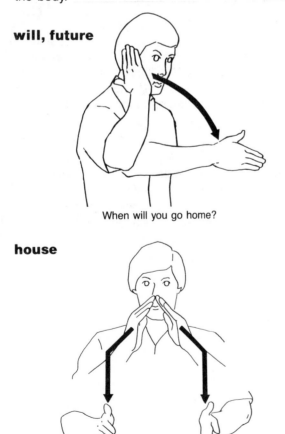

Will you eat at my house?

Solid double pointed arrows and **circles** indicate repeated motion parallel to the body.

ice cream

She went home to get ice cream.

here, present

She will be here soon.

Black and white arrows show that the hand(s) move either forward or backward away from the body.

boat

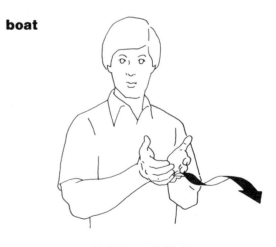

He is here with his boat.

Indian

I like Indian jewelry.

Black and white double pointed arrows and **circles** show repeated motion away from the body.

airplane

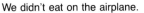

We didn't eat on the airplane.

swim

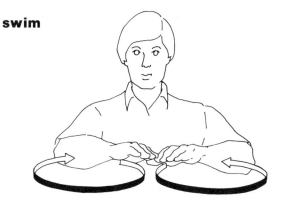

We will swim near the boat.

One black and white arrow together show the hands moving in opposing or alternating directions while the movement is repeated.

court

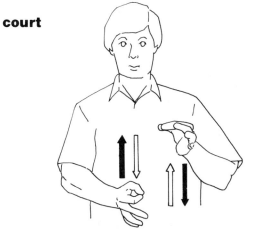

The police officer was in court.

Shaded and solid black areas show that there is contact or that body parts touch. Most instances of body contact are obvious.

police officer, cop, *detective

I saw the police officer in court.

cry, tears

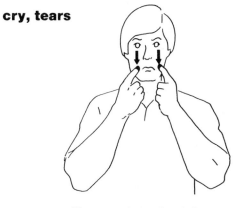

She was crying on the airplane.

Inflections

Almost all of the inflections that follow are used only in MCE. They are added to the root word or sign to convey plurality, tense, or a change in a part of speech.

Inflections can be added to English words to indicate that the word refers to a person (e.g., -er, -or, -ist, -an). Sign markers can be added to signs for the same purpose. This inflection is referred to as the -er sign.

-er, -or, -ist, -an

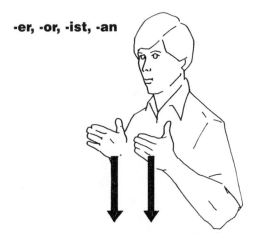

player, instructor, artist, American

Some nouns represent people, but are not inflected. These nouns do not use the -er sign (e.g., doctor, nurse, dentist, priest, member, king).

priest

Is the priest on the plane?

-'s and **-s'** show possessives

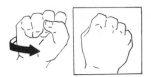

students' books, Grant's tomb

-er and **-est** show comparatives

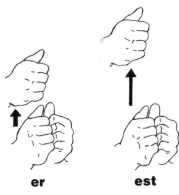

er **est**

fatter, sadder, slowest, slickest

-d shows past tense for regular verbs

played, learned, baked

Finish shows past tense for irregular verbs

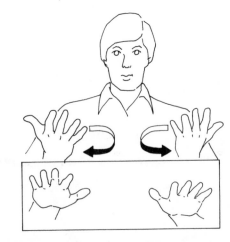

wrote (write + finish), felt (feel + finish), got (get + finish)

20

-s shows plurals

boy*s*, girl*s*, house*s*

-ing shows progressive tense

runn*ing*, walk*ing*, throw*ing*

-ment shows concrete results

develop*ment*, amaze*ment*

-ness shows state, quality, degree, or condition

deaf*ness*, sad*ness*, good*ness*

-ly shows likeness, manner, or time

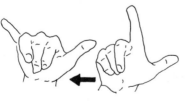

father*ly*, slow*ly*, hour*ly*

-n shows participles

sadd*en*, brok*en*, spok*en*

-un, -il, -dis, -in, -im show negatives

*im*possible, *un*willing, *il*legal, *dis*please, *in*expensive

Adapted Signs

Adapted signs are initialized signs. Initialized signs are formed from traditional signs for the purpose of clarity. The traditional movement is incorporated into the adapted sign, but the handshape is determined by the first letter of the word. These adapted signs are used to convey a one-to-one correspondence of English and sign vocabulary. These signs are used in MCE. They are marked in this book with an asterisk (*).

*duty

The police officer's duty was done.

If the adapted sign is based on a traditional sign, then the traditional sign is shown in parentheses. Additional words are also shown and may or may not have an asterisk.

*duty (work), ***industry**

My duty is to stay here.

Most of the signs in the book are traditional signs. If a synonym (in English) for that sign can be initialized, it is marked with an asterisk (*). The student has the option of signing these either in the traditional way or the adapted way.

work, *duty, *industry

I will go to work later.

A dagger (†) marks a word that is a multi-sign word. The sign used depends on the context of the sentence. Sentences using these words can be found in the Multi-sign Word Appendix.

†about (almost)

It is about time to leave.

†about (about)

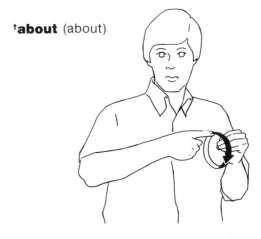

I heard about the accident.

Lesson 1

The Structure of the Referent

1
†house

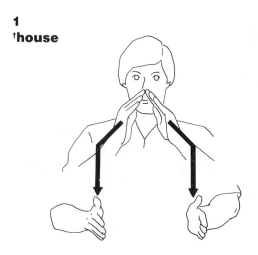

Your hands outline the house's roof and frame.

2
boat

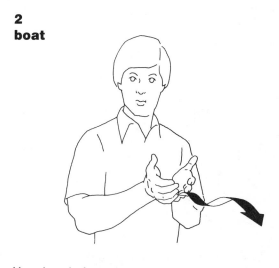

Your hands form the hull of the boat.

23

3
airplane

Your fingers and thumb represent the nose and wings of the airplane.

4
butterfly

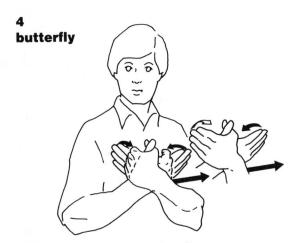

Your hands represent the moving wings of a butterfly.

5
tree

Your arm is the tree's trunk and your fingers form the branches.

What the Referent Wears

6
police officer, cop, *detective

Your hand represents a police officer's badge.

7
Indian

Your fingers represent head feathers.

8
boy

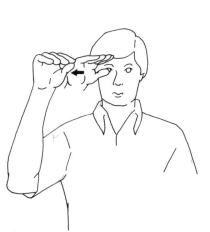

Your hand represents the bill of a cap.

9
girl

Your thumb represents the string of a bonnet.

10
priest

Your hand represents the priest's collar.

Symbolic Referent

11
hour

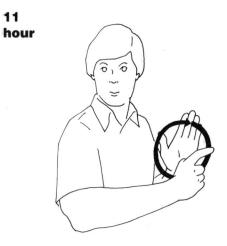

Your finger represents the minute hand circling the clock.

12
†judge,
justice

Your hands represent the scales of justice.

13
morning

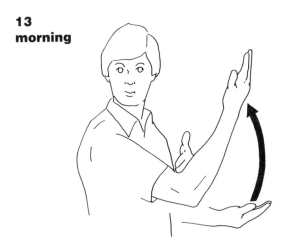

Your arm represents the horizon and your hand represents the rising sun.

14
noon

Your hand represents the sun's position at noon.

15
night

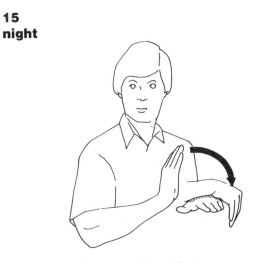

Your hand represents the setting sun.

16
day

Your hand represents the sun moving across the sky.

17
afternoon

Your hand represents the sun beginning to set.

18
devil

Your fingers represent the devil's horns.

What You Do with the Referent

21
ice cream

You lick ice cream.

19
flower

You smell a flower.

22
baby, infant

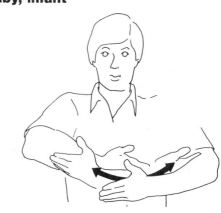

You rock a baby in your arms.

20
bicycle, bike

You pedal a bicycle.

23
swim

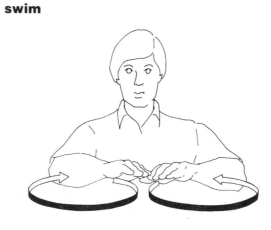

You move your arms while swimming.

24
eat,
***food**

You put food in your mouth.

25
drink

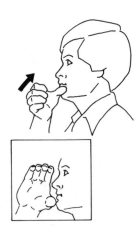

You put a drink to the mouth.

26
pie

You cut a pie into wedges.

27
basketball

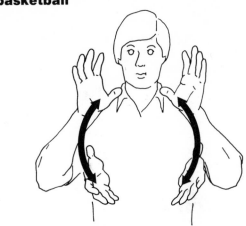

You throw a basketball.

28
†cry

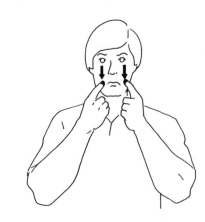

You have tears streaming down your face.

29
buy

You pass money from one person to another.

30
speak,
say,
talk,
†speech

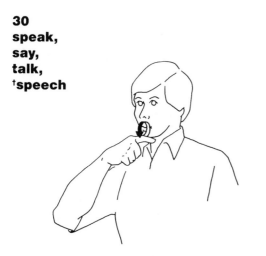

You move your lips when talking.

What the Referent Does

31
doctor

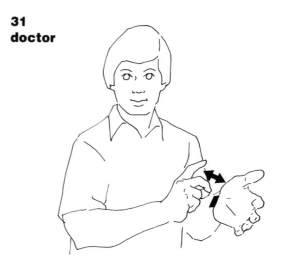

A doctor takes your pulse.

32
nurse

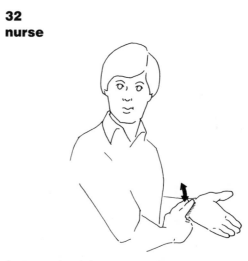

A nurse also takes your pulse.

33
carpenter

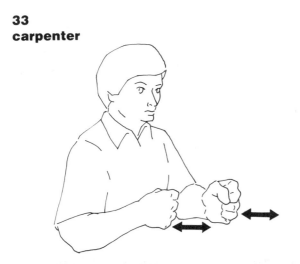

A carpenter uses a plane.

34
writer,
write

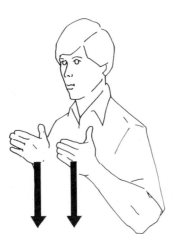

A writer writes.

35
artist,
art, †*draw

An artist draws on canvas.

30

Spatial Referent

38
†come

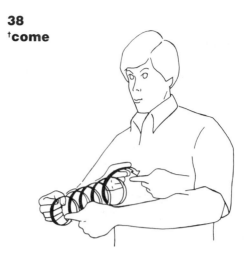

Something is coming toward you.

36
meet,

Two things come together to meet.

39
go

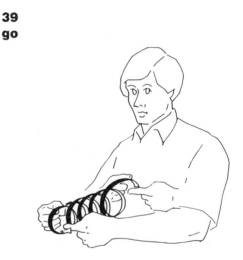

Something is going away from you.

37
separate,
†part

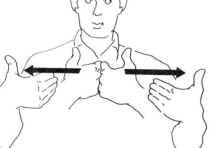

Two things go apart to separate.

40
†above, †over

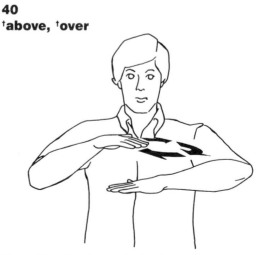

Something is above the horizon.

31

41
†below, under

Something is below the horizon.

42
here,
†present

Something is near the body.

43
there

A place that is indicated by pointing to it.

44
present,
now, this

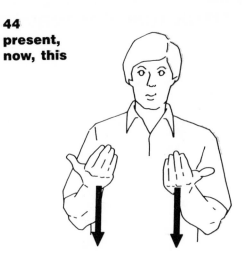

The area near your body indicates present time.

45
will, *future

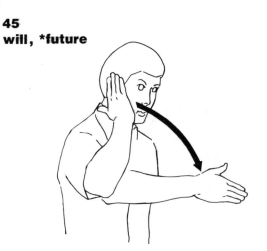

Forward motion away from the body indicates future time.

46
past, previous

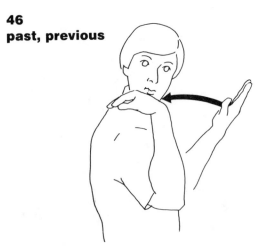

Backward motion away from the body indicates past time.

Practice Sentences

1. *The* baby swims *every* morning.

2. *The* carpenter *has a* house boat.

3. *A* priest *is* eating ice cream now.

4. *The* doctor bought *a* basketball.

5. *The* artist met *a* writer *and a* nurse.

6. *The* Indian will *be* here *in* two hours.

7. *The* boy *and* girl *are sleeping in the* airplane.

8. *A* doctor *was chasing* butterflies this noon.

9. *The* detective *picked* flowers *from the* tree.

10. *The* doctor *put the picture* below *the clock.*

11. There is *my* doctor's bicycle.

12. *The* girl *and* boy spoke *to the* nurse.

13. *The* basketball *team plays at* night.

14. *The* doctor ate *and* drank *with the* artist.

15. This afternoon *they* will *be* separated.

16. *The* Indian *lived in the* past.

17. *The* baby cried *all* day *and* night.

18. *The* doctor spoke *standing* above *the crowd.*

19. Will *the* priest come *again* this morning?

20. *The* artist drew *a* devil.

Vocabulary

house	afternoon	nurse
boat	devil	carpenter
airplane	flower	writer, write
butterfly	bicycle, bike	artist, art, *draw
tree	ice cream	meet
police officer, cop, *detective	baby, infant	separate, part
Indian	swim	come
boy	eat, *food	go
girl	drink	above, over
priest	pie	below, under
hour	basketball	here, present
judge, justice	cry	there
morning	buy	present, now, this
noon	speak, say, talk, speech	will, *future
night	doctor	past, previous
day		

Additional Signs and Notes

Lesson 2

47
cat

A cat *meows.*

48
dog

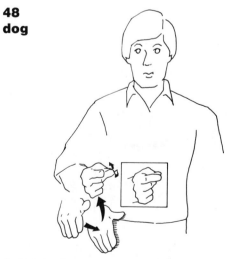

A dog *barks.*

49
†like

Boys like dogs.

50
don't like

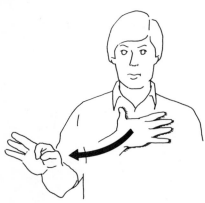

Dogs don't like cats.

51
and

Dogs and cats like trees.

52
*the

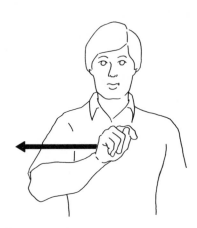

The cat doesn't like the dog.

53
*a

A baby cries.

54
this, that, it,
†which

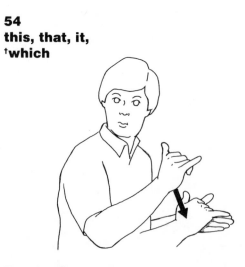

This dog likes *to* eat.

36

55
*this

This cat likes ice cream.

56
†have, own, possess

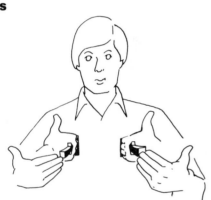

Police officers have dogs.

57
I

I have a cat and dog.

58
me

The dog doesn't like me.

59
we

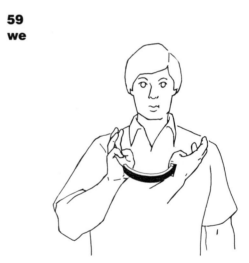

We have two bicycles.

60
us

The cats like us.

61
my, mine

My doctor came *to* the house.

62
our

That *is* our boat.

63
**you, he, she,
it, him, her,
†point**

You have my bicycle.

64
**they, them,
those, these**

They have our basketball.

65
your, his, her, hers (singular)

I met your priest.

66
yours, their, theirs (plural)

They have their drinks.

67
*he

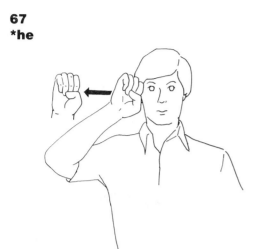

He came here this morning.

68
*she

She has seven flowers.

69
*him

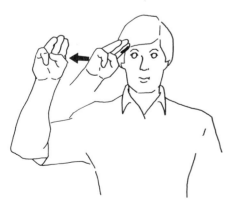

The nurse likes him.

70
*her, *hers

Her baby doesn't like me.

71
*his

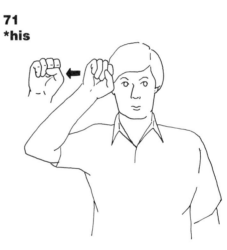

He ate his ice cream.

72
*it

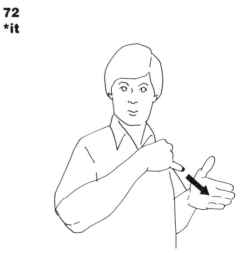

Her dog doesn't like it.

73
*they

They like our house.

74
*them

We will meet them *in* two hours.

75
himself,
herself,
itself,
yourself

He bought himself a boat.

76
themselves

They came *by* themselves.

77
myself

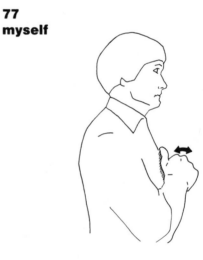

I like myself.

78
ourselves

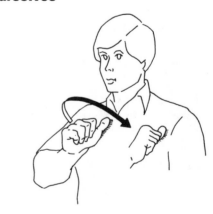

We like ourselves.

40

Practice Sentences

1. The dog *chased* the cat *up* the tree.

2. They will judge him themselves.

3. We *can do* that ourselves *in* the morning.

4. Our baby doesn't like this *kind of* ice cream.

5. *Both* he and she *got* flowers *from* them.

6. They like my doctor and his nurse.

7. Her priest spoke *with* her himself.

8. I *cannot* go *by* myself.

9. The police officer said it *was* yours *or* mine.

this
44

10. The nurse *saw* us this afternoon.

11. I have her flowers *in* my house.

12. They don't like your *blue* bicycle.

13. They will *all* go there *at* noon.

14. We don't like that tree *in* our *yard*.

15. They *often* buy *milk for* their baby.

this
44

16. We *had to* separate them this morning.

17. They come and go *when* they *wish*.

18. Our dog likes going *on* our boat.

19. You *may* swim *with* them.

20. My dog likes *to* go *in* the boat.

Mind Ticklers

Make the sign _____	and think about . . .

cat 47	a cat's whiskers
dog 48	calling a dog
like 49	positive emotions from the heart
don't like 50	pushing away negative feelings
have, own, possess 56	holding something to yourself
I 57	pointing to yourself with an *i* handshape
me 58	pointing to yourself
we 59	making a sweeping motion to include everyone and yourself
us 60	making the sign for *we* with a *u* handshape

POSSESSIVES:	my 61	mine 61	your 65	yours 66	moving your hand toward the person(s) or object(s) being referred to
		his 65	her 65	hers 65	
	our 62	ours 66	their 66	theirs 66	

PRONOUNS:	you 63	he 63	she 63	it 63	pointing to the appropriate person(s) or object(s)
			him 63	her 63	
	they 64	them 64	these 64	those 64	

ADAPTED PRONOUNS:		*he 67	*she 68	initializing the last letter of the pronoun and moving the hand out slightly from the male or female position (top or bottom of the head, respectively)
		*him 69	*her 70	
ADAPTED PRONOUNS:		*they 73	*them 74	a sweeping motion ending in the last letter of the word

Vocabulary

cat	me	*she
dog	we	*him
like	us	*her, *hers
don't like	my, mine	*his
and	our	*it
*the	you, he, she, it, him, her	*they
*a		*them
this, that, it, which	they, them, those, these	himself, herself, itself, yourself
*this	your, his, her, hers	themselves
have, own, possess	yours, their, theirs	myself
	*he	ourselves

Additional Signs and Notes

Lesson 3

79
**to be, am, are,
is, was, were,
will be**

He is here.

80
***is**

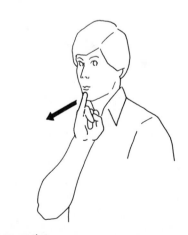

She is an artist.

81
*am

I am crying now.

82
*are

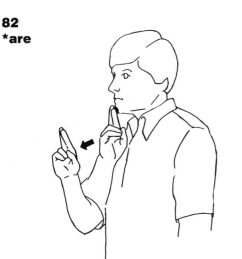

The boys are under the tree.

83
*was

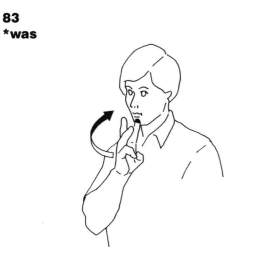

The boat was theirs.

84
*were

They were nurses.

85
*be

She will be a doctor.

86
color

I like that color.

87
purple

He has a purple butterfly.

88
green

She liked the green bicycle.

89
†blue

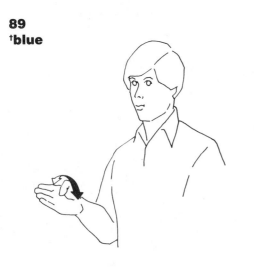

We have a blue *car*.

90
yellow

The flower was yellow.

91
orange

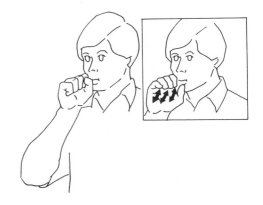

A basketball is orange.

92
white

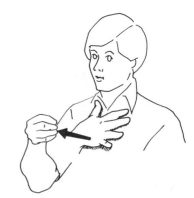

They have a white boat.

93
†black

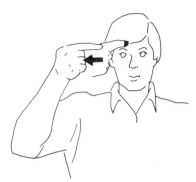

I like the black and white dog.

94
brown

The cat is white and brown.

95
red

The boat is red and blue.

96
pink

She has a pink flower.

97
gray

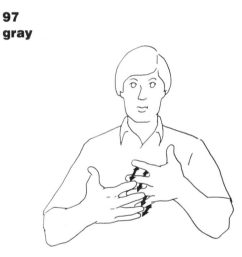

The gray airplane is ours.

98
money

Money is green and black.

99
guess

I guess she is a doctor.

100
†call, telephone

The doctor is calling you.

101
†call, summon

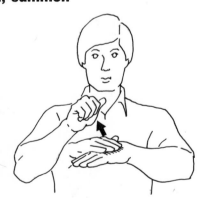

The judge called *for* the detective.

102
†call, yell, †cry

The girl yelled *at* the baby.

103
†call, †named

They called her dog *Spot.*

104
yesterday

The priest was here yesterday.

She will meet me tomorrow night.

**106
real, true,
*really, sure,
†original**

Is the money real?

**107
isn't, don't,
doesn't,
didn't, †won't**

I don't have your money.

Practice Sentences

1. He likes that green and blue bicycle.

2. *What* color is your telephone?

call
100

3. They were *asked to* call him *at home.*

4. I don't really have a purple and black *car.*

call
102

5. She called *for* her dog *all* night.

6. Yesterday was *when* I *got* my money.

7. I am red and pink *from all* that *sun.*

call
103

8. They were *determined to* call their dog *Spot.*

call
100, 101

9. The nurse called *each patient for* the doctor.

10. I guess they will *paint* their house brown and yellow.

11. Tomorrow, we are going *without* her.

12. There were orange, gray, and white colored *pencils.*

call
100, 101

13. Are we *to* call the artist *for dinner?*

14. Here are the pink flowers I *promised* you.

15. We don't like you *to* yell *at* us.

16. I really don't cry *much.*

call
100

17. I guess we *should* call *home* tomorrow.

call
101

18. We don't like the *teacher to* call *on* us.

19. Will you be here tomorrow *at* noon?

20. Yesterday was a *dark,* gray day.

Mind Ticklers

    and think about . . .

TO BE:	***is** 80	***am** 81	***are** 82	initializing the signs; the direction of the sign indicates the verb tense
	*was 83	***were** 84	***be** 85	

                                                    color 86   children putting crayons in their mouths

COLORS:	**purple** 87	**green** 88		**blue** 89	**yellow** 90

initializing the first letter of each color

orange 91 — squeezing an orange

white 92 — wearing a white shirt

black 93 — black eyebrows

brown 94 — people being tan or brown

red 95 — the lips being red

pink 96 — the lips sometimes being pink

money 98 — money piling up in the hand

guess 99 — grabbing at what is in the head

call, telephone 100 — putting a telephone receiver to your ear

call, summon 101 — tapping and grabbing someone to get their attention

call, yell 102 — calling for someone

yesterday 104 — time that is behind you

tomorrow 105 — time that is ahead of you

real, true 106 — speaking straight out

isn't, don't, doesn't, didn't, won't 107 — "hands-off"

Vocabulary

to be	blue	call, telephone
*is	yellow	call, summon
*am	orange	call, yell, cry
*are	white	call, named
*was	black	yesterday
*were	brown	tomorrow
*be	red	real, true, *really, sure, original
color	pink	
purple	gray	isn't, don't, doesn't, didn't, won't
green	money	
	guess	

Additional Signs and Notes

52

Lesson 4

108
yes

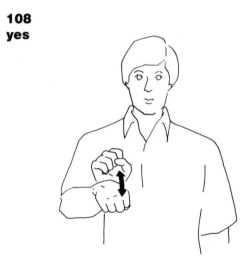

Yes, I like red flowers.

109
†no

No, it isn't ice cream.

110
†no, none

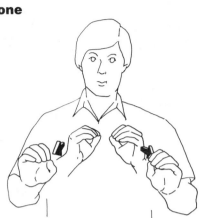

There are no drinks.

111
not

He is not here now.

112
nothing

Nothing is colored pink.

113
now, †present,
†at once

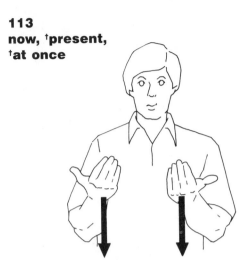

Now I have nothing.

114
today

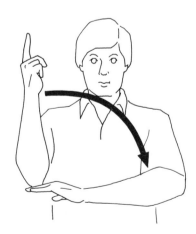

Yes, telephone him today.

54

115
tonight

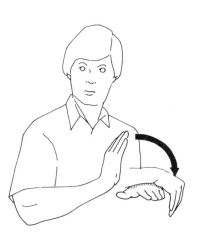

Yes, the doctor will come tonight.

116
first,
†original

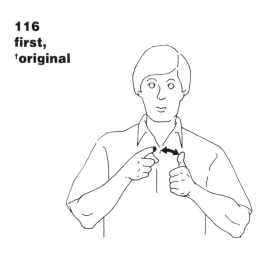

Yes, today is my first day.

117
†second

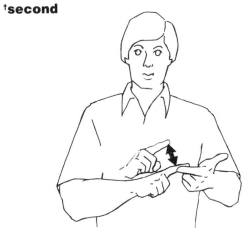

She is our second baby.

118
third

No, it is not the third day.

119
then

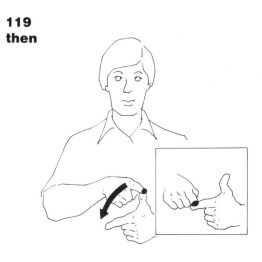

First, call me, then call *dad.*

120
†time
o'clock

It is time *to* go now.

121
†time, period

I don't like my second period *class*.

122
minute, moment,
†second,
in a minute,
†wait a minute

You have 11 minutes *to* eat.

123
hour

We will go *in* three hours.

124
later, after a while

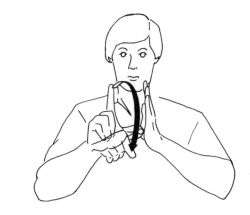

Really, call me later.

125
†can, able,
possible, may

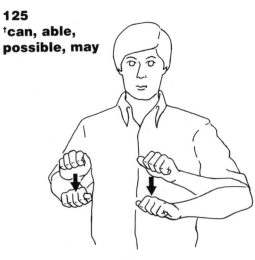

Can we go ourselves?

126
cannot, can't

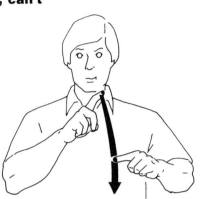

They cannot come here.

127
†to (preposition)

They will go to the yellow house.

128
†get, become

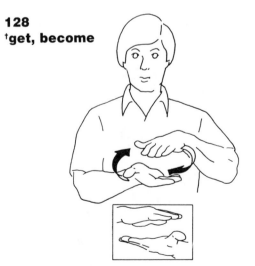

He gets sick *often*.

129
†get, arrive,
†reach

He reached the house first.

130
†get, obtain,
receive, acquire

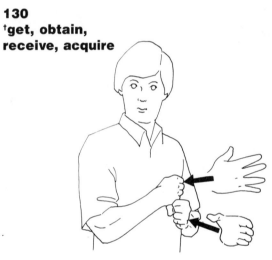

She will get a white dog.

131
in, inside

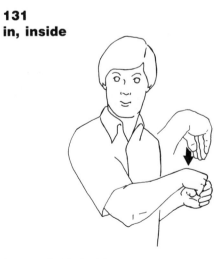

I guess he is inside.

57

132
into, enter, entrance

They went into the house.

133
†out, outside

It is time *to* go outside.

134
come

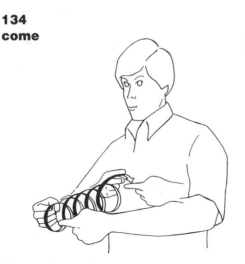

You can come inside now.

135
go

We can go later.

136
all, whole, †total, †complete

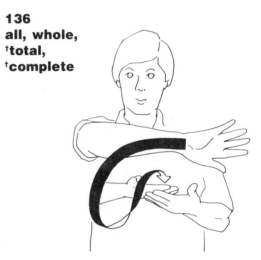

We have all the dogs.

137
†see, †vision

Can you see her now?

Practice Sentences

time	**get**
120	129

no
110
no
109
get
130

get
128

time
120

time
121
get
130

1. Yes, today is the day I buy you flowers.

2. *What* time will you get *home* tomorrow?

3. My third period class *met* outside.

4. I cannot see you later today.

5. Tonight, there will be no money *for* you.

6. No, I was not there *for* the whole hour.

7. Go into the house and get the yellow flowers.

8. We will see you in a minute *if* we can.

9. Come in first, then you can see the doctor.

10. Nothing is *wrong* now.

11. This is my second house in five *years*.

12. She gets sick *for* hours and hours.

13. We can see nothing above us.

14. They *may* go to the *farm* tomorrow.

15. None *of* us can go *at* that time.

16. *An* hour later they all went *home*.

17. *Christmas* time can be *exciting*.

18. They cannot get *any more* money.

19. Tonight, we will see her first.

20. Can we enter *through* here?

Mind Ticklers

| *and think about . . .*

yes 108	the head nodding in agreement
no 109	spelling the word—n + o
no, none 110	both hands holding nothing
nothing 112	the idea that what is coming from the mouth is dropped, that it is not of any great importance
now 113	the present being immediately in front of you
today 114	the idea that *now* the sun is going across the sky
tonight 115	the idea that *now* the sun is going over the horizon
first 116	the thumb as being your first digit
second 117	your index finger as being your second digit
third 118	your middle finger as being your third digit
then 119	doing something in sequence—first and second
time 120	tapping a watch
time 121	an indefinite number of hours on a clock
minute 122	the minute hand moving around the clock
hour 123	the minute hand going completely around the clock
later 124	showing 20 minutes on a clock
to 127	an object moving from one place to another
get, become 128	something going from the top to the bottom
get, arrive 129	coming from the past to the present
get, obtain 130	grabbing something and pulling it toward you
in 131	putting something in a box
into 132	going all of the way into something
out 133	taking something out of a box
come 134	something coming toward you
go 135	something going away from you
all 136	gathering everything in front of you and putting it all in one pile
see 137	the eyes seeing outward

Vocabulary

yes	time, o'clock	get, arrive, reach
no	time, period	
no, none	minute, moment, second, in a minute, wait a minute	get, obtain, receive, acquire
not		in, inside
nothing		into, enter, entrance
now, present, at once	hour	out, outside
today	later, after a while	come
tonight	can, able, possible, may	go
first, original		all, whole, total, complete
second	cannot, can't	
third	to	see, vision
then	get, become	

Additional Signs and Notes

Lesson 5

138
how

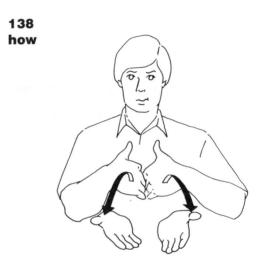

How is she today?

139
when

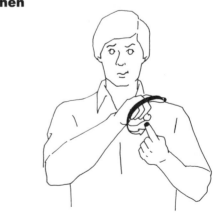

When can you see me?

140
where

Where are they going?

141
why

Why are you outside?

142
who, whose

Who is in my house?

143
†which

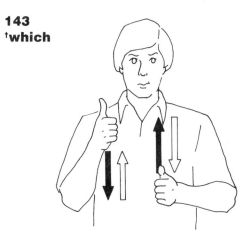

Which telephone is mine?

144
what

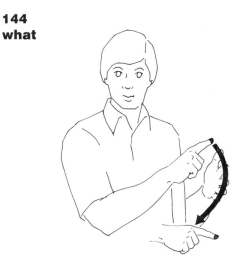

What time is it now?

145
†name

What is your name?

63

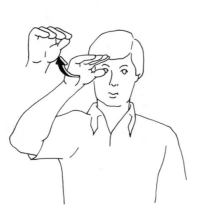

Which man is coming here?

**147
woman, lady**

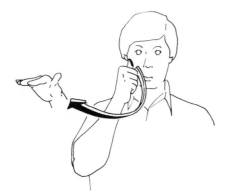

That woman went outside.

**148
mother, mom**

Which woman is your mother?

**149
father, dad**

Which man is your father?

**150
*parents** (mother, father)

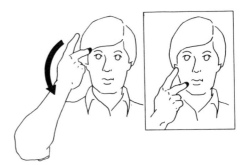

When are your parents coming?

**151
marry, marriage**

My parents were married in *May.*

64

152
wedding

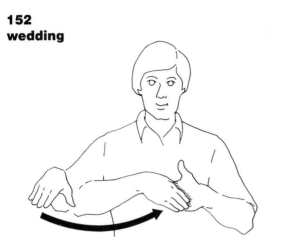

Why was the wedding outside?

153
wife

Where is my wife today?

154
husband

Who is her husband?

155
son

Which son is married?

156
daughter

Which daughter is home now?

157
†**same,**
†**like**

We have the same parents.

**158
sister**

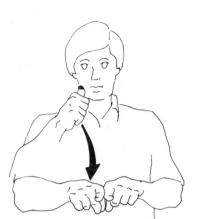

How is your sister now?

**159
brother**

Where is my brother?

**160
grandmother**

Whose grandmother is that?

**161
grandfather**

Is your grandfather here?

**162
child**

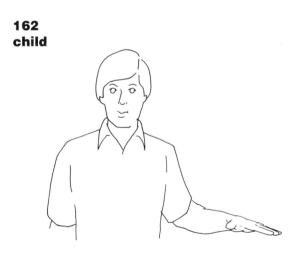

That is my sister's child.

**163
children**

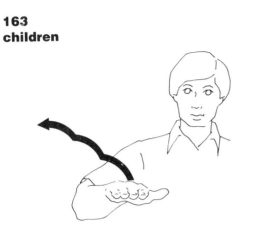

Which children are yours?

**164
aunt**

My aunt is not coming.

**165
uncle**

Where are your aunt and uncle?

**166
niece**

She is my sister's niece.

**167
nephew**

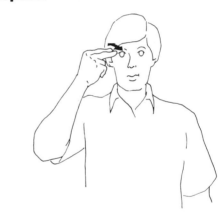

His nephew is outside.

**168
cousin**

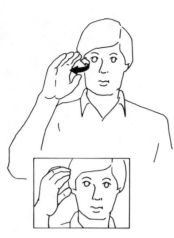

Is your cousin coming?

**169
friend**

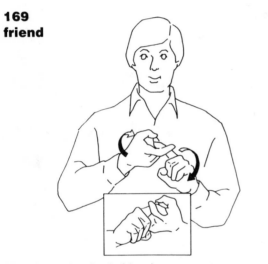

That is my brother's friend.

**170
divorce**

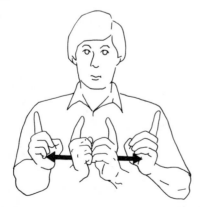

When was his sister divorced?

Practice Sentences

1. They didn't say who, when, where, *or* how.

2. Which man is your grandfather?

3. His aunt and uncle are divorced now.

4. How *old* are your nieces and nephews?

5. What is the name *of* your sister's friend?

call
103

6. What *do* your parents call the baby?

7. That woman married my brother.

8. Is one *of* those children your cousin?

get
128

9. My mother and that man are getting married.

10. Is dad going to the wedding tomorrow?

11. She *has* had the same husband *for* 52 *years*.

call
100

12. My daughter and son don't call *often*.

13. She doesn't like my grandmother's *cooking*.

14. Is your wife really *planning* the whole wedding?

15. Where will your husband *plant* the flowers?

16. Why is that child outside in the *cold*?

time
120

17. What time is the second wedding?

18. My uncle cannot come *until* later.

get
129

19. They won't get there tonight *or* tomorrow.

20. None *of* the sisters are coming now.

Mind Ticklers

Make the sign _____ | *and think about . . .*

when 139	the point in time when something happens
where 140	trying to put your finger on something
who 142	pointing to the lips
which 143	weighing two choices
what 144	the items in a list
man 146	a man being taller than a boy
woman 147	a woman being taller than a girl
parents 150	the initialized *p* handshape representing both mother and father
marry 151	two people embracing when they are married
wedding 152	the bride and groom joining hands
wife 153	a girl who is married
husband 154	a boy who is married
son 155	a boy being rocked in the arms
daughter 156	a girl being rocked in the arms
same 157	two things that are alike
sister 158	girls being in the same family
brother 159	boys being in the same family
grandmother 160	a previous mother
grandfather 161	a previous father
child 162	the height of a child
children 163	the height of several children
aunt 164	making an *a* handshape in the female head position
uncle 165	making a *u* handshape in the male head position
niece 166	making an *n* handshape in the female head position
nephew 167	making an *n* handshape in the male head position
cousin 168	making a *c* handshape
divorce 170	two people becoming unmarried

Vocabulary

how	father, dad	grandmother
when	*parents	grandfather
where	marry, marriage	child
why	wedding	children
who, whose	wife	aunt
which	husband	uncle
what	son	niece
name	daughter	nephew
man	same, like	cousin
woman, lady	sister	friend
mother, mom	brother	divorce

Additional Signs and Notes

Lesson 6

171
for

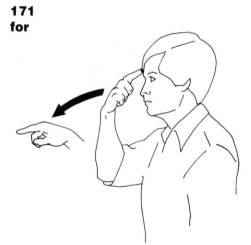

She is here for the wedding.

172
†but,
however

I came, but I didn't see you.

173
different

We arrived *at* different times.

174
†same,
alike,
†like

They like the same house.

175
†same,
common,
similar,
standard

Yes, they are all the same.

176
†on, upon,
onto

She is on his bicycle.

177
†right,
all right,
privilege

We all have the right to speak.

178
†right,
†correct,
appropriate

My friend is right.

179
†right (direction)

Go through the *door* on the right.

180
†left (direction)

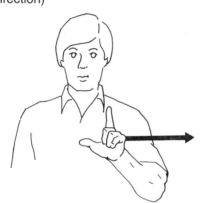

The blue house is on the left.

181
**†left,
depart,
†leave,
†gone**

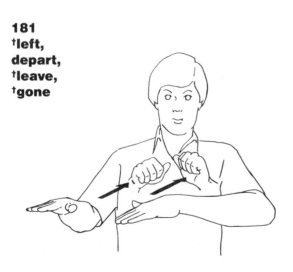

Our uncle left yesterday morning.

182
**†left,
abandon,
†leave**

When was that left here?

183
good, *well

They left *at* a good time.

184
bad, †poor

The *weather* was bad yesterday.

**185
with**

They left with their mother.

**186
without**

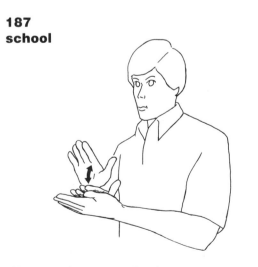

They went without my friend.

**187
school**

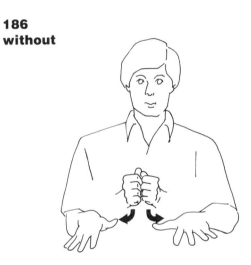

We go to the same school.

**188
college**

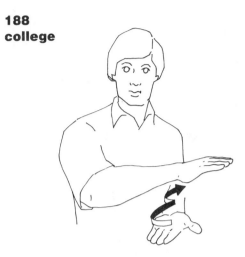

I went to my dad's college.

**189
person, human,
one**

That person is a good friend.

**190
people**

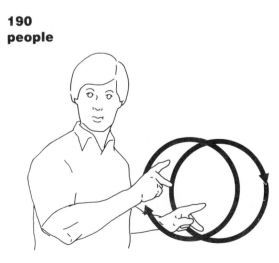

Those people are my friends.

191
individual

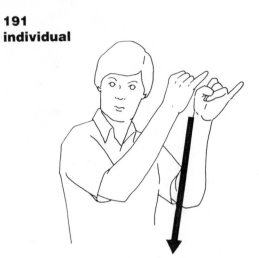

He is a bad individual.

192
†tell

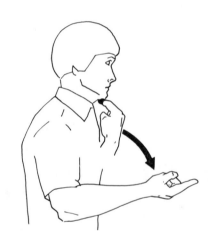

When can you tell her?

193
†tell me

Tell me when you leave.

194
†talk,
conversation

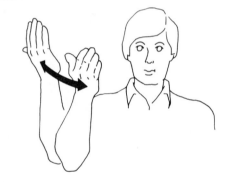

Father was talking with her.

195
†talk,
lecture,
†speech

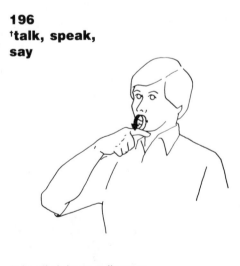

The talks are all the same.

196
†talk, speak,
say

It is all right *to* talk now.

197
maybe, perhaps,
may, might

Maybe it is different now.

198
any

Do you have any money?

Practice Sentences

	talk 196	3. Tell her it is all right *to* talk.

1. Maybe you can tell me *about* your brother.

2. My sister went to college for six *years.*

3. Tell her it is all right *to* talk.

4. The school lecture was really bad.

5. *Do* all the babies *look* the same?

6. Maybe the school is on the left.

7. Our conversations are *always* different.

8. That person was left without any friends.

9. All the people *thought* they were right.

10. You *turn* right *at* the white house.

11. That individual left without a *word.*

12. She was right, but he didn't like it.

13. Our individual rights were *threatened.*

14. No, we didn't *think* he was the same person.

15. What time is tonight's talk?

16. Any person who *wishes* may talk now.

17. Grandfather left his money *at home.*

18. Don't say the same *thing* tomorrow.

19. Really, how good is that college?

20. They talked *about* the good times and the bad.

Margin word/number references (left to right of each sentence):

- 3. **talk** 196
- 5. **same** 175
- 6. **left** 180
- 8. **left** 182
- 9. **right** 178
- 10. **right** 179
- 11. **left** 181
- 12. **right** 178
- 13. **right** 177
- 14. **no** 109 **same** 174
- 15. **time** 120 **talk** 195
- 16. **talk** 196
- 17. **left** 182
- 20. **talk** 194 **time** 121

Mind Ticklers

Make the sign _____ | *and think about . . .*

but 172	leaving something open for discussion
different 173	the opposite of the sign for same
same, alike 174	two things matching or being similar
on, upon 176	putting one thing on top of another
right 179	an *r* handshape moving to the right
left 180	an *l* handshape moving to the left
left, depart 181	moving from one place to another
left, abandon 182	leaving something behind by emptying the hands
good 183	offering something good to someone
bad 184	turning something that is bad away from the mouth
with 185	two things being side by side
without 186	emptying your hands
school 187	a teacher clapping her hands to get the students' attention
college 188	the idea that college is on a higher level than school
person, human 189	outlining the body with *p* handshapes
people 190	initialized *p* handshapes as being people moving around
individual 191	outlining the body with *i* handshapes
tell 192	words coming from the mouth
tell me 193	words coming from the speaker to the receiver
talk, conversation 194	words going between two people
talk, lecture 195	a lecturer gesticulating while giving a talk
talk 196	words rolling out of the mouth
maybe 197	weighing an action before doing it

Vocabulary

for	left	people
but, however	left, depart, leave	individual
different	left, abandon, leave	tell
same, alike, like		tell me
	good, *well	talk, conversation
same, common similar, standard	bad, poor	talk, lecture, speech
on, upon, onto	with	
	without	talk, speak, say
right, all right, privilege	school	
		maybe, perhaps, may, might
right, correct, appropriate	college	
right	person, human, one	any

Additional Signs and Notes

Lesson 7

199
never

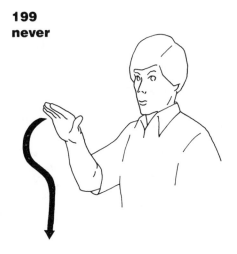

They never said that yesterday.

200
than

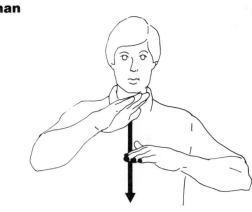

It is later than you *think*.

201
†wait

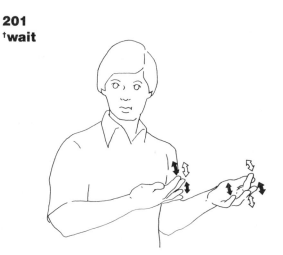

Maybe you can wait for me.

202
help,
assist

Tell me how *to* help your uncle.

203
†kind,
gentle,
gracious

Those people are never kind to us.

204
†kind,
type

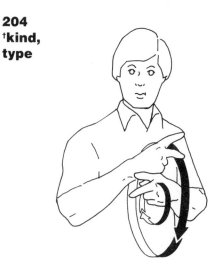

What kind *of* person is your mother?

205
up, upstairs

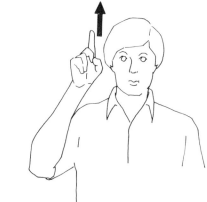

I went upstairs with my grandfather.

206
down,
downstairs

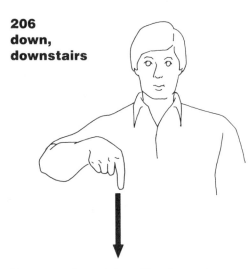

Never go downstairs without me.

207
**watch, look at,
observe**

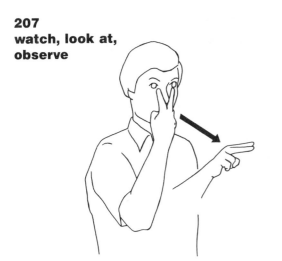

We watched the children *play* with the cats.

208
**†watch me,
†look at me**

Watch me help that man.

209
†watch

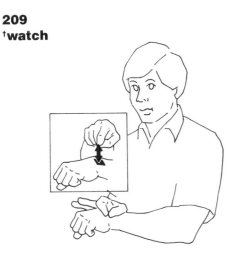

Where is your watch?

210
windy, wind

Why is it windy today?

211
†hot

It is not *as* hot today *as* it was yesterday.

212
warm

Today is warmer than yesterday.

213
†cold, chilly,
***winter**

Father said it was cold in here.

214
***weather** (cold)

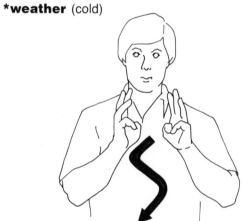

The weather is warm and windy.

215
†cold,
handkerchief

I have a bad cold.

216
some, section, *part

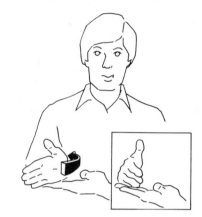

Some *of* us got colds on the *trip.*

217
some thing

I have some things *to* tell you.

218
†class,
***group,**
***family**

My class is first in school.

84

219
*family (class)

Our family *car* is green.

220
*group (class)

My friends are in that group.

221
*team (class)

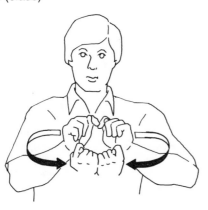

The team has its ups and downs.

222
†association (class)

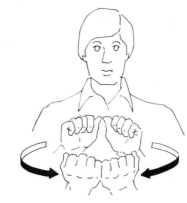

Our association helps people.

223
home

His family has a *nice* home.

224
table

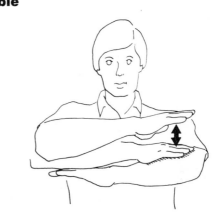

We never saw the brown table.

225
bed

The baby goes to bed at 7:00.

226
floor

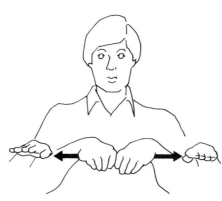

The baby is *crawling* on the cold floor.

227
*room (box)

This room is not cold tonight.

228
window

Is the window up *or* down?

229
door

The doors and windows are white.

230
television, TV

May we watch TV later?

231
mirror

They bought a mirror for the bedroom.

232
furniture

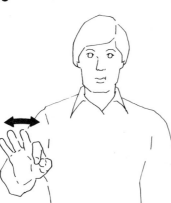

I have *new* furniture in my room.

Practice Sentences

cold 215	1. Mom and Dad both have bad colds.
cold 213	2. The weather is hot, then cold, then hot *again.*
	3. My sister likes warm days and chilly nights.
	4. Some *of* my family will help them *move.*
watch 207	5. The whole team went *to* watch.
this 54, 55	6. Watch me *put* this up the tree.
watch 209	7. I never saw your watch on the table.
kind 203	8. It was kind *of* you *to* help me home.
	9. The whole group is down on the floor.
	10. My class can't wait *more* than 33 minutes.
kind 204	11. What kind *of* a bed *do* you have?
left 182	12. I left some things in my morning class.
	13. Our association helps *needy* people.
	14. The table and bed are in the house.
	15. We never saw *such* a windy day.
kind 203	16. It was kind *of* you *to watch* my baby.
cold 213	17. The home team was cold all night.
	18. Wait a minute, and I will help you.
like 174	19. I never *heard* you lecture like that.
kind 204	20. What kind of weather are you having?
no 110	21. The bedroom has no windows.
	22. That furniture goes up in my room.
cold 213	23. I never *open* the door on cold days.
	24. Our mirror is above the TV.
watch 207	25. They all watched the TV *special.*

Mind Ticklers

Make the sign _____ | *and think about . . .*

never 199	making a question mark; never is always questionable
wait 201	a group of impatient people
help 202	giving a helping hand to someone
kind 203	an act of kindness coming from the heart
up 205	the natural gesture of pointing up
down 206	the natural gesture of pointing down
watch, look up 207	the fingers as representing the eyes swinging outward to look at something
watch me 208	someone looking at you
watch (noun) 209	pointing to a wristwatch
windy, wind 210	the movement of the wind
hot 211	pushing away something too hot to put into the mouth
warm 212	the warm air coming from the mouth
cold 213	the natural gesture of shivering
cold, handkerchief 215	wiping a runny nose
some 216	cutting a part from a whole object
*family 219 ***group** 220 ***team** 221 ***association** 222	a group of people in a circle
home 223	the place where you eat and sleep
table 224	the top of a table
bed 225	putting your head on a pillow
floor 226	the flatness and broadness of floors
door 227	the opening and closing of a door
window 228	the opening and closing of a window
mirror 231	holding a mirror in your hand and looking into it

Vocabulary

never	windy, wind	*team
than	hot	*association
wait	warm	home
help, assist	cold, chilly, *winter	table
kind, gentle, gracious	*weather	bed
		floor
kind, type	cold, handkerchief	*room
up, upstairs		
	some, section, *part	window
down, downstairs		door
	some thing	
watch, look at, observe		television, TV
	class, *group, *family	mirror
watch me, look at me	*family	furniture
watch	*group	

Additional Signs and Notes

Lesson 8

233
†mean, unkind,
†rough

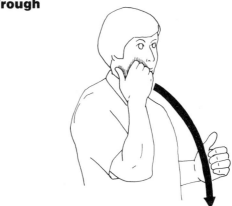

Father is never mean to me.

234
†mean, intend

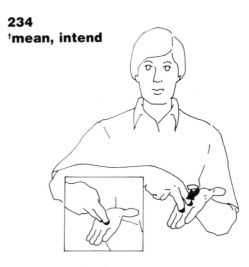

That is not what I mean.

235
know

We know my aunt is kind.

236
don't know

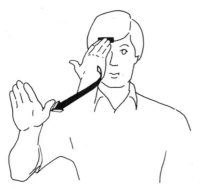

Her mother doesn't know us.

237
forget

The whole class forgot *to study* for the *test*.

238
think,
thought,
†mind, †sense

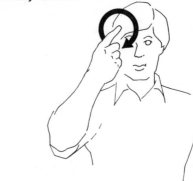

My sister thinks she's right.

239
think over,
consider,
ponder

Think over what I told you.

240
knowledge,
aware, familiar

You get knowledge in school.

**241
idea,
*opinion**

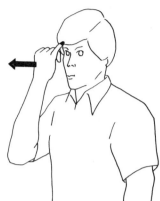

That is a good idea!

**242
imagine,
imagination**

I imagine he is in bed.

**243
understand,
comprehend,
realize**

He thinks he understands.

**244
misunderstand**

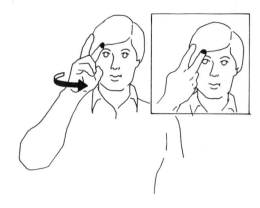

He misunderstood what I said.

**245
hope,
expect,
anticipate**

They hope you understand me.

**246
trouble,
†anxious, *worry**

The children were in trouble.

**247
predict,
foretell,
forecast**

Who can predict the future?

**248
wise, wisdom**

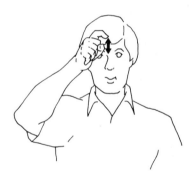

She is a wise person.

**249
*concept** (idea)

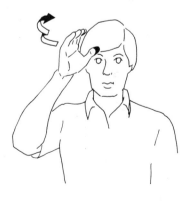

Who understands that concept?

**250
sorry,
apologize,
unfortunate**

Are you sorry you didn't buy that table?

**251
please**

Please forget that idea.

**252
satisfy,
†content**

Are you satisfied now?

94

**253
complain,
†mind, care,
†object**

It isn't wise *to* complain all the time.

**254
eager, †anxious,
motivated,
enthusiastic**

He is eager *to* satisfy father.

**255
†poor, pity,
sympathy,
compassion**

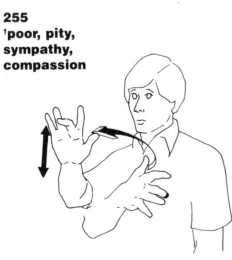

That poor child has no mother.

**256
†poor, poorly,
impoverished,
inadequate**

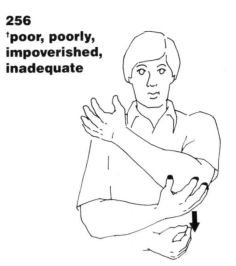

That family is poor.

**257
reason**

I don't know a good reason.

**258
happy, glad**

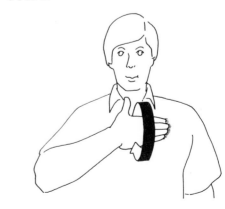

They imagine he is happy.

**259
enjoy,
pleasure,
enjoyable**

We hope you enjoy yourself.

**260
dream, †vision**

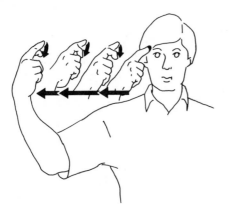

He cannot predict your dreams.

Practice Sentences

mean
233

poor
256

kind
203

time
121

mean
234

poor
255

mean
234

talk
195

poor
255

no **one**
110 189

kind **mean**
203 233

1. We don't know how his parents could be mean.

2. In a dream, he predicted his family would be poor.

3. I know he will forget our kindness.

4. Think over my idea and *let* me know.

5. I'm sorry, but I think you misunderstood me.

6. Mom has good reason to be happy.

7. My brother complains all the time.

8. We are eager to satisfy your friends.

9. We hope your troubles are not *too* bad.

10. I think I understand what you mean.

11. I imagine we have all we *need.*

12. The poor child *lost both of* her parents.

13. Please, *relax* and enjoy yourself.

14. That is not the same concept I mean.

15. I predict his talk will be *boring.*

16. When he *heard* the bad *news,* the poor *kid* cried.

17. No one could imagine his reasons.

18. You never know when he will be kind or mean.

19. We hope all your dreams are happy.

20. Sorry, the weather is not *very* warm.

Mind Ticklers

Make the sign _____	*and think about . . .*
know 235	patting the head as if to indicate knowledge
don't know 236	pushing knowledge out of your head
forget 237	wiping away knowledge
think, thought 238	turning something around in the mind
think over 239	turning over something in the mind
knowledge 240	the sign for *know*
idea 241	the initialized *i* handshape as a thought coming out of the head
understand 243	a flicker of light going on in the head
misunderstand 244	a thought that is turned around
predict 247	the eyes looking into the future
wise, wisdom 248	a depth of knowledge
please 251	rubbing the chest when something is good
satisfy 252	everything in the body being relaxed and satisfied
complain 253	getting something off your chest
eager, anxious 254	rubbing your hands to get ready for a task
poor 256	holes in the elbow of someone's shirt
reason 257	making the sign for *think* with an *r* handshape
happy, glad 258	the heart fluttering with happiness
enjoy 259	rubbing the heart and stomach to show pleasure

98

Vocabulary

mean, unkind, rough	understand, comprehend, realize	satisfy, content
mean, intend		complain, mind, care, object
know	misunderstand	
	hope, expect, anticipate	eager, anxious, motivated, enthusiastic
don't know		
forget	trouble, anxious, *worry	poor, pity, sympathy, compassion
think, thought, mind, sense		
	predict, foretell, forecast	poor, poorly, impoverished, inadequate
think over, consider, ponder		
	wise, wisdom	reason
knowledge, aware, familiar	*concept	happy, glad
	sorry, apologize, unfortunate	enjoy, pleasure, enjoyable
idea, *opinion		
imagine, imagination	please	dream, vision

Additional Signs and Notes

99

Lesson 9

261
happen, occur, *result

I am sorry that happened to us.

262
†find, discover, find out

See *if* you can find it.

263
thank you,
thanks, thank

Thank you for finding my *wallet*.

264
†hold, grip,
†keep

Please hold my watch.

265
†keep an eye on,
watch,
take care of

Will mother keep our dog?

266
†keep,
continue,
†last

That will not keep six nights.

267
†last, past,
ago, †used to,
†before

That happened last night.

268
†last, †final

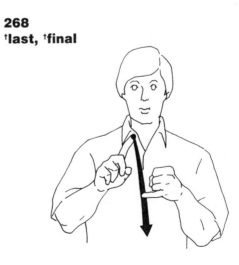

Her sister is my last hope.

**269
anything**

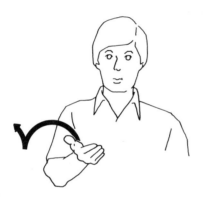

Can you find anything?

**270
*try** (attempt),
***effort**

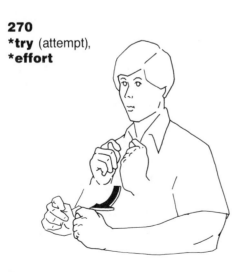

Try taking care of her for a day.

**271
†work, job,
†play, †trade**

Continue working inside for now.

**272
better**

Anything is better than that.

**273
best**

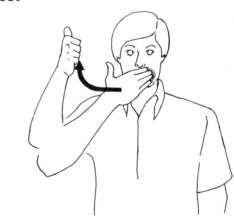

She is the best friend I have.

274
†long, †length

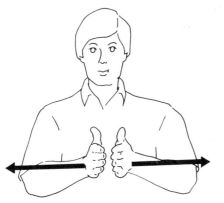

How long is their boat?

275
†long, †length

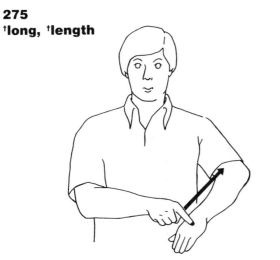

How long will you work?

276
†need,
necessary,
should

You should call the doctor.

277
†have to, must

I have to try that for you.

278
†old, age

How old is your sister?

279
young

They have a young child.

280
open

Try *to* open that for me.

281
†close,
shut

I have to close it now.

282
†close,
near, by

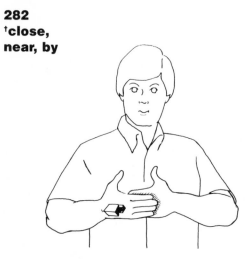

How close is your aunt's house?

283
†act, *do,
***behave,**
***did, action**

Young people act happy.

284
act, perform,
performance,
†show

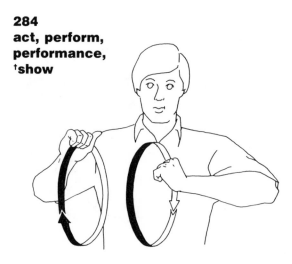

He performed for the group.

285
†tie, even,
equal, †fair,
†draw

He thought the *game* was tied.

286
†tie, knot

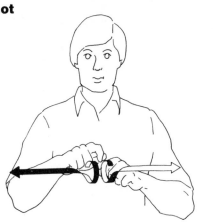

Thank you for tying that.

287
†away, go away

The young boy had to go away.

Practice Sentences

1. We have to go away *before* tomorrow.

2. Can you find anything *to* tie this?

3. Try *to* keep the better *of* the two televisions.

4. How long is the third act?

5. That old woman is holding your mirror.

6. Don't open that one *until* last.

7. The young people need *more* time *to* work.

8. No, I'm sorry, I saw nothing happen.

9. It continued for eight hours and was *still* a tie.

10. I really don't think it will last *very* long.

11. Thank you, but last night was *enough* for me.

12. Tell me, how long is your *new sail* boat?

13. She never found out how *to* open it.

14. At best, it will *only* last three weeks.

15. Why are you acting *so* happy?

16. He *has* not worked here for the last *several* days.

17. My aunt used to *live* close to us.

18. How long *do* you have to work tomorrow?

19. You need *to* get some money.

20. That *sounds* fair to us.

Mind Ticklers

Make the sign _____   *and think about . . .*

find 262	retrieving something from under or beneath an object
hold 264	the natural gesture of holding something
keep, watch 265	watching something with four eyes
keep, continue 266	something moving into the future
last, past 267	time that is behind you
last, final 268	your pinky finger as being the last of your digits
work, job 271	working with one's hands
long, length 274	measuring the length of something
long 275	measuring a length of time on the arm
have to 277	hooking something that you must have
old, age 278	an old man's beard
young 279	excitable children
open 280	opening the flaps of a box
close, shut 281	closing the flaps of a box
close, near 282	two things being in close proximity
tie, even 285	two things being on the same level
tie, knot 286	the gesture of tying a bow
away, go away 287	pushing someone or something away

Vocabulary

happen, occur, *result

find, discover, find out

thank you, thank, thanks

hold, grip, keep

keep an eye on, watch, take care of

keep, continue, last

last, past, ago, used to, before

last, final

anything

*try, *effort

work, job, play, trade

better

best

long, length

long

need, necessary, should

have to, must

old, age

young

open

close, shut

close, near, by

act, *do, *behave, *did, action

act, perform, performance, show

tie, even, equal, fair, draw

tie, knot

away, go away

Additional Signs and Notes

Lesson 10

**288
pretty,
beautiful,
lovely**

Their daughter is *very* pretty.

**289
†ugly**

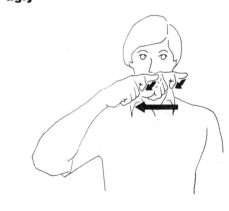

The ugly dog is not mine.

290
†make, create,
***produce, form**

She can make the room pretty.

291
†make,
force

Father made him work *at* home.

292
many,
†a large number

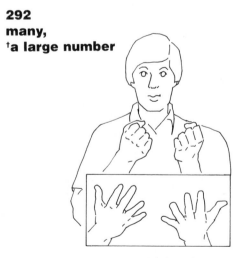

Many people made *donations* to the group.

293
few,
several,
†a number of

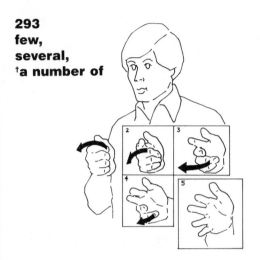

He has several friends *at* school.

294
again,
†over

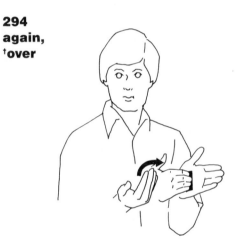

Please come *to* see me again.

295
†problem (math)

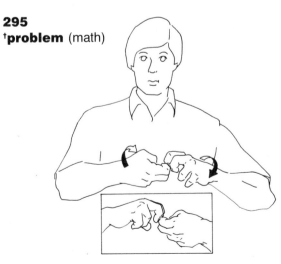

There are many long problems in that *chapter*.

296
†problem,
difficult,
†hard, †rough

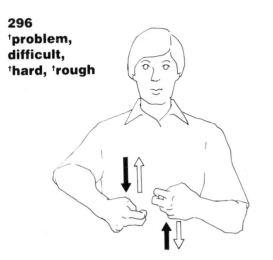

Her problems won't go away.

297
kid, child

My kid is not ugly.

298
kidding,
tease

They continue teasing him.

299
†before

Tell me before you leave.

300
†before, †past, ago

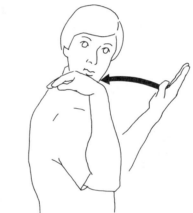

He had that problem before.

301
†before,
†in front of,
confront, †face

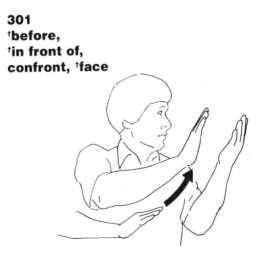

He lectured before the whole group.

302
†next

Next time I will know better.

303
†next,
†turn

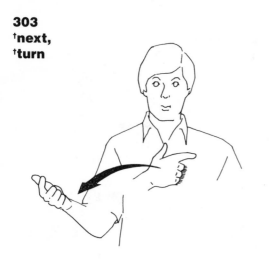

I think you are next.

304
†turn off,
†turn on

Make him turn off the TV.

305
beside,
†next to

The kid is beside her mother.

306
believe

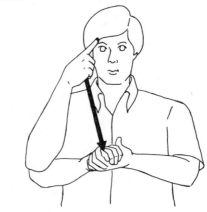

I believe it is your turn.

307
mad, angry,
†cross, †hot

That kid made me mad.

308
sad, morose

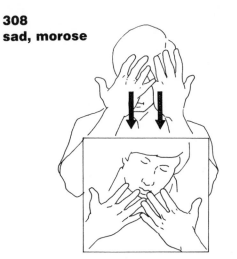

I believe you are sad today.

309
I love you

I love you.

310
love

Love makes us happy.

311
†after, chase

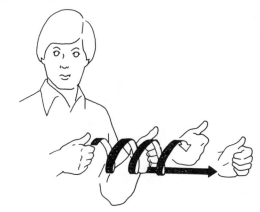

The boy chased the cat.

312
†after (succession)

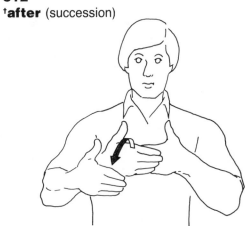

What day is after tomorrow?

313
†after, finish,
†over, †complete,
†had, †through

See me after work.

**314
car, *drive,
*bus, *truck**

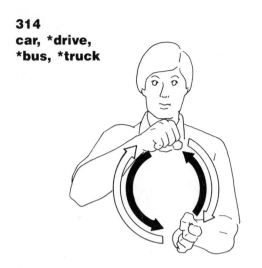

They love your yellow car.

**315
gasoline**

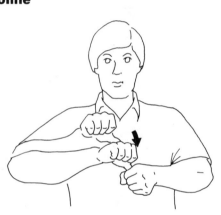

I believe you need gasoline.

Practice Sentences

			problems
			295

		made	before
		290	299

	kid	next	after
	297	303	312
			after
			311
		next	over
		302	313

no	one	make	problem
110	189	291	296

			before
			299

			made
			291

		talk	after
		194	313
			next
			303

			next to
			305
		before	left
		299	181
		before	leave
		301	181

1. Dad is teasing Mike again.

2. I can't understand a few problems.

3. I believe I love you *more* and *more*.

4. They made him mad before he came here.

5. Many *of* the ugly *dolls* were *thrown* in the box.

6. That kid is next, after you.

7. I think the police are after you.

8. The next *thing* I knew, it was over.

9. No one can make him *solve* his problem.

10. I believe he was *standing* in front of the car.

11. My grandmother knew it before I *did*.

12. *Do* you really like *living* beside your mother?

13. He was sad because they made him turn off the TV.

14. *Did* you *put* gasoline in the car?

15. Can we talk after we eat tonight?

16. When my sister is finished, you are next.

17. Her dog *looks* sad *most of the* time.

18. I believe you *sit* next to me in school.

19. She was really angry before she left.

20. They all *stood* before the group *refusing to* leave.

Mind Ticklers

Make the sign _____ | *and think about . . .*

Make the sign	and think about . . .
pretty 288	outlining the face
ugly 289	a distorted face
make 290	putting something together with the hands
many 292	all your fingers as representing a large quantity
few, several 293	counting one, two, three, four, and five
kid, child 297	a kid wiping a runny nose
before 299	the area in front of a stationary point
before, past 300	time that is behind you
before, in front of 301	something appearing in front of you
next 302	moving over one object to become next
next, turn 303	the thumb as the first person and the index finger as the second or third person in a sequence
turn off, turn on 304	the natural gesture of turning something on or off
beside, next to 305	something being beside the body
believe 306	holding on to something that you think
mad 307	the face wrinkling in anger
sad, morose 308	putting the head down in dejection
I love you 309	combining *i*, *l*, and *y* handshapes
love 310	hugging the person you love
after, chase 311	one person chasing another
after 312	the area in back of a stationary point
after, finish 313	dropping what was in the hands
car 314	the natural gesture of driving
gasoline 315	putting the gasoline nozzle into a gas tank

Vocabulary

pretty, beautiful, lovely	kidding, tease	mad, angry, cross, hot
	before	sad, morose
ugly	before, past, ago	I love you
make, create, *produce, form	before, in front of, confront, face	love
make, force		after, chase
many	next	after
few, several	next, turn	after, finish, over
again, over	turn off, turn on	car, *drive, *bus, *truck
problem	beside, next to	gasoline
problem, difficult	believe	
kid, child		

Additional Signs and Notes

Lesson 11

**316
week**

See me again in two weeks.

**317
†next week**

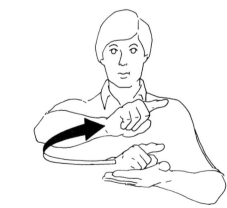

Please see me next week.

**318
last week**

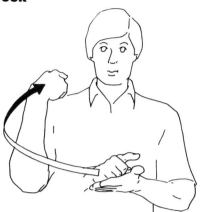

Last week it was cold.

**319
month**

They will work next month.

**320
monthly**

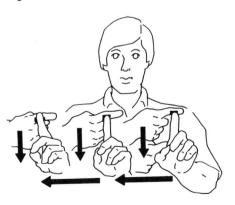

Try *to* do that monthly.

**321
year**

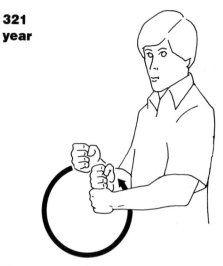

They were mad all year.

**322
†next year**

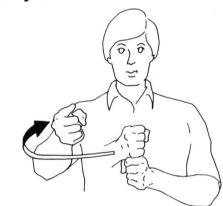

Next year will be a better year.

**323
last year**

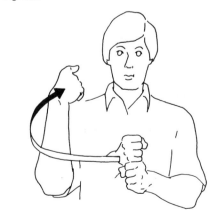

Last year was a good year.

119

324
*world (year),
*universe,
*international

The world has a few problems.

325
†complete, full,
†fill, †total

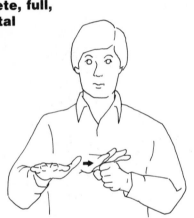

You have one full year.

326
complete,
finish,
already, done

Will you complete the work?

327
enough, plenty,
sufficient

One year is enough time.

328
†play, †act, drama

The play lasted six years.

329
†play

My brother is outside playing.

330
†through,
passage

I drive through here monthly.

331
†through,
finish, did

She was through in a month.

332
new, †original

Today is a new day.

333
interest,
interesting

The new play is interesting.

334
bored, †dry

The play was boring.

335
†*part (some), **piece**

Which part was the best?

121

336
†put, †place

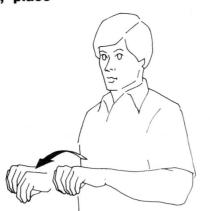

Put that there for me.

337
†place,
position,
†location

That place is interesting.

338
†ask, request

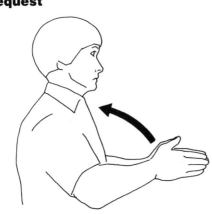

Ask for part *of* your money now.

339
†ask, question,
†quiz

Why ask him for that?

340
†word

That is *an* interesting word.

341
vocabulary

Is your vocabulary good?

122

342
want, ⁺need,
⁺wish

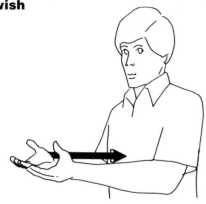

What *do* you want *to* ask him?

343
don't want

They don't want *to* work now.

Practice Sentences

		complete 326	1. We have eight full weeks *to* complete the work.
		kid 297	2. They don't want your kid playing here.
did 331	**ask** 339	**mean** 234	3. Did you ask what that word means?
		play 328	4. My sister said the play was boring.
		through 330	5. They drive through the new section monthly.
		complete 326	6. Last week we completed the new book.
		through 331	7. I am through putting that where you want it.
			8. How can we *improve* our vocabularies?
			9. My brother has a *very* interesting position.
		ask 338, 339	10. Please ask me that again next week.
			11. Last year was good; next year will be better.
		did 331	12. Which year did you *travel around* the world?
		time 121	13. One year was not enough time *to* do the *project*.
		ask 338	14. *Remember*, tomorrow ask for more money.
		play 328	15. *Only* parts *of* the play were interesting.
		act 284	16. My sister doesn't want *to* act.
	next 302	**through** 330	17. Next month we will go through the *museum*.
	did 331	**get** 128	18. Did your father get mad last week?
			19. Last year there was not enough money.
			20. Her new vocabulary is interesting.

Mind Ticklers

Make the sign _____	and think about . . .
week 316	seven days across a calendar
next week 317	a week in the future
last week 318	a week in the past
year 321	the earth revolving around the sun
next year 322	a year in the future
last year 323	a year in the past
*world 324	making the sign for *year* with a *w* handshape
complete, full 325	liquid running down the arm from a full cup
enough 327	leveling off a specific measure
through, passage 330	passing between two objects
bored 334	having your nose to the grindstone
*part 335	making the sign for *some* with a *p* handshape
put, place 336	putting something down
place, position 337	drawing the boundaries of a place
ask, request 338	praying or pleading for something that you desire
ask, question 339	drawing a question mark in the air
word 340	the approximate length of a word
vocabulary 341	making the sign for *word* with a *v* handshape
want 342	pulling something that you desire towards you
don't want 343	holding something and then rejecting or dropping it

Vocabulary

week	complete, finish,	bored, dry
next week	already, done	*part, piece
last week		put, place
month	enough, plenty, sufficient	place, position, location
monthly	play, act, drama	
year		ask, request, quiz
next year	play	
last year	through, passage	ask, question
*world, *universe, *international	through, finish, did	word
		vocabulary
complete, full, total	new, original	want, need, wish
	interest, interesting	don't want

Additional Signs and Notes

Lesson 12

344
while, during

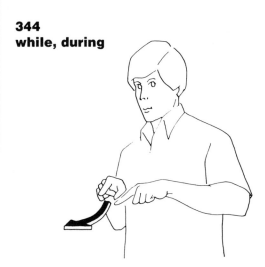

I get bored while waiting.

345
everyday, daily,
every day

I have classes every day.

**346
listen**

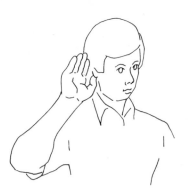

Listen while he tells you.

**347
hear, *sound**

They hear him every day.

**348
speech,
speechread,
lipread**

Can you speechread me?

**349
hard of hearing**

Who is hard of hearing?

**350
hearing impaired**

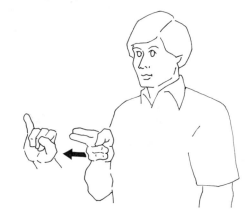

They are not hearing impaired.

**351
hearing aid,
aid**

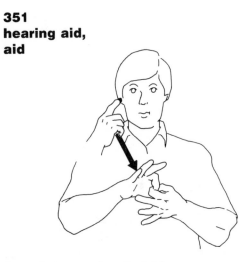

I can hear your hearing aid.

128

352
hearing (person)

Are you a hearing person?

353
deaf

I am deaf.

354
†**look for,**
search, †**hunt**

Look for your hearing aid.

355
†**look,**
look at,
watch, observe

Look and listen daily.

356
†**look,** †**appear,**
appearance,
†**face**

Why *do* you look bored?

357
under, beneath,
†**below**

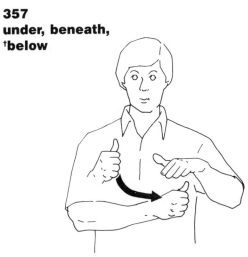

We found the aid under the bed.

358
**†below, under,
less than**

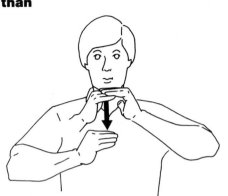

That is less than I have.

359
**increase, †gain,
†add, †jump,
†raise**

Will it increase next year?

360
*less (reduce),
*least

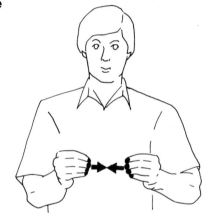

It will be less next year.

361
more

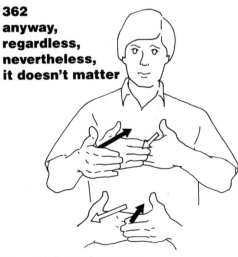

They need more time.

362
**anyway,
regardless,
nevertheless,
it doesn't matter**

He can't lipread anyway.

363
each, every

Every deaf person watched the show.

364
everything

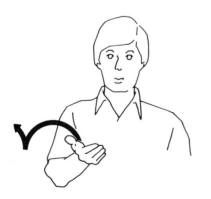

Everything is increasing.

365
everyone

Is everyone under the tree?

366
obey, †mind

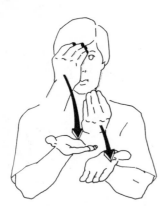

Please mind the police officer.

367
think, †mind,
wonder

Do you have an idea in mind?

368
†mind, complain,
object

I don't mind waiting for you.

Practice Sentences

1. Father, listen *to* your daughter's vocabulary.

2. Everyone thought he was deaf.

3. Everything will be *fine* regardless *of* what happens.

4. My sister is looking for her hearing aid.

5. Please write every day while I am *gone*.

6. That hard of hearing person speechreads well.

7. I think my dog will obey you.

8. *Do* you mind *if* I look at your hearing aid?

9. I think each person wanted more money.

10. *Instead of an* increase, you can expect less.

11. Tell the hearing person *to* search for it later.

12. Did you put the *gift* under the tree?

13. The *fine* was less than I expected.

14. I heard something under the house.

15. Each person here will listen to everything said.

16. Did you put the mirror below the window?

17. I think she can buy it below *cost*.

18. He is hard of hearing; she is deaf.

19. Listen, can you hear it better now?

20. His mind is not like it was before.

Mind Ticklers

Make the sign _____	*and think about . . .*
everyday, daily, every day 345	repeating the sign for tomorrow
listen 346	cupping your ear to help you listen better
hear 347	pointing to the ear
speech, speechread 348	reading lips with the eyes
hard of hearing 349	using an *h* handshape to indicate the abbreviation for *h*ard of *h*earing
hearing impaired 350	using *h* and *i* handshapes as an abbreviation for *h*earing *i*mpaired
hearing aid 351	the earmold of a hearing aid
hearing person 352	the idea that a hearing person can speak
deaf 353	the ears being closed to sound
look for 354	the French word *chercher*, which means *to search*
look, look at 355	the eyes swinging outward to look
look, appear 356	showing what the face looks like
under, beneath 357	putting one object under another
below, less than 358	showing that something is below the average
increase, gain 359	building or adding onto something
less 360	a reduced amount
more 361	adding one amount to another
obey, mind 366	putting the hands out to indicate respect

Vocabulary

while, during	deaf	more
everyday, daily, every day	look for, search, hunt	anyway, regardless, nevertheless
listen	look, look at, watch, observe	each, every
hear, *sound	look, appear, appearance, face	everything
speech, speechread, lipread		everyone
hard of hearing	under, beneath, below	obey, mind
hearing impaired	below, under, less than	think, mind, wonder
hearing aid, aid	increase, gain, jump, raise	mind, complain, object
hearing	*less, *least	

Additional Signs and Notes

Lesson 13

**369
begin, start,
commence**

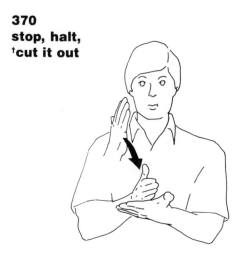

School will begin today.

**370
stop, halt,
†cut it out**

Stop complaining *about* everything.

371
heavy

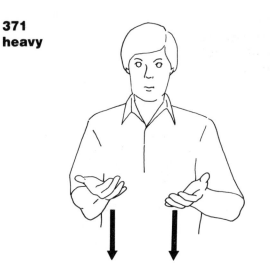

The old table is heavy.

372
†light (weight)

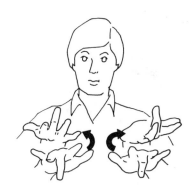

The new furniture is light.

373
†light, bulb

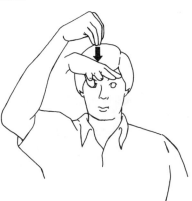

Please turn off the light.

374
bring

Bring your hearing aid.

375
†carry

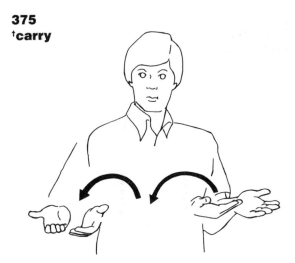

Carry everything you can.

376
†move, †motion

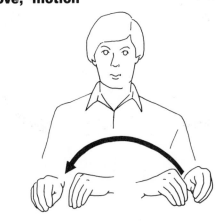

She moved the furniture again.

377
†give, †hand, †grant

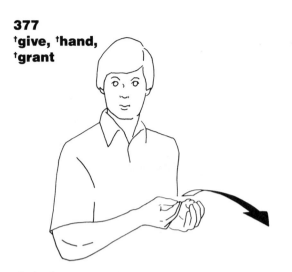

A deaf man gave it *to* her.

378
†give up, †drop, quit

She had to give up playing.

379
surrender, †give up

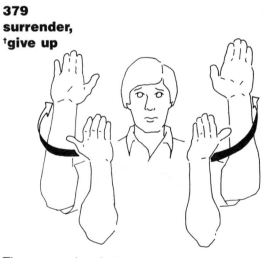

They surrendered *at* noon.

380
obvious, clear, †bright, †light, light color

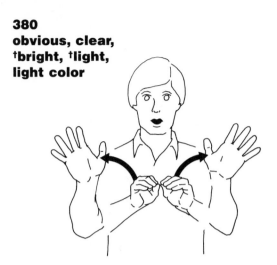

It was obvious that they gave up.

381
†bright, clever, gifted, intelligent

Everything he says is clever.

382
†bright, shiny, silver, †sharp

The floor was shiny.

383
silly, foolish,
fool, †cut up,
ridiculous

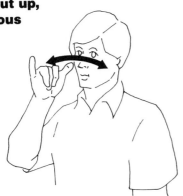

It was silly *to* start now.

384
funny,
humorous

She is silly, but funny.

385
fun

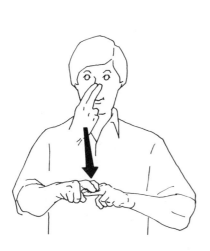

Every day is a fun day.

386
†prefer,
preference,
rather

They prefer playing *tennis* in the morning.

387
†little bit,
little

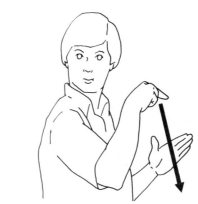

Bring a little bit *of* money.

388
kill, murder

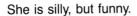

Stop; don't kill the cat.

389
feel, *emotions,
†sense

Tell me how you feel.

390
refuse, †won't,
†decline

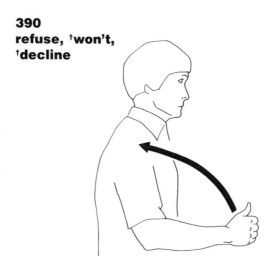

They refuse *to* surrender.

391
†point

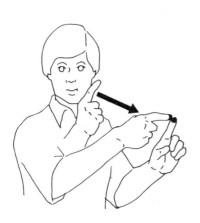

That's a silly point *to* make.

392
†order, †command

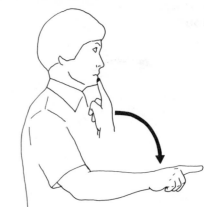

Who ordered us *to* stop?

393
dismiss, laid off,
†excused, †release

I refuse *to* dismiss him.

394
†excuse, pardon,
forgive

Excuse me, what's your point?

140

395
†clean

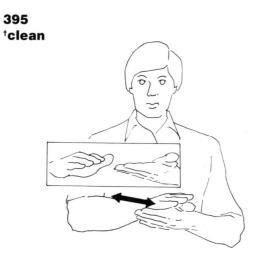

It's time *to* clean the lights.

396
nice

That was nice *of* you.

Practice Sentences

1. Before we could start, they stopped us.

2. They refused *to* obey the order *to* kill the *animals*.

3. It was silly *to* dismiss him for that.

4. That funny child is *very* bright.

5. It may *take* several men *to* carry the heavy table.

6. Why *did* they make you give up football?

7. You mean the whole army gave up?

8. Your nice sister cleaned the whole boat.

9. Excuse me, but I would like *to* make a point.

10. We hope your uncle feels a little bit better.

11. It was obvious they all had fun.

12. He cleaned the floor *until* it shined.

13. They couldn't give him enough *to* move again.

14. Don't forget *to* bring a good light.

15. He refused *to* excuse himself for the *mistake*.

16. She will bring a little bit *of* her light beer.

17. I stopped everything when the deaf man left.

18. We will start *at* eight o'clock and stop *at* eleven-thirty.

19. Regardless *of* what you say, I will look for it.

20. The hearing people are beginning *to* come daily now.

Mind Ticklers

Make the sign _____ | *and think about . . .*

Make the sign	and think about . . .
begin 369	inserting a key to start something
stop 370	putting up a barrier to stop something
heavy 371	having something heavy in your hands
light 372	something being so light it floats upwards
light, bulb 373	overhead lights shining
bring 374	having something in your hands
carry 375	carrying a heavy object
move 376	picking something up and putting it down elsewhere
give 377	handing something to someone
give up 378	throwing something down that you will not attempt again
surrender 379	putting both hands up in a gesture of defeat
obvious, clear 380	something opening up before your eyes
bright, shiny 382	rays shining up from something
funny, humor 384	clowns with funny noses
little bit 387	making a little motion
kill 388	stabbing a knife into something
feel 389	feelings being located around the heart
order, command 392	an order being stated and then written down
clean 395	brushing the floor with a broom
nice 396	something being smooth and neat

Vocabulary

begin, start, commence	surrender, give up	little bit, little
stop, halt, cut it out	obvious, clear, bright, light	kill, murder
heavy	bright, clever, gifted, intelligent	feel, *emotions, sense
light	bright, shiny, silver, sharp	refuse, won't, decline
light, bulb		point
bring	silly, foolish, fool, cut up, ridiculous	order, command
carry		dismiss, laid off, excused
move, motion	funny, humorous	excuse, pardon, forgive
give, hand, grant	fun	clean
give up, drop, quit	prefer, preference, rather	nice

Additional Signs and Notes

144

Lesson 14

397
a lot, much,
amount

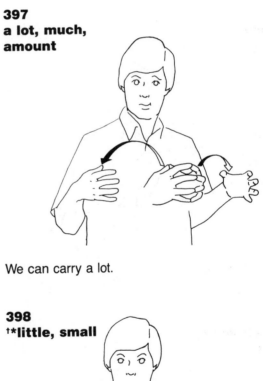

We can carry a lot.

398
†*little, small

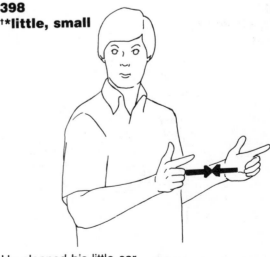

He cleaned his little car.

**399
big, huge**

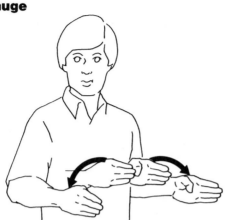

It was a big house *to* clean.

**400
†stand**

Don't stand here a long time.

**401
sit, sit down,
seat**

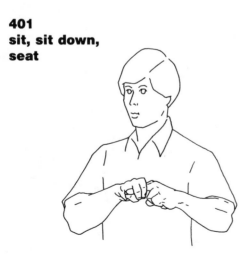

Sit down for a little bit.

**402
get up,
†stand up**

Why *do* you refuse *to* get up?

**403
great,
wonderful,
marvelous,
*fantastic**

What a great idea!

**404
*great** (a lot),
***big**

He is in great trouble with his father.

405
†fine, cost,
†charge, tax

The fine was $35.

406
†fine, well

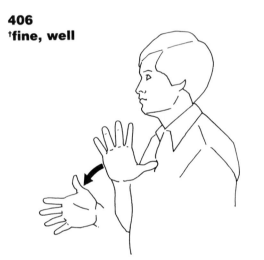

You look fine today.

407
don't care,
†don't mind

They don't care where you stand.

408
don't believe,
†doubt,
disbelieve

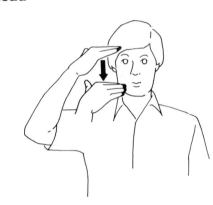

I don't believe I said that.

409
†head

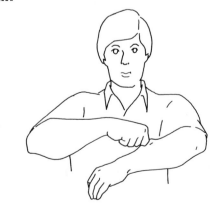

My head is better now.

410
skin

Your skin looks yellow.

147

411
arm

How long is your arm?

412
mouth

Is her mouth red?

413
teeth

She has pretty teeth.

414
†hand

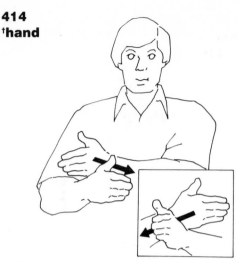

Grandfather has big hands.

415
hair

What nice red hair you have.

416
eye

Yes, I have blue eyes.

417
heart

Her heart is fine now.

418
†back

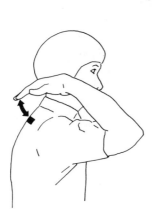

My back feels marvelous now.

419
voice

He has a fantastic voice!

420
†hard, difficult, problem

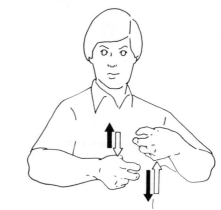

It is hard *to* think now.

421
†hard

Your head is really hard.

422
early

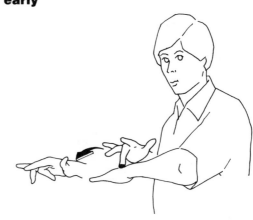

We arrived early yesterday.

423
ready

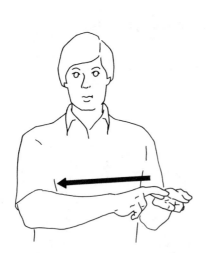

Are you ready *to* get up?

424
almost, †about

The baby can almost stand up.

425
big, †tall

My son is really big.

426
small, †little

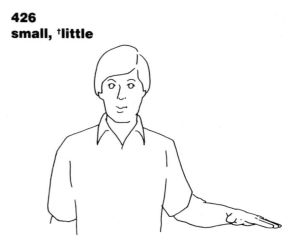

That girl is not small.

150

Practice Sentences

speech
195

fine
405

fine
406

hard
421

great
404

gave　**problem**
377　296

this
44

little
387

small
398

1. The hair on his arms and hands is red.

2. Are you ready for a wonderful speech?

3. We don't care how much the fine is.

4. Sit down; don't stand in front of us.

5. Her mouth and teeth are fine now.

6. I don't believe he almost got up *to fight* again.

7. Her yellow hair and blue eyes are beautiful.

8. They said he had a hard head.

9. Her great voice *frightened* the children.

10. His bad heart gave him problems.

11. He *hurt* his back first and his head later.

12. The big house was cleaned earlier this month.

13. All the children have beautiful white teeth.

14. My brother had a lot *of* difficulty in school.

15. How much *did* he charge for *fixing* the car?

16. What is that on your mouth and teeth?

17. Will you be ready *to* go *at* eleven o'clock?

18. Her aunt had a little money with her.

19. I would like a small piece *of* pie.

20. They don't care when we finish.

151

Mind Ticklers

Make the sign _____ | *and think about . . .*

QUANTITIES:				
	a lot	**much**	**little**	gesturing the size of something
	397	397	398	
	small	**big**	**huge**	
	398	399	399	
			stand	the legs being in a standing position
			400	
		sit, sit down		the legs being draped over a chair
		401		
		get up, stand up		the legs moving from a reclining position to a standing position
		402		
		don't care		not being interested in putting your nose into something
		407		

BODY PARTS:				
	head	**skin**	**arm**	pointing to the different body parts
	409	410	411	
mouth	**teeth**	**hands**	**hair**	
412	413	414	415	
	eye	**heart**	**back**	
	416	417	418	
			voice	sound coming from the voice box and out the mouth
			419	
			hard	knuckles tapping on something hard
			421	
			ready	making the sign for *plan* with *r* handshapes
			423	

HEIGHT:	**big**	**tall**	**small**	**little**	gesturing the height of something
	425	425	426	426	

Vocabulary

a lot, much	don't care, don't mind	heart
*little, small		back
big, huge	don't believe, doubt, disbelieve	voice
stand		hard, difficult, problem
	head	
sit, sit down	skin	hard
get up, stand up	arm	early
wonderful, great, marvelous, *fantastic	mouth	ready
	teeth	almost, about
*great, *big	hand, hands	big, tall
fine, cost, charge, tax	hair	small, little
fine, well	eye	

Additional Signs and Notes

Lesson 15

**427
sometimes,
†once in a while,
occasionally**

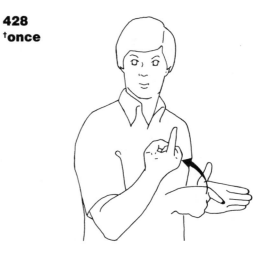

Sometimes my back is fine.

**428
†once**

She was almost fined once.

429
since,
†has been,
up to now,
all along

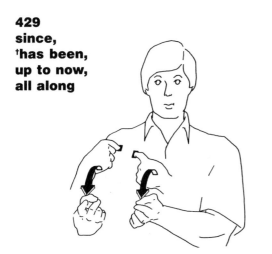

He has been here nine years.

430
snow

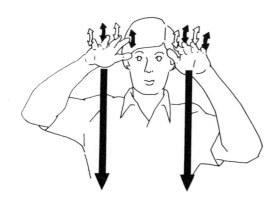

It snows here once in a while.

431
rain

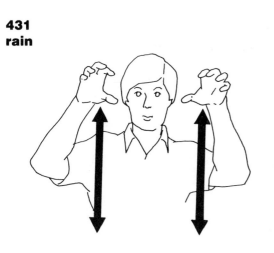

It rains there all the time.

432
†fire, †cut, expel

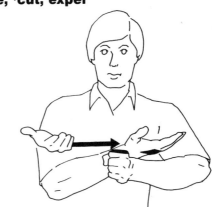

They had to fire more people.

433
†cut, scissors, cut out

Please cut this for me.

434
†cut (knife)

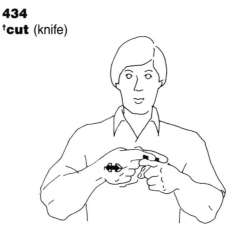

This is hard; I can't cut it.

155

435
†cut, †miss,
absent, †gone

She cut class again.

436
send, *refer

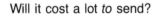

Will it cost a lot *to* send?

437
paper

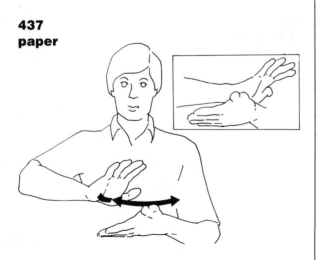

Please cut the paper once.

438
most

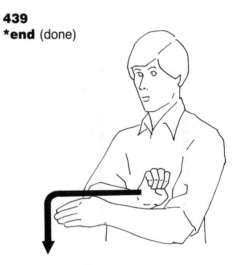

I have most *of* the paper.

439
***end** (done)

Is this the end?

440
†course, †subject, lesson

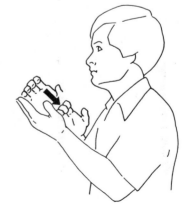

She cut her *favorite* course.

156

441
†check, check off

My paper has more checks.

442
†check (money)

Please send her check.

443
**†check,
investigate,
inspect,
†look over**

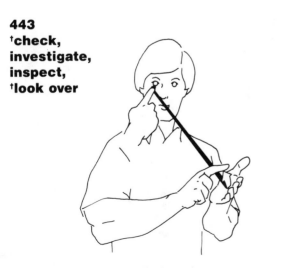

The police checked the house.

444
**†correct,
criticize,
cancel,
call off, †check**

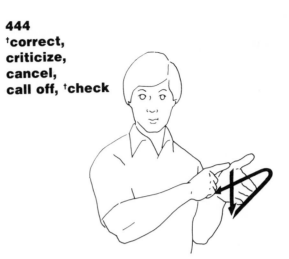

Yes, I corrected your papers.

445
both

Both people were fired.

446
**live, life,
*address**

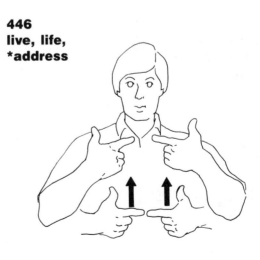

He lived here for two years.

447
together

My dad and I live together.

448
†run away,
escape, flee,
take off, run off

We ran away together.

449
†run, control,
manage, †direct,
govern, †charge,
†rule

I will run the investigation.

450
†run, jog

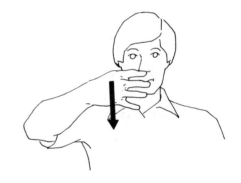

We all run every morning.

451
†run (nose)

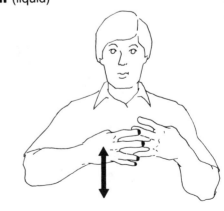

My nose is running again.

452
†run (liquid)

I hear *water* running.

453
**†run, compete,
contest, race**

Will everyone run today?

454
**†run off,
duplicate,
crank, †turn**

Please run off 200 papers.

Practice Sentences

	jog 450	1. Both *of* my parents jog every day.
	time 120	2. Sometimes it snows at *strange* times.
	check 442	3. My sister sent me a bad check.
	run off 454	4. We have eleven different papers *to* run off.
		5. My *history* course ends next week on *Wednesday*.
	checks 441	6. Did you see all the checks on my paper?
		7. My father was never fired *from* his work.
	has been 429	8. Her grandmother has been living here for years.
	miss 435	9. We missed class *because of* the rain.
cut 434	**hard** 421	10. How can we cut this hard *apple* in half?
little 426	**cut** 433	11. The little girl was cutting out paper *dolls*.
big 425	**run** 453	12. Our big son runs in *marathons*.
		13. Most *of* our classes were cancelled again.
	check 443	14. I will try *to* check that address tomorrow.
	run 451	15. My child's nose is always running.
left 182	**run** 452	16. He left the *water* running for two days.
run 449	**this** 54	17. Who is supposed to be running this place?
		18. He will correct both papers in *an* hour.
	long 275	19. How long ago since you saw your parents?
		20. Father doesn't compete *very often* anymore.

160

Mind Ticklers

Make the sign _____ | *and think about . . .*

sometimes 427	repeating the sign for *once*
once 428	something happening just one time
since, has been 429	moving from a point in time in the past to the present
snow 430	snow flakes floating down
rain 431	raindrops falling
fired, cut 432	cutting off someone's hold on something
cut, scissors 433	cutting with a pair of scissors
cut (knife) 434	slicing something with a knife
cut, miss 435	missing one out of the five school days
paper 437	paper running through a machine
course 440	the lessons in a book
check, check off 441	making a check mark on a paper
check (money) 442	the shape and size of a check
check, investigate 443	looking at something closely
correct 444	putting an *X* on something
both 445	putting two things together
run, control 449	taking the reins in hand and taking control
run (nose) 451	having a runny nose
run (liquid) 452	water coming out of a faucet
run, compete 453	running against someone in a race
run off 454	turning the crank of a duplicating machine

Vocabulary

sometimes,
once in a while,
occasionally

once

since.
has been,
up to now,
all along

snow

rain

fire, cut, expel

cut, scissors,
cut out

cut

cut, miss,
absent, gone

send, *refer

paper

most

*end

course, subject,
lesson

check, check off

check

check,
investigate,
inspect,
look over

correct, criticize,
cancel, call off,
check

both

live, life,
*address

together

run away,
escape, flee,
take off, run off

run, control,
manage, direct,
govern

run, jog

run (nose)

run (liquid)

run, compete,
contest, race

run off,
duplicate, crank,
turn

Additional Signs and Notes

Lesson 16

455
water

Most *of* the water is cold.

456
wine

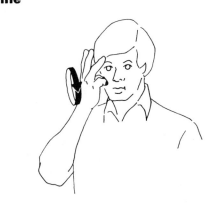

The red wine is like water.

**457
beer**

I like both beer and wine.

**458
liquor,
whiskey**

All the liquor is *at* home.

**459
†take,
remove**

You take the liquor and beer.

**460
†take,
take up**

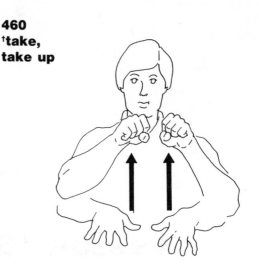

I will take a good course.

**461
†sentence,
caption,
*language**

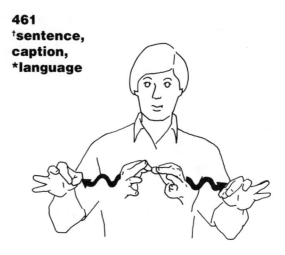

Correct those sentences now.

**462
story**

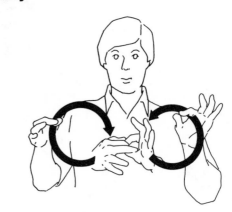

This is the story I heard.

164

463
*language (sentence)

She loves *to study* different languages.

464
†rest, relax

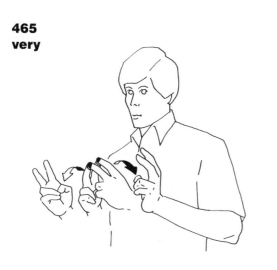

White wine makes us relax.

465
very

That was a very good story.

466
until

Don't go until you rest.

467
asleep, sleep

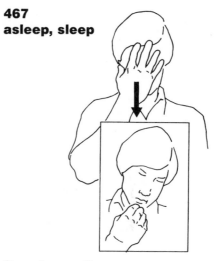

Sleep here until noon.

468
awake, wake up

Is your brother awake?

**469
surprise**

What a very nice surprise!

**470
hungry, starve**

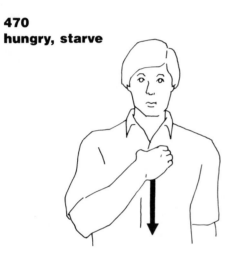

He is hungry when he wakes up.

**471
wish, desire,
†long for**

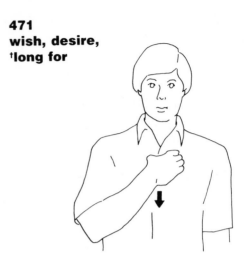

How long *do* you wish *to* sleep?

**472
preach,
minister,
preacher**

I wish a minister were here.

**473
pray**

Pray for all *of* us.

474
Jesus

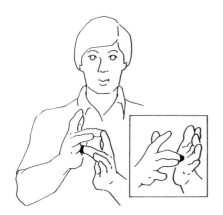

Jesus prayed for the people.

475
God

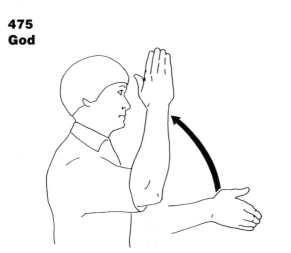

She preached God's words.

476
heaven

He wished *to* go to heaven.

477
Bible (Christian)

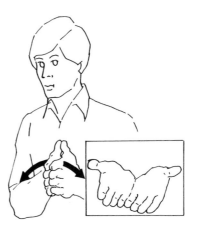

Children enjoy Bible stories.

478
temple

The temple is very old.

480
Jewish

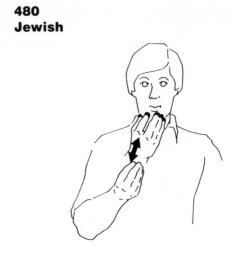

The Jewish temple is open.

479
church

Is your church closed today?

481
religion

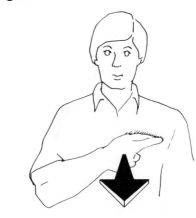

He took up a new religion.

Practice Sentences

take
459

had to   **take**
277   460

take up
460

watch
207

play
329

1. Our church has wine during *communion*.

2. People pray in churches and temples.

3. The minister preached *about* God and Jesus.

4. Please take all the beer and wine with you.

5. They drank a lot *of* whiskey and went *to* sleep.

6. Which sentence do you wish *to remove?*

7. Some Jewish people are good *at* telling a story.

8. Religion is very *important to* our families.

9. Our baby *always* wakes up hungry.

10. He preached *from* the Bible every Sunday.

11. We had to take a language in college.

12. You should rest here until tomorrow.

13. He told the children *about* heaven.

14. Were you surprised the whiskey was *gone?*

15. Her religious stories were enjoyable.

16. I wish we could take up *golf.*

17. Why *did* you put water in the beer?

18. Deaf people enjoy watching captioned TV.

19. The children are playing in the water.

20. They didn't surprise him until later.

Mind Ticklers

Make the sign —————	*and think about . . .*
water 455	water trickling down the chin
wine 456	the cheeks becoming red after drinking
beer 457	the cheeks becoming red after drinking
liquor 458	measuring a drink with your fingers
take, remove 459	reaching out and taking something
take, take up 460	beginning something new or taking up a project
sentence 461	stringing words together
story 462	stringing sentences together
*language 463	making the sign for *sentence* with *l* handshapes
asleep 467	closing the eyes and lowering the head
awake 468	opening the eyes
surprise 469	your eyes and face lighting up
hungry 470	the path food takes going down into the stomach
pray 473	folding the hands reverently
Jesus 474	nail holes in the hands
heaven 476	the vastness of heaven
Bible (Christian) 477	the sign for *Jesus* and the sign for *book*
Jewish 480	the goatee worn by some members of this religion
religion 481	religious feelings coming from the heart

Vocabulary

water	rest, relax	pray
wine	very	Jesus
beer	until	God
liquor, whiskey	asleep, sleep	heaven
take, remove	awake, wake up	Bible (Christian)
take, take up	surprise	temple
sentence, caption, *language	hungry, starve	church
	wish, desire, long for	Jewish
story		religion
*language	preach, minister, preacher	

Additional Signs and Notes

Lesson 17

482
store

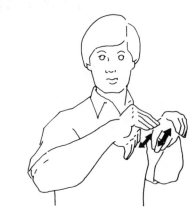

I think the store is open.

483
sell

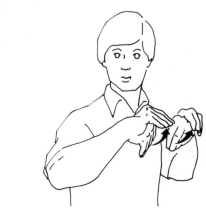

The store will not sell that.

484
pay

Can you pay for that today?

485
dollar

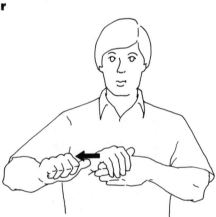

She has several dollars left.

486
money, *funds, *economy

The store made more money this year than last year.

487
buy

He is eager *to* buy more.

488
expensive, costly

That Bible is very expensive.

489
spend, waste

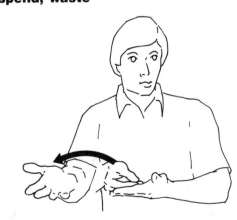

Don't waste your money.

490
shopping

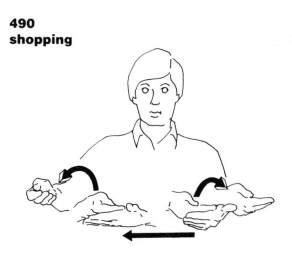

Go shopping with me later.

491
shoes, *boots

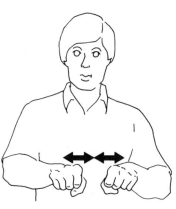

Those blue shoes are pretty.

492
skirt

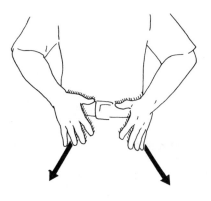

Where is my purple skirt?

493
socks

I can't find two socks.

494
pants

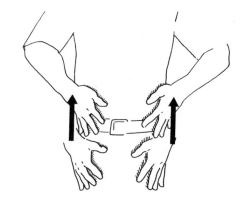

His pants are very old.

495
necktie, †tie

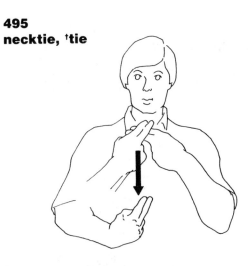

Surprise him with a tie.

496
clothes,
†dress (verb)

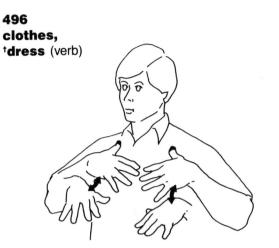

We buy clothes *at* that store.

497
†dress (noun)

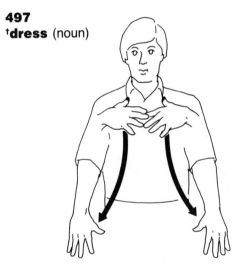

She wishes her dress were new.

498
hat, cap

He bought several hats.

499
pocketbook,
purse,
suitcase

What *an* expensive purse!

500
allow,
†*permit, *let

Allow me *to* buy that please.

501
†*let (allow),
***permit**

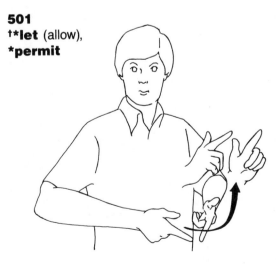

Don't let us waste any more time.

502
read,
†go through

Please read the Bible to me.

503
dance

Who paid for this dance?

504
party

The party costs ten dollars.

505
walk, †step

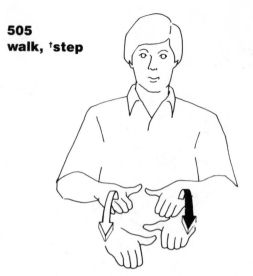

Walk to the store with me.

506
always, †ever

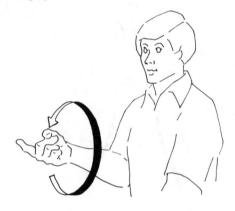

They always spend a lot.

507
†against,
sue, oppose

Are you opposed to paying them?

176

508
far

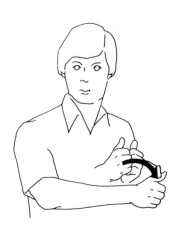

How far is the store?

509
ahead

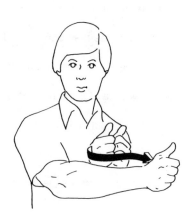

Allow me *to* walk ahead.

Practice Sentences

take
460

have
56

dress
497

1. I am going to the store later.

2. She always takes walks with a hat on.

3. We cannot read ahead in our story.

4. That store sells very expensive clothes.

5. We went to the party in new dresses.

6. Don't dance in here with your hat on.

7. Please, let me carry your suitcase.

8. Are you allowed *to wear* pants in school?

9. All the boys are expected *to* have on neckties.

10. We bought new shoes and socks for the baby.

11. Mom and my sister went shopping for skirts.

12. Father spent less than $55 yesterday.

13. *Do* you have any money *to* buy that?

14. How will you pay for the hat and shoes?

15. She *wore* a beautiful red and white dress.

16. Let me read several sentences for you.

17. His new blue car was expensive; it cost *about* $11,000.

18. They are against shopping on Sunday.

19. He tries *to* buy *low* and sell *high.*

20. Mom's pocketbook is on the table.

Mind Ticklers

Make the sign _____ | *and think about . . .*

store 482	taking clothes off a rack and shaking them
sell 483	trying to push something to increase sales
pay 484	pushing money out of the hand
dollar 485	counting out dollar bills
money 486	money piling up in your hand
buy 487	taking money from your hand to give it to someone else
expensive 488	something that seems to make money fly away
spend, waste 489	throwing money away
shopping 490	giving out money in several different places where you shop
shoes 491	hitting your shoes together to knock off the dirt
skirt 492	the fullness of a skirt
socks 493	knitting socks
pants 494	pulling on a pair of pants
necktie, tie 495	tying a tie
dress 497	the outline of a dress
hat, cap 498	tipping your hat
pocketbook 499	carrying a pocketbook
read 502	the eyes scanning a page
dance 503	the fingers as feet and legs moving while dancing
party 504	making the sign for *play* with *p* handshapes
walk 505	putting one foot in front of the other
always 506	an unending circle
against 507	an object encountering a barrier
far 508	putting one hand out far from the other one
ahead 509	putting one hand ahead of the other

179

Vocabulary

store	skirt	read, go through
sell	socks	dance
pay	pants	party
dollar	necktie, tie	walk
money, *funds, *economy	clothes, dress	always, ever
buy	dress	against, sue, oppose
expensive, costly	hat, cap	far
spend, waste	pocketbook, purse, suitcase	ahead
shopping	allow, *permit, *let	
shoes, *boots	*let, *permit	

Additional Signs and Notes

Lesson 18

510
another,
other, *else

Is another person going?

511
***else** (another)

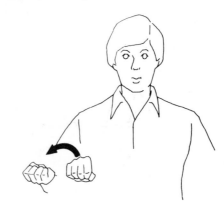

What else can you do?

512
†grow, †raise, grown

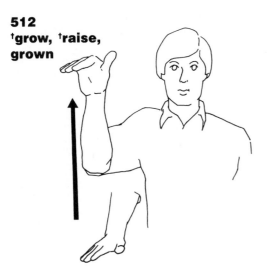
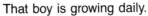

That boy is growing daily.

513
†grow, †raise, grown, †*plant (noun)

Will you grow flowers again?

514
lead, guide, †head

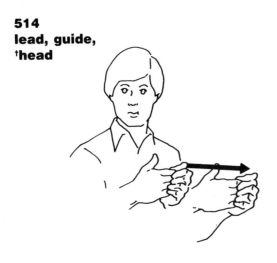

Will you lead us there?

515
boss, coach, captain, †head, officer

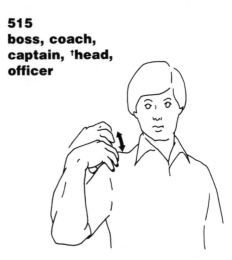

The boss wastes his money.

516
†hit, punch, beat, †strike

I am against hitting people.

517
†hit, success, †finally, achievement, at last

The play was a real hit.

182

518
shoot, gun,
rifle, †hunt

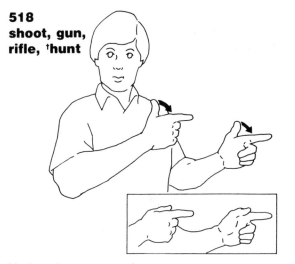

He bought an expensive gun.

519
†pull, †draw

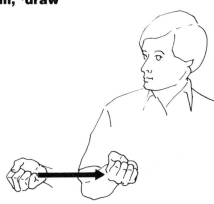

I pull my sister's *wagon* with my bike.

520
late, not yet,
yet, †have not

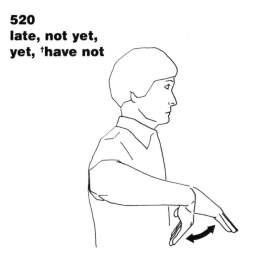

Yes, she is late again.

521
go ahead,
get along,
along, proceed,
†go on

Go ahead, tell the coach.

522
towards, approach,
toward

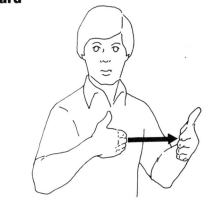

Is he walking towards her?

523
test, exam,
examination,
†quiz

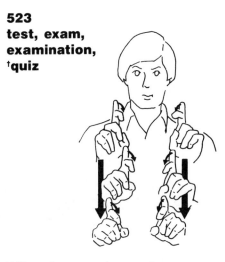

Will we have another test?

183

524
†show, movie, film

We have not seen that show.

525
†show, *illustrate, *represent, †reveal, *demonstrate

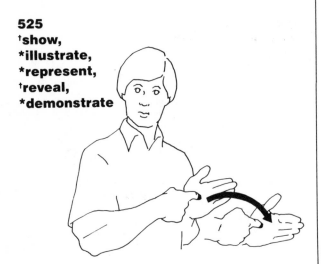

Let me show you something.

526
***example** (show), ***symbol**

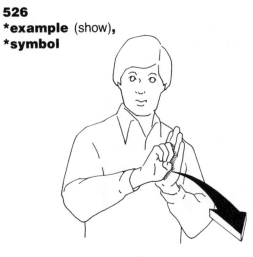

Here are several examples.

527
confuse, mix up, mix, †disturb

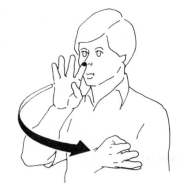

I think the boss is confused.

528
ignore, neglect

Why *do* they ignore him?

529
†about, around, approximate

Tell me about our first guide.

184

530
†around,
vicinity,
near, †about

Do you live around here?

531
†around, round

Run around the house with me.

532
catch, get

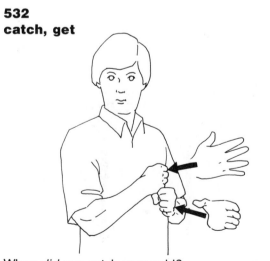

When *did* you catch your cold?

533
†catch,
apprehend,
arrest

You will never catch him now.

534
catch

See *if* you can catch this.

535
†cover, blanket

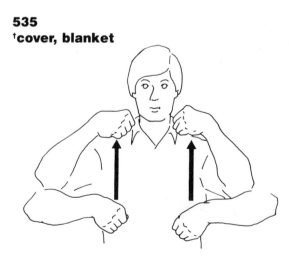

You need another blanket.

536
†cover, go over

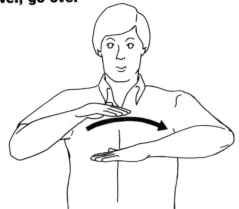

Can you cover that idea later?

537
†cover up,
vague,
unclear, obscure

Don't cover up your *mistakes*.

538
street, *road,
***path, *way,**
†trail

Is your street around here?

539
***way** (street),
procedure,
***method, †course**

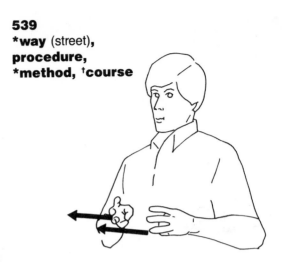

Which way is the best?

540
book

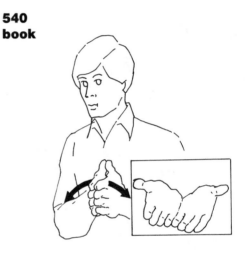

Let me show you my book.

541
stay, remain

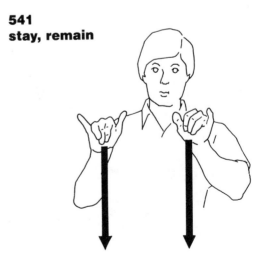

Please stay around here.

186

Practice Sentences

	around 530	1. Another friend *of* mine lives around here.
		2. *Do* you understand now *or* is it *still* vague?
		3. There was some mix-up about the test day.
show 525	**which** 143	4. Show us which street *to* walk on.
	show 524	5. Go ahead; we will see you *at* the show.
	grown 512	6. They have six grown children *at* home.
	around 530	7. I know that green book is around here.
grow 513	**this** 54	8. What else will you grow this year?
	head 515	9. She is the head *of* our association.
	catch 533	10. The police couldn't catch the *thief.*
play 328	**hit** 517	11. The play about Indians was a big hit.
caught 532	**cold** 215	12. He went outside while hot and caught a cold.
ran 450	**around** 531	13. He ran around the *track* until he became exhausted.
		14. Father neglected his guns, and they *rusted.*
		15. It is not *too* late *to* lead us to your house.
		16. Don't pull the car now; I'll tell you when.
	hit 516	17. You can stay, but don't hit me again.
	cover 535	18. She covered the baby with the blanket.
	catch 534	19. When she *throws* it, you catch it.
		20. She approached the dog *slowly,* but it fled.

187

Mind Ticklers

Make the sign _____	*and think about . . .*
another 510	pointing to someone else with your thumb
***else** 511	making the sign for *other* with an *e* handshape
grow 512	gesturing how much or high something has grown
grow 513	something growing up from the ground
lead 514	taking someone by the hand and leading or guiding them
boss 515	having epaulets on the shoulders to indicate rank
hit 516	hitting something with your fist
shoot 518	holding a gun or rifle
pull 519	the natural gesture of pulling something
late 520	being behind in time
go ahead 521	moving forward with someone
towards 522	moving towards a stationary point
test 523	a page full of questions
show, movie 524	a film going through sprockets
show 525	pointing to something in the hand you are going to show someone
***example** 526	making the sign for *show* with an *e* handshape
confuse 527	things being mixed up
ignore 528	turning your nose away from something
around 530	outlining an area
around 531	making a circular motion around something
catch 532	grabbing and bringing something to yourself
catch 533	grabbing hold of someone
catch 534	the natural gesture of catching a ball
cover 535	pulling up a blanket
cover up 537	rubbing something to make it unclear
street 538	the width of a street
book 540	opening the covers of a book
stay 541	holding something down with the hands

Vocabulary

another, other, *else	late, not yet, yet, have not	around, vicinity, near
*else	go ahead, get along, along, proceed	around, round
grow, raise, grown		catch, get
grow, raise, grown, *plant	toward(s), approach	catch, apprehend, arrest
lead, guide, head	test, exam, examination, quiz	catch
boss, coach, captain, head, officer	show, movie, film	cover, blanket
hit, punch, beat, strike	show, *illustrate, *represent, reveal, *demonstrate	cover, go over
		cover up, vague, unclear, obscure
hit, success, finally, achievement, at last	*example, *symbol	street, *road, *path, *way, trail
		*way, procedure, *method, course
shoot, gun, rifle, hunt	confuse, mix up, mix	book
pull	ignore, neglect	stay, remain
	about, around, approximate	

Additional Signs and Notes

189

Lesson 19

542
west, western

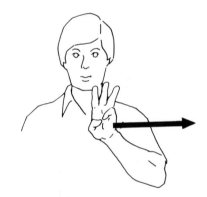

I lived in the West before.

543
east, eastern

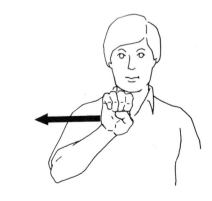

Now you live in the East.

544
north, northern

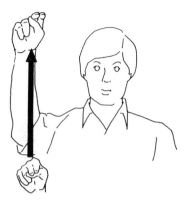

They caught him up North.

545
south, southern

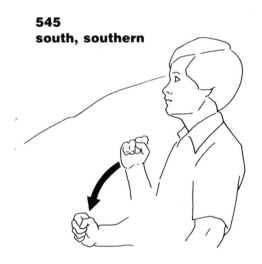

Everyone enjoys the South.

546
wide, expand,
broad, *general

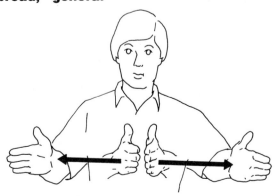

How wide is the blanket?

547
small, †short
***little, †reduce**

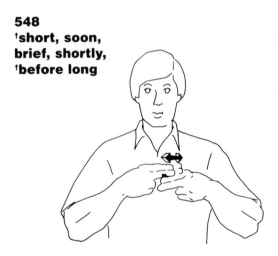

That blanket is *too* short.

548
†short, soon,
brief, shortly,
†before long

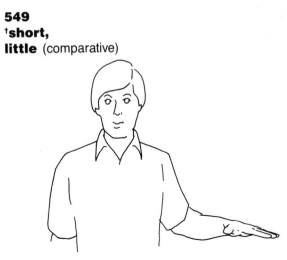

I can stay a very short time.

549
†short,
little (comparative)

I am short like my mother.

191

550
soft

The small cat is soft.

551
†line, major,
*field,
*profession,
†trade

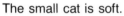

What is your line *of* work?

552
*field (line of work)

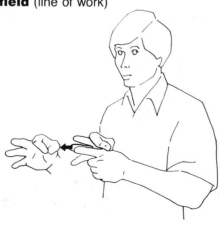

She doesn't like her field.

553
†line, string

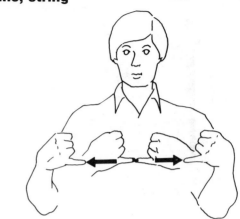

She put the clothes on the line.

554
hate, dislike

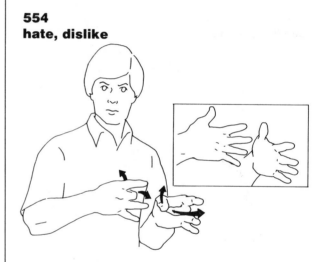

They hate staying here.

555
expression,
make faces

He *signs* with a lot of expression.

192

556
easy,
simple,
†light

The boss gave me an easy job.

557
box,
***room**

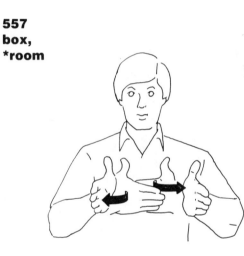

It's easy to make a small box.

558
awful, terrible, horrible,
danger, †ugly

What an awful expression!

559
†break

Don't break the string.

560
†appears, seems,
apparently

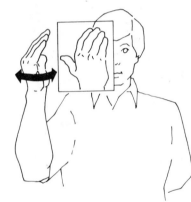

It appears we are late.

561
†appear,
†show up,
†come up

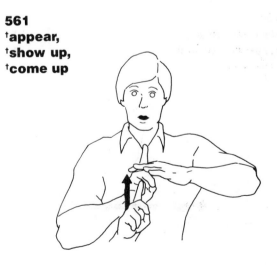

You didn't appear on time.

562
†appear, look,
appearance

He appears to be angry.

563
often

He often makes it look easy.

564
prepare, plan,
arrange, †in order,
organize

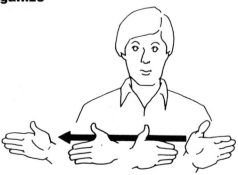

Will you prepare for class?

565
profit, benefit,
advantage, †gain

The store made a good profit.

566
cherish,
miserly,
stingy

She cherished his love.

567
revenge,
get back at

He had a desire for revenge.

**568
country, farm,
county, †land**

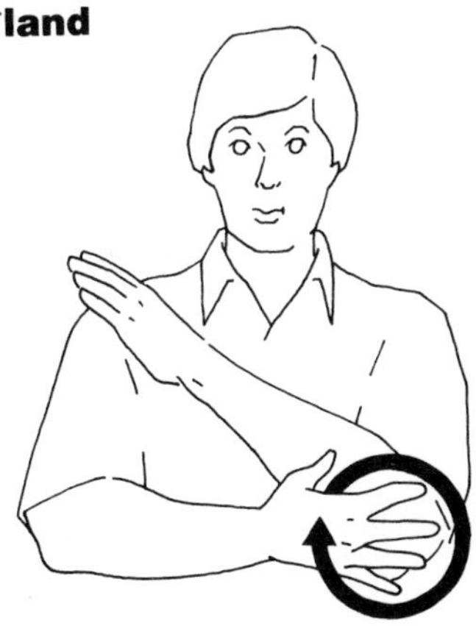

Country living is easy.

**569
depend,
†count on,
rely**

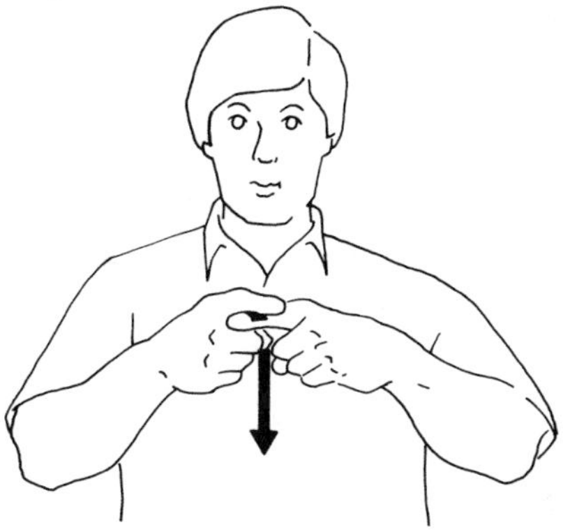

We depend on you *to* show up.

Practice Sentences

give up
378

line
551

shortly
548

short   **this**
547   54, 55

appears   **liked**
560   49

appear
561

finally   **got**
517   532

looks   **like**
562   174

counting on   **make**
564 or 569   290

took
460

this
54, 55

showed up   **left**
561   181

show up
561

short
549

1. She refused *to* give up something she cherished.

2. *Do* you know why he hates that line *of* work?

3. They will be going out west shortly.

4. We lived in the southern part *of Florida*.

5. I need a short piece of string for this box.

6. It appears her facial expressions are not liked.

7. How often *does* he appear *at* his grandmother's *to* eat?

8. It was awful, but he finally got his revenge.

9. He looks like he lives in the country.

10. She is counting on making a *quick* and easy profit.

11. While planning the party, we took a break every hour.

12. Why *did* your father move *from* the East *Coast*?

13. Her clothes always look soft and *smell* good.

14. That is a good field *to* start working in.

15. When he shows up, we can begin our planning.

16. Try *to* find a box wide enough for this book.

17. Apparently, he showed up early and left late.

18. Many young people showed up in western clothes.

19. If you clean the box, it might break.

20. She is very short for her age.

196

Mind Ticklers

Make the sign _____   *and think about . . .*

DIRECTIONS:	**west** 542	**east** 543	**north** 544	**south** 545

moving initialized handshapes in the appropriate direction

WIDTH:	**wide** 546	**small** 547

gesturing how wide, narrow, or small something is

short 549 — gesturing the height of something

soft 550 — feeling something soft

major 551 — moving in a specific direction

hate 554 — shooting arrows at something you dislike

expression 555 — changing the shape of the face for different expressions

box 557 — forming the outline of a box

awful 558 — something that causes your hair to stand on end

break 559 — the natural gesture of breaking a stick

appears 560 — a side-view reflection

appear 561 — a person popping up out of nowhere

appear 562 — drawing attention to the face so someone will notice how you look

often 563 — repeating the sign for again

prepare 564 — putting everything into its proper place

profit 565 — putting money into your pocket

revenge 567 — picking on someone

country 568 — farmers wearing the elbows of their shirts thin

depend 569 — putting a burden on someone else's shoulders

197

Vocabulary

west	*field	appear, look, appearance
east	line, string	
		often
north	hate, dislike	
		prepare, plan, arrange, in order, organize
south	expression, make faces	
wide, expand, broad, *general	easy, simple	
		profit, benefit, advantage, gain
small, short, *little	box, *room	
		cherish, miserly, stingy
short, shortly, soon, brief, before long	awful, terrible, horrible, danger	
	break	revenge, get back at
short, little	appears, seems, apparently	country, farm, county
soft		
line, major, *field, *profession, trade	appear, show up, come up	depend, count on, rely

Additional Signs and Notes

Lesson 20

570
Monday

Monday is in two days.

571
Tuesday

Tuesday is after Monday.

572
Wednesday

Will he show up on Wednesday?

573
Thursday

Thursday was *an* awful day.

574
Friday

Friday is the last work day.

575
Saturday

Saturday is our planning day.

576
Sunday

Sunday we go to church.

577
Easter

Easter Sunday is soon.

578
Christmas

Christmas was on Monday.

579
Valentine

Valentine's Day is tomorrow.

580
†step, walk,
†prints

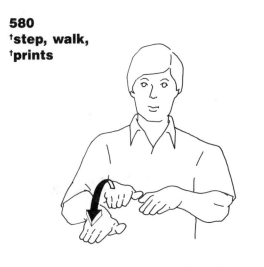

Don't step on the box.

581
steps

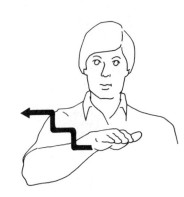

Our *front* steps are broken.

582
toilet,
bathroom

The toilet is up the steps.

583
stamp

I saw the new Christmas stamp.

584
letter

The letter is on the steps.

585
mail

No mail comes on Sunday.

586
†present,
†offer,
propose,
suggest,
***recommend,**
†motion,
†raise, †move

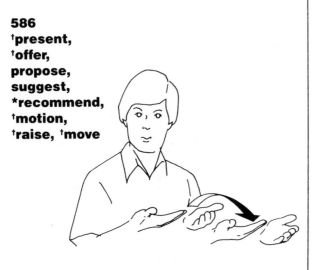

I have an idea *to* present.

587
†present,
introduce

I want *to* present my dad to you.

588
†present, gift

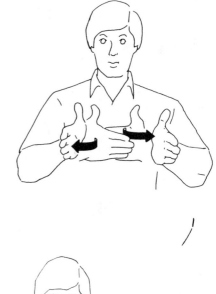

I got a Valentine present.

589
**†present,
now, this**

He isn't living in the present.

590
†present, here

Is everyone present now?

591
***environment,
*situation,
*circumstances**

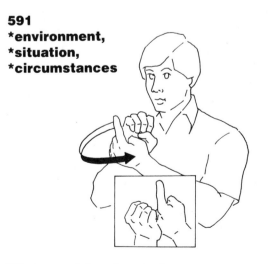

What *an* awful environment.

592
**dead, die,
death, †gone**

She died on Sunday.

593
system

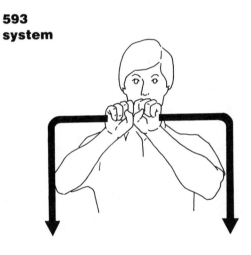

She proposed a better system.

594
behind

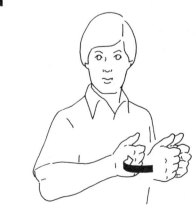

The gift is behind my bed.

595
bother, hinder,
annoy, †disturb

Who bothered us last night?

596
†associate,
mingle,
each other

We cannot associate with him.

597
tolerate, †bear,
endure, †patient,
†put up with,
†stand, †take

How can you tolerate him?

598
suffer, anguish

He didn't suffer before dying.

599
secret,
confidential,
private, †close

This new system is a secret.

600
protect,
defend, guard,
†save

I have to protect the system.

601
between

We kept the secret between us.

602
decide,
decision,
†figure out,
†judgment, †name,
†make up one's mind

When will you decide?

Practice Sentences

1. You must decide what kind *of* gift *to* buy.

2. Yes, next Monday is Valentine's Day.

3. Before you mail the letter, put three stamps on it.

4. All *of* our mail comes between Sunday and Thursday.

5. The bathroom is up the steps, then to the right.

6. Who will introduce your parents *at* the party?

7. She is really suffering in her present work.

8. I suggest we not buy Christmas presents.

9. She needs all *of* us *to* be present on Wednesday.

10. Father can't tolerate the new system at work.

11. They offered *to* protect him until death.

12. He stepped on the gift and broke it.

13. I am late *in* buying presents this year.

14. Easter Sunday the family will eat together.

15. We don't bother each other *so* we get along fine.

16. My brother is keeping his new system a secret.

17. *At* the present time, we are eleven hours behind *schedule*.

18. Where is your new bathroom?

19. They decided not *to* bother the environment.

20. I think my grandmother died in 1969.

21. Who will recommend him for that position?

22. Saturday's mail is on the black table.

23. We enjoy associating with different people.

24. No, you never introduced us before.

25. Don't bother us until next Saturday.

Mind Ticklers

Make the sign _____ | *and think about . . .*

DAYS OF THE WEEK: **Monday**   **Tuesday** | initializing the first letter of each day, except Thursday
570   571 | (an *h* handshape)

Wednesday   **Thursday**   **Friday**   **Saturday**
572   573   574   575

Make the sign	and think about . . .
Sunday 576	palm leaves for Easter Sunday
Easter 577	making the sign for *Sunday* with an *e* handshape
Christmas 578	the shape of one-half of a Christmas wreath
Valentine 579	the shape of a heart
steps 580	the configuration of a flight of steps
stamp 583	licking and putting a stamp on an envelope
letter 584	licking and putting a stamp on a letter
mail 585	repeating the sign for *letter*
offer 586	offering something in your hands to someone
introduce 587	bringing two people together
gift 588	giving something to someone
present 589	the area directly in front of the body
dead 592	the act of rolling over and dying
system 593	the structure of a system
behind 594	putting one object behind another
associate 596	people mingling together
tolerate 597	suffering without saying anything
secret 599	your lips being sealed
protect 600	throwing your hands up in front of yourself in self-defense
between 601	putting something between two objects

Vocabulary

Monday	letter	bother, hinder, annoy, disturb
Tuesday	mail	
Wednesday	present, offer, propose, suggest, *recommend, motion	associate, mingle, each other
Thursday		tolerate, bear, endure, patient, put up with
Friday		
Saturday	present, introduce	
Sunday		suffer, anguish
Easter	present, gift	
Christmas	present, now, this	secret, confidential, private
Valentine	present, here	protect, defend, guard, save
step, walk, prints	*environment, *situation, *circumstances	between
steps	dead, die, death	decide, decision, judgment, make up one's mind
toilet, bathroom	system	
stamp	behind	

Additional Signs and Notes

208

Lesson 21

603
animal

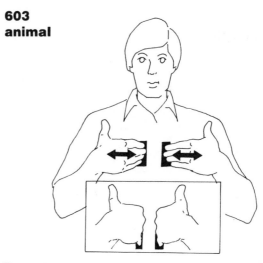

The animals are hungry.

604
insect, bug

That is a small insect.

605
deer

The deer live in the *woods.*

606
cow, cattle

Where are the cows?

607
donkey, mule

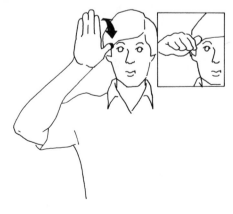

What color is the donkey?

608
horse

That horse is not very old.

609
wolf

The wolf was chasing the deer.

610
snake

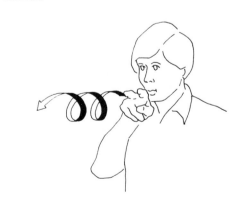

A snake is in that box.

210

611
chicken, bird

We will have chicken tonight.

612
duck

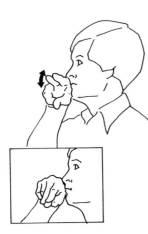

Why *do* you dislike duck?

613
rat

That was a big brown rat.

614
pig, hog

Where is his pig farm?

615
fox

The red fox is beautiful.

616
elephant

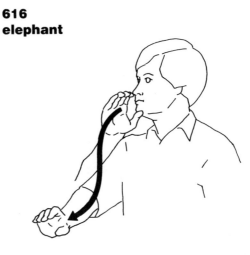

That elephant is very big.

617
turkey,
Thanksgiving

She shot several turkeys.

618
monkey

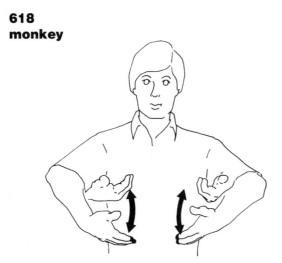

A monkey was in the street.

619
lion

The hungry lion escaped.

620
worm

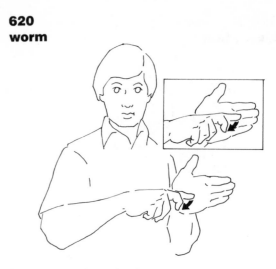

The worm looked dead.

621
turtle, tortoise

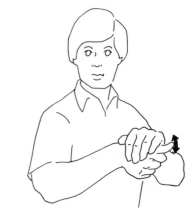

Was the turtle green *or* brown?

622
spider

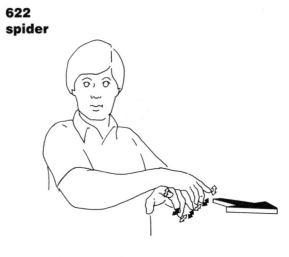

Most spiders are ugly.

623
squirrel

No, I don't like squirrels.

624
rabbit,
bunny,
hare

Is there an Easter rabbit?

625
†fly

Flies are an awful bother.

626
sheep, lamb

Sheep and cows live together.

627
fish

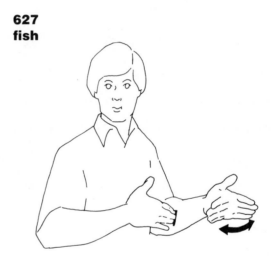

I saw many fish in the water.

628
†bear

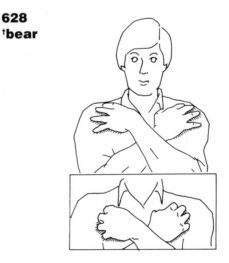

The brown bear was eating.

213

Practice Sentences

1. Every Saturday, we have chicken for *dinner.*

2. We bought five white rabbits on Easter.

same
174

3. The donkey and horse are the same color.

4. The red fox was eating our big white duck.

around
530

5. Snakes can control the *number of* rats around here.

6. My sister hates spiders and insects.

7. The *circus* had lions and elephants.

8. Tell me, is that a black *or* brown bear?

9. The fish were eating flies.

10. There were both black and white sheep.

11. We *gathered* worms for the fish.

12. The cows and pigs stayed together.

13. Deer are pretty animals, but they are *destructive.*

after
311
did
331

14. The wolf was after all the turkeys.

15. Did you hear about the tortoise and hare race?

16. My grandparents love eating squirrel.

17. The turkeys were in the big tree.

18. Where *did* you say you saw the rats?

have to	**take**	**small**	**steps**
277	460	547	580
		act	**like**
		283	174

19. Elephants have to take small steps.

20. My kids often act like monkeys.

Mind Ticklers

Make the sign _____ | *and think about . . .*

animal 603	how an animal's rib cage moves while breathing
insect 604	an insect's antennae
deer 605	a deer's antlers
cow 606	a cow's horns
donkey 607	a donkey's big ears
horse 608	a horse's small ears
wolf 609	a wolf's long nose
snake 610	a snake's forked tongue
chicken 611	a bird's bill or beak
duck 612	ducks having wider bills than birds
rat 613	a rat's nose twitching
pig 614	pigs being in mud up to their chins
fox 615	the fox's pointed nose
elephant 616	an elephant's long trunk
turkey 617	a turkey's wattle hanging down
monkey 618	a monkey scratching itself
lion 619	a lion's mane
worm 620	a worm crawling on the ground
turtle 621	a turtle in its shell
spider 622	a spider's eight legs
squirrel 623	a squirrel holding a nut
rabbit 624	a rabbit's ears
fly 625	the act of trying to catch a fly
sheep 626	shearing a sheep's wool
fish 627	how a fish moves in water
bear 628	a bear scratching a tree trunk

215

Vocabulary

animal	duck	turtle, tortoise
insect, bug	rat	spider
deer	pig, hog	squirrel
cow, cattle	fox	rabbit, bunny, hare
donkey, mule	elephant	
horse	turkey	fly
wolf	monkey	sheep, lamb
snake	lion	fish
chicken, bird	worm	bear

Additional Signs and Notes

Lesson 22

629
***fruit**

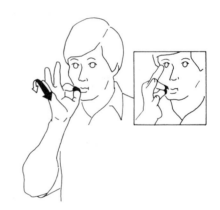

Monkeys love fruit.

630
apple

The white horse ate an apple.

631
peach

Which animal eats peaches?

632
lemon

The lemon pie is good.

633
strawberry

Do rabbits eat strawberries?

634
grapes

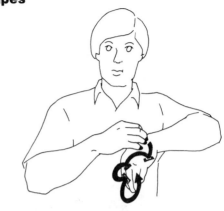

Can the fox get the grapes?

635
pear

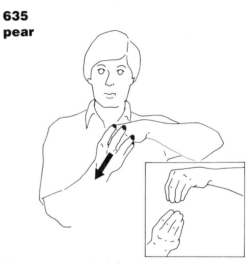

The pear tree is dying.

636
pumpkin, melon

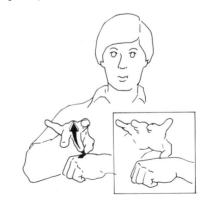

Who made the pumpkin pie?

637
watermelon

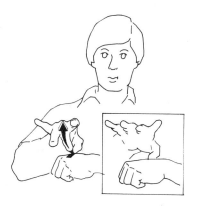

They love watermelon.

638
banana

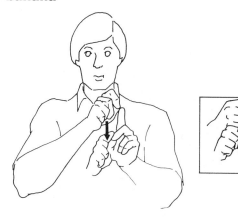

Which animal loves bananas?

639
***dessert**

We never eat dessert.

640
sandwich

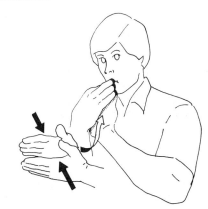

Did you eat a banana sandwich?

641
hamburger

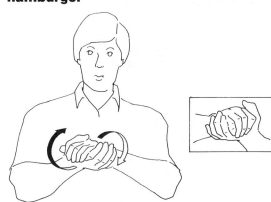

I really want a hamburger.

219

642
sausage,
hot dog,
bologna

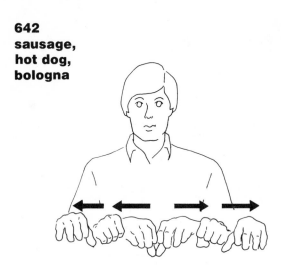

Sausage is made from pigs.

643
bacon

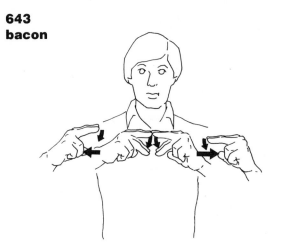

Is the bacon done now?

644
corn-on-the-cob

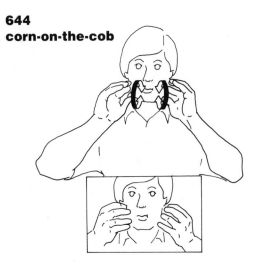

Do we have more corn-on-the-cob?

645
spaghetti

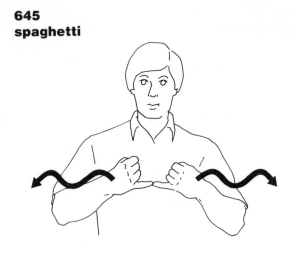

Her dog ate our spaghetti.

646
egg

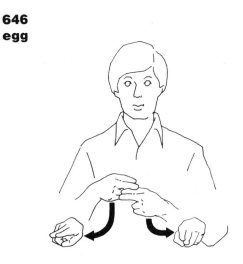

Where are the duck eggs?

647
milk

The brown cow gave no milk.

648
popcorn

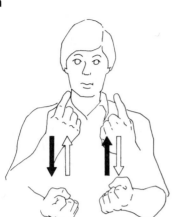

The squirrel ate the popcorn.

649
coffee

I don't like milk in my coffee!

650
cracker,
biscuit

Mix the crackers and eggs.

651
jelly, †jam,
preserves

My mother made the peach jelly.

652
butter

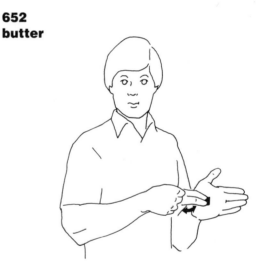

He put butter on the popcorn.

653
potato

Please give me a small potato.

221

654
toast

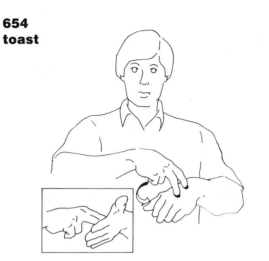

I had some toast and coffee.

655
tea

Do you drink a lot *of* tea?

656
meat

Lions eat a lot *of* meat.

657
gravy,
grease, oil

We have no more gravy.

658
corn

Give the cows some corn.

659
bread

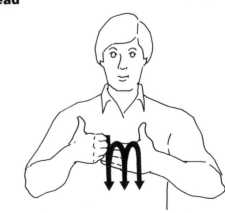

The bread is on the table.

660
tomato

I am growing some tomatoes.

661
soup

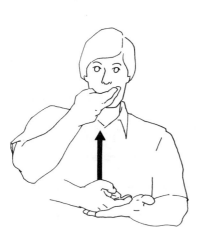

Was *there* any tomato soup left?

Practice Sentences

like
49

has been
429

no
110

make
290

great
403

like
49

like
49

watch
207

no
110

make
290

made
291

kind
204

cold
213

no
110

1. Mother told us *to* eat a lot *of* fruit.

2. Which *do* you like better, apple or peach pie?

3. They put lemons, grapes, pears, and bananas in our *basket*.

4. The strawberry dessert was fantastic.

5. Pumpkin pie has been my *favorite* for years.

6. My brother loves sausage sandwiches.

7. No tomato on my hamburger, please.

8. Soup and a sandwich will be enough for me.

9. My sister makes great gravy and bread.

10. Watermelons now cost about three dollars each.

11. I like bacon, eggs, toast, and coffee in the morning.

12. Would you like buttered popcorn while watching TV?

13. There is no jelly or butter on the biscuits.

14. She puts milk in her potatoes *to* make them soft.

15. The chickens are not *laying* big eggs.

16. Can you imagine, our cat doesn't like milk?

17. Grandmother made us eat that awful turtle meat.

18. Some kind *of* bug is eating our watermelons.

19. Yes, both bacon and sausage come from pigs.

20. We can't have both spaghetti and corn-on-the-cob.

21. I don't like corn when it is cold.

22. Where can I buy some good grapes and apples?

23. Tomato soup is *exactly* what you need.

24. There is no milk in your coffee.

25. Nothing is better than hot bread with butter on it.

Mind Ticklers

Make the sign _____ | *and think about . . .*

apple 630	cheeks being red like an apple
peach 631	the fuzz on the face being similar to peach fuzz
lemon 632	making the sign for *bitter* with an *l* handshape
strawberry 633	holding strawberries by the stem while biting off the berry
grapes 634	a clustering of grapes
pear 635	the shape of a pear
pumpkin 636	thumping a melon to see if it's good
watermelon 637	signing *water* + *melon*
banana 638	peeling a banana
sandwich 640	putting two pieces of bread together
hamburger 641	making a hamburger patty
sausage 642	showing the links of sausage
bacon 643	how wrinkled bacon looks when it's cooked
corn-on-the-cob 644	eating corn-on-the-cob
spaghetti 645	very thin strands of spaghetti
egg 646	hitting an egg to crack and separate it
milk 647	milking a cow
popcorn 648	how popcorn pops
coffee 649	grinding coffee in a coffee grinder
cracker 650	the superstition of breaking crackers on the elbows for good luck
jelly 651	spreading jelly on bread with a *j* handshape
butter 652	buttering bread
potato 653	sticking a fork into a potato
toast 654	sticking a fork into toast to turn it
tea 655	stirring tea with a spoon
meat 656	meat hanging from a hook

225

Mind Ticklers

Make the sign _____   *and think about . . .*

gravy 657	gravy dripping off of meat
corn 658	shucking corn off the cob
bread 659	cutting a loaf of bread
tomato 660	slicing red tomatoes
soup 661	bringing soup to the mouth

Vocabulary

*fruit	sandwich	jelly, jam, preserves
apple	hamburger	butter
peach	sausage, hot dog, bologna	potato
lemon		toast
strawberry	bacon	tea
grapes	corn-on-the-cob	meat
pear	spaghetti	gravy, grease, oil
pumpkin, melon	egg	corn
watermelon	milk	bread
banana	popcorn	tomato
*dessert	coffee	soup
	cracker, biscuit	

Additional Signs and Notes

227

Lesson 23

662
cake

Who made the lemon cake?

663
cookie

Did you bring those cookies?

664
vanilla

Is that vanilla ice cream?

665
chocolate

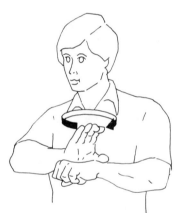

The chocolate cake is mine.

666
pizza

Get us a sausage pizza.

667
pop, soda

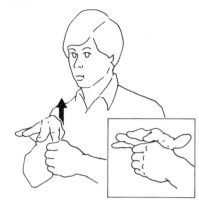

What kind *of* pop is that?

668
salt

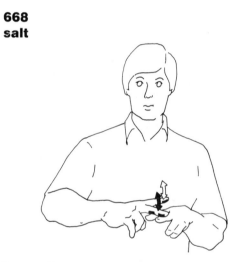

Do you like salt on watermelon?

669
pepper

Don't pepper the pizza.

670
onion

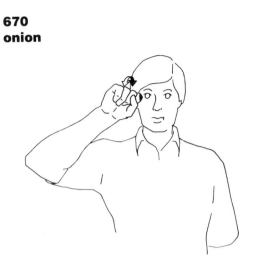

Onions make me cry.

671
sugar, sweet

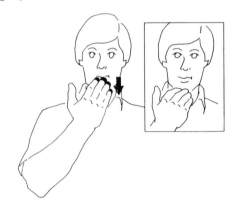

All animals love sugar.

672
vinegar

I don't like the *taste of* vinegar.

673
candy

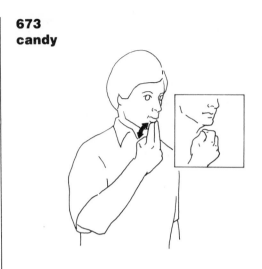

He gave the horse some candy.

674
†nuts, peanuts

The candy has nuts in it.

675
spring

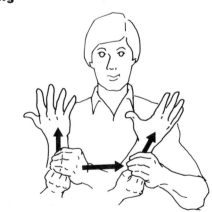

Spring is always beautiful.

230

676
summer

We work during the summer.

677
†**fall, autumn**

This fall I will go to college.

678
*****winter** (cold)

We make candy every winter.

679
*****breakfast** (eat)

Are there eggs for breakfast?

680
breakfast (eat + morning)

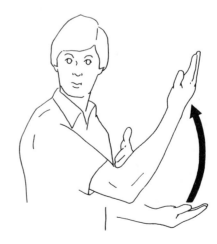

He eats pizza for breakfast.

**681
cook,
*kitchen,
bake**

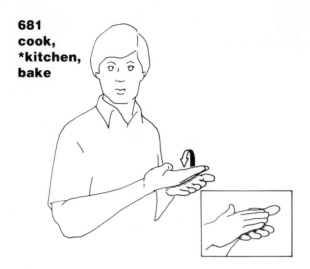

Who cooks breakfast every day?

**682
*lunch** (eat)

Lunch is always late.

**683
lunch** (eat + noon)

We had spaghetti for lunch.

**684
slow, slowly**

Eat your lunch slowly.

232

685
*dinner (eat)

I want coffee with dinner.

686
dinner,
supper (eat + night)

They had soup for dinner.

687
thirsty, †dry

Lemons make me thirsty.

688
†hang, hang up

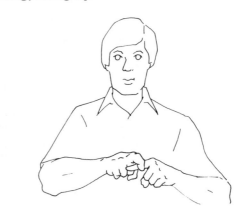

Did you hang up your coat?

689
†hang

When will they hang him?

Practice Sentences

big
399

small
398

hangs
688

get
128

hang
689

make
290

time
120

like
174

1. I will bring the chocolate cake.

2. We always cook candy very slowly.

3. These cookies are *too* sweet for me *to* eat.

4. Which *do* you want, vanilla or chocolate ice cream?

5. During the winter we eat a lot *of* pizza.

6. My parents eat a big lunch and a small dinner.

7. We ate *an* onion and sausage pizza yesterday.

8. *If* you are thirsty, drink some pop.

9. I never put salt and pepper in anything I cook.

10. Father always hangs his deer for several days.

11. In the summer we eat breakfast on the *porch*.

12. They always have peanuts when drinking beer.

13. Hot chocolate milk in the fall is nice.

14. Eat slowly, *or* you will get sick.

15. It was awful that they hanged him.

16. My mother makes a good cake with vinegar in it.

17. Why *do* you eat all those awful onions?

18. I'm thirsty; let's drink something.

19. I never have time *to* eat much breakfast.

20. Mother loves sweets like cookies, cake, and candy.

Mind Ticklers

Make the sign _____ | *and think about . . .*

cake 662	a cake rising
cookie 663	cutting cookies with a cookie cutter
pizza 666	cutting pizza into wedges with a *p* handshape
pop 667	the popping sound made when a soda bottle is opened
salt 668	tapping salt off a salt knife
pepper 669	shaking pepper out of the shaker
onion 670	crying when you peel onions
sugar 671	licking something sweet
vinegar 672	making the sign for *water* with a *v* handshape
nuts, peanuts 674	peanut butter sticking to the roof of the mouth
spring 675	plants growing
summer 676	wiping perspiration from the forehead
fall 677	leaves piling at the base of a tree in the fall
*winter 678	making the natural gesture of shivering with *w* handshapes
cook 681	turning food over in a skillet
thirsty 687	water trickling down the throat
hang 688	hanging up a clothes hanger
hang 689	a person hanging by the neck

Vocabulary

cake	vinegar	cook, *kitchen, bake
cookie	candy	*lunch
vanilla	nuts, peanuts	lunch
chocolate	spring	slow, slowly
pizza	summer	*dinner
pop, soda	fall, autumn	dinner, supper
salt	*winter	thirsty, dry
pepper	*breakfast	hang, hang up
onion	breakfast	hang
sugar, sweet		

Additional Signs and Notes

Lesson 24

690
ability, skill,
talent,
expertise,
proficient

How are your cooking skills?

691
list, itemize

She wrote a shopping list.

**692
advise,
influence,
counsel,
advice**

What advice can you give me?

**693
*background** (below)

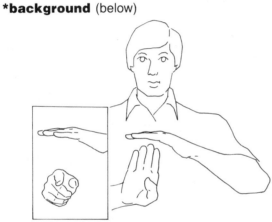

Your work background is good.

**694
lose, lost**

He lost his ability *to* talk.

**695
accept, adopt,
†follow,
†take on, †take**

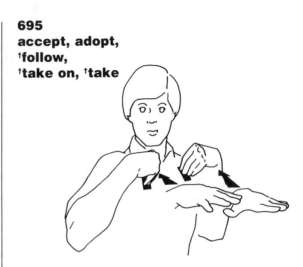

You should accept his advice.

**696
responsible,
responsibility,
obligate,
†charge**

Are you responsible for that?

**697
†miss,
†disappoint**

I miss your parents.

238

698
†miss,
cut,
absent

Did you miss class again?

699
†miss,
didn't get

All *of* us missed lunch.

700
†missing,
gone,
absent

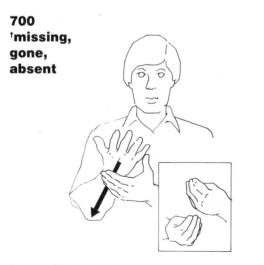

My apple pie is missing.

701
†follow, †by,
†take, †trail

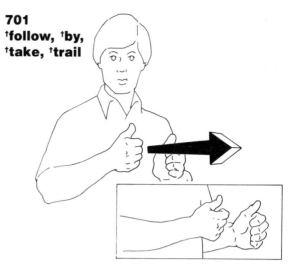

When will you follow me?

702
alone

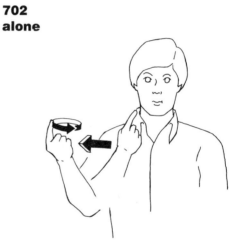

I am alone and I miss you.

703
study

Do you often study alone?

239

704
afraid, fear,
frighten,
scare

I am afraid *to* follow you.

705
farm

My uncle raised farm animals.

706
†sign, signing

How often *do* you study signs?

707
†sign, poster,
square

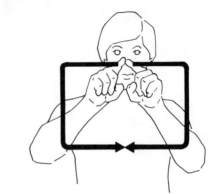

You missed seeing the sign.

708
†sign,
signature

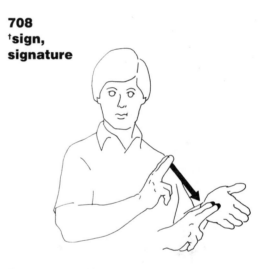

Please sign this paper.

709
fingerspell,
spell

Fingerspell the word *farm*.

**710
moon**

Is the moon out tonight?

**711
sun,
sunshine,
†light**

The sun is nice and warm.

**712
*free** (safe),
***liberty,
*independent,
†release,
†save,
†turn loose**

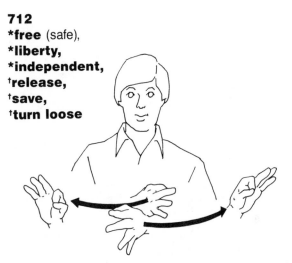

You are free *to* leave *at* 3:00.

**713
†save**

I saved all the old signs.

**714
exact, precise,
†*perfect, †just**

She gives precise advice.

**715
experience**

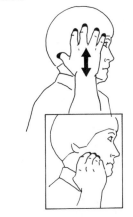

Do they have any experience?

241

**716
exchange,
†trade,
substitute**

Will you exchange cars?

**717
†knock**

I knocked, but he was gone.

**718
pride, proud**

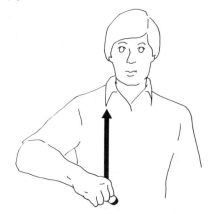

She is proud *of* her singing ability.

Practice Sentences

		sign 706
make 290	**like** 174	**show** 525
	past 300	**present** 589
		signs 707
		miss 697
		miss 698
		sign 706
	looked 354	**miss** 700
	still 266	**miss** 699
	sign 708	**save** 713
		give 377
		light 373
	short 548	**time** 120
		sign 707
		save 713
	achievements 517	
		miss 699

1. Now I can sign and fingerspell my name.

2. Making candy like that shows real ability.

3. Write your work background from the past to the present.

4. They are your responsibility *so* don't lose the signs.

5. She decided to accept her father's advice.

6. We really miss not having a car.

7. Try *to* be precise when telling him everything.

8. Don't tell me you are missing class again.

9. I want *to* go alone *so* don't follow me.

10. You should be proud *of* your signing ability.

11. We looked and looked, but he was missing.

12. We studied all night and still missed the point.

13. Are you afraid *to* walk alone *at* night?

14. He has experience working on a farm.

15. I knocked on the door, but there was no *answer*.

16. Sign this paper and save it for later.

17. I give you the responsibility *of* exchanging my shoes.

18. *Wow*, the sun is really hot today!

19. We can go sit in the moonlight.

20. They freed all the people in a short time.

21. Where did you put most *of* the signs?

22. Dad decided *to* save his money and not buy a car.

23. His parents are proud *of* his achievements.

24. America sent men to the moon in 1969.

25. Your daughter missed the school bus today.

Mind Ticklers

Make the sign _____ | *and think about . . .*

list 691	putting things down on paper
lose 694	dropping something that was in your hands
accept 695	pulling something towards you
responsible 696	having a burden on your shoulders
miss 698	referring to one of the five days you miss something
miss 699	being unable to catch or get something
missing 700	something that is no longer around
follow 701	one person following another
alone 702	going off by yourself
study 703	looking at a book with your eyes
afraid 704	all your bones shaking from fear
farm 705	the generalization that farmers used to have beards
sign 706	moving your hands around to form signs
poster 707	the shape of a poster
sign, signature 708	putting your name on paper
fingerspell 709	moving your fingers when spelling
moon 710	the crescent shape of the moon
sun 711	the sun being a circle of light
*free 712	breaking hand shackles to gain freedom
save 713	protecting what you are holding
experience 715	gray hair at the temples indicating experience with age
knock 717	a fist knocking on a door
pride 718	your buttons popping off as your chest swells with pride

Vocabulary

ability, skill, talent, expertise, proficient

list, itemize

advise, influence, counsel, advice

*background

lose, lost

accept, adopt, follow, take

responsible, responsibility, obligate, charge

miss, disappoint, bitter

miss, cut, absent

miss, didn't get

missing, gone, absent

follow, trail

alone

study

afraid, fear, frighten, scare

farm

sign, signing

sign, poster, square

sign, signature

fingerspell, spell

moon

sun, sunshine, light

*free, save, release, *liberty, *independent

save

exact, precise, *perfect, just

experience

exchange, trade, substitute

knock

pride, proud

Additional Signs and Notes

245

Lesson 25

719
trip,
travel

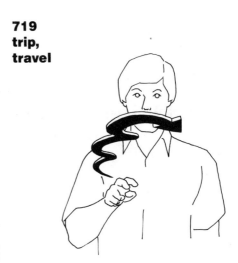

Save your trip for summer.

720
announce,
announcement,
†word

I will announce my trip soon.

721
famous,
outstanding

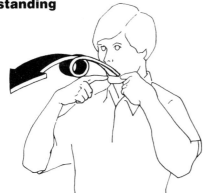

We know a famous person.

722
teach,
***educate,**
***instruct**

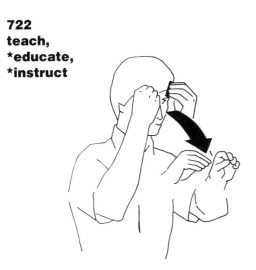

Teach her how *to* fingerspell.

723
inform, news,
information,
†let know

Inform her about the trip.

724
building

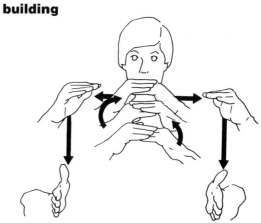

That is a famous building.

725
build,
***construction,**
***construct,**
†make

When can you build it?

726
***basic** (below),
***elementary,**
basis, †grounds

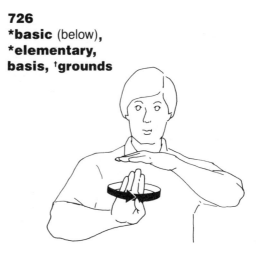

That is basic information.

727
serve, service,
†wait, wait on

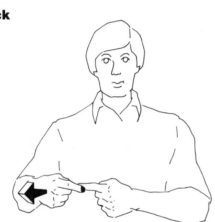

He was proud *to* serve us.

728
†block

We walked for three blocks.

729
†block, stuck,
†catch, †jam

Her hair blocked the *drain*.

730
†block, prevent

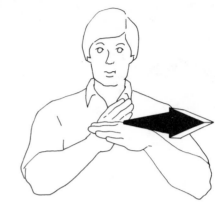

The defense blocked the kick.

731
corner

My building is on the corner.

732
†admit, *welcome,
***invite, *hire**

We will admit two people.

733
†admit, confess,
†grant

I admit that you are right.

734
remember,
remind

Remember, we are leaving *at* 12:30.

735
†nuts, crazy,
†out of one's head

He informed them I was crazy.

736
†over, across,
cross

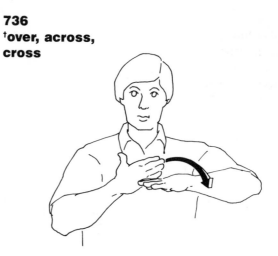

He walked across the road.

737
over, †above

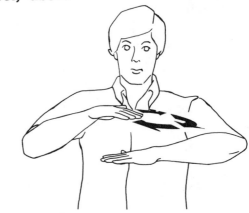

The birds *flew* over the house.

738
over, finish,
have, done

Yes, my announcement is over.

739
†decline,
decrease,
reduce,
lower, less,
†drop

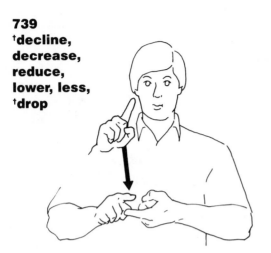

My enthusiasm is decreasing.

740
†figure,
†count, †add

I can figure this for you now.

741
†figure,
shape, †prints

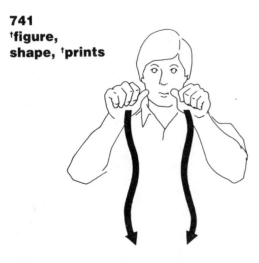

I am losing my figure.

742
measure, size,
inch, †rule

Teach him how *to* measure.

743
government,
***federal,**
***politics**

She works for the government.

744
law, lawyer,
attorney

The government makes many laws.

250

745
†rule,
regulations

I can't count all the rules.

746
area, *†place

Measure all *of* this area.

Practice Sentences

has	had	problem	before
738	56	420	300

			has
			56
		light	over
		373	737
			figure
			741
		done	figure
		738	740

			problem
			295
get up		run	block
402		450	728
have to		admit	this
277		733	54, 55

			kind
			204
			this
			54, 55
			get
			130
			have
			738
			this
			54, 55

			did
			331

1. Yes, he has had problems before.

2. Remember, we need *to* announce our travel plans.

3. Our crazy teacher became a lawyer.

4. The government has *so* many rules you can't count them all.

5. A huge light was put over the building.

6. Mother thinks she is losing her figure.

7. When you are done, figure what I *owe* you.

8. Good news is always welcomed here.

9. I am stuck on this problem.

10. Mother gets up early and runs 16 blocks.

11. I have to admit, this is not what I expected.

12. Everything my father builds becomes famous.

13. In what kind *of* basic service are you interested?

14. The army prevented people *from* entering this area.

15. Go to the corner and get some candy.

16. Yes, I have invited your cousin to the wedding.

17. This is a government area, closed to the public.

18. It is a basic law understood *by* everyone.

19. The bus was stuck in the *mud* for hours.

20. Did you announce the building plans?

Mind Ticklers

Make the sign _____ | *and think about . . .*

trip 719	going from one place to another
announce 720	telling something far and wide
famous 721	becoming well known by word of mouth
teach 722	taking knowledge from your head and putting it into someone else's head
inform 723	taking knowledge from your head and sharing it with others
build 725	placing one block upon another
basic 726	the foundation or base of something
serve 727	carrying a tray
block 728	measuring a city or street block
stuck 729	something sticking in the throat
prevent 730	putting up a shield for protection
corner 731	forming the area where two streets come together
welcome 732	pulling someone towards you in a welcoming gesture
confess 733	confessing something to get it off your chest
remember 734	tacking up something as a reminder
crazy 735	everything being mixed up in the head
over 736	going over a barrier
above 737	the natural gesture of indicating that something is over the horizon
decrease 739	showing the size of something diminishing
count 740	counting numbers on an abacus
figure 741	outlining a person's figure
measure 742	measuring something with rulers
government 743	the head of the country
law 744	listing laws on the pages of a book
rule 745	listing rules on the pages of a book
area 746	outlining the boundaries of an area

253

Vocabulary

trip, travel

announce, announcement

famous, outstanding

teach, *educate, *instruct

inform, news, information, let know

building

build, *construction, *construct

*basic, *elementary, grounds

serve, service, wait on

block

block, stuck

block, prevent

corner

admit, *welcome, *invite, *hire

admit, confess

remember, remind

nuts, crazy

over, across, cross

over, above

over, finish, have, done

decline, decrease, reduce, lower, less, drop

figure, count

figure, shape

measure, size, inch

government, *federal, *politics

law, lawyer, attorney

rule, regulations

area, *place

Additional Signs and Notes

Lesson 26

747
†add, addition,
additional,
†come to,
†total

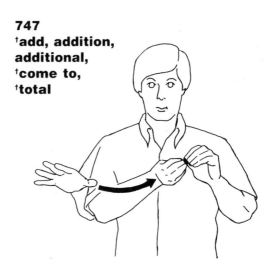

Please add this for me.

748
†number

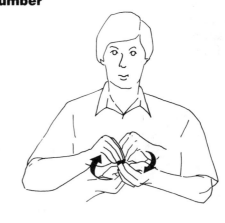

Try to think of a number between 1 and 50.

255

749
machine,
factory,
†plant

They added two new machines.

750
special,
except,
particular,
†but

We got a special machine.

751
come here,
†come over,
come back,
†drop over,
†return

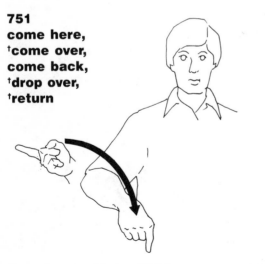

Come here and help add this.

752
bridge

We will go over the bridge.

753
average,
medium,
†mean

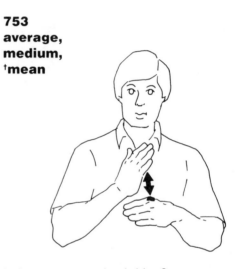

Is it an average-size bridge?

754
practice,
†*train,
***rehearse,**
***drill**

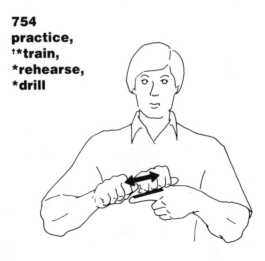

Can he practice on my machine?

256

**755
answer, *reply,
*respond**

Come here and answer this.

**756
born, birth**

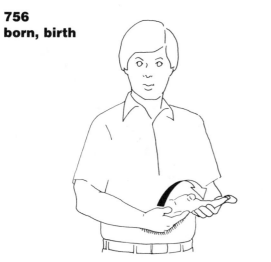

Were you born on a Monday?

**757
birthday**

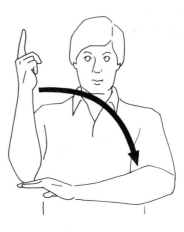

My birthday is next week.

**758
paint, †apply,
spread**

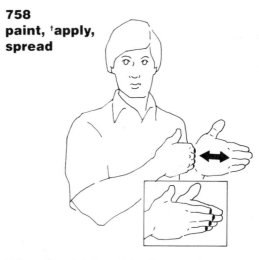

Who will paint the bridge?

257

759
†fall (over),
†drop,
†knock down

Don't fall on me.

760
quit, get out,
†drop out, †give up

I quit working *at* the factory.

761
rock, stone

That machine breaks rocks.

762
mountain

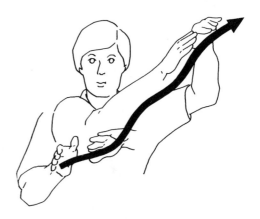

I was born in the mountains.

763
pass, †by,
†past

We pass the mountain daily.

258

**764
include,
involve**

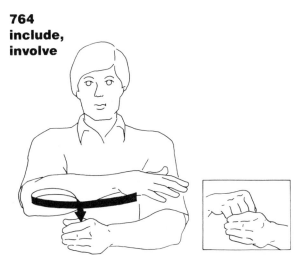

Include me in your practice.

**765
science,
chemistry,
*biology**

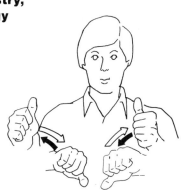

Science class is cancelled.

**766
arithmetic,
multiply,
math,
*calculus,
*algebra**

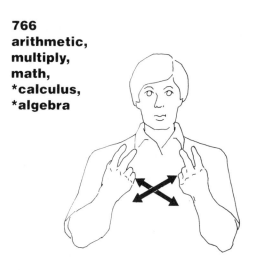

Arithmetic class is over now.

**767
history**

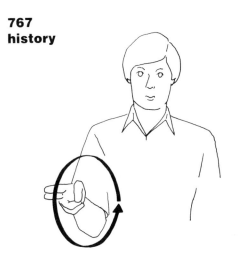

History is my *favorite* class.

**768
fat, obese**

I don't think she is fat.

**769
thin**

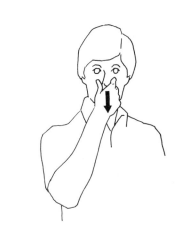

She is really thin!

**770
thick**

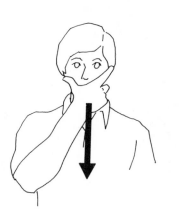

Put the paint on thick.

**771
push, shove,
†knock down**

Help me push this machine.

**772
honest,
truthful**

Honest, it's my birthday!

Practice Sentences

get
130

this
54, 55

got
130

has
56

had to
277

which
143

time
120

1. He put the paint on *too* thickly.

2. Add all the numbers and see what you get.

3. Will you help us push this machine?

4. Honest, I got *an* "A" in history class.

5. My mother is thin and my father is fat.

6. Come here; dad has something special for you.

7. They practiced their arithmetic without enthusiasm.

8. I had to quit science class.

9. The mountain was *only* average in size.

10. He fell on the bridge in the rain.

11. We tried *to* include you in the birthday party.

12. My cousin walks past here daily.

13. Several rocks fell *from* the mountain onto the road.

14. When the telephone *rings,* please answer it.

15. Can you remember on which day you were born?

16. The new machine was painted green.

17. The boys were *throwing* average-size rocks.

18. Don't push; there is plenty *of* time.

19. Are you involving me in your plans?

20. Arithmetic, science, and history are my best classes.

Mind Ticklers

Make the sign _____ | *and think about . . .*

add
747 | adding one amount to another

machine
749 | the cogs of a machine meshing together

special
750 | one thing standing out from the rest

come here
751 | motioning a person towards you

bridge
752 | the supports under a bridge

average
753 | something being right in the middle

practice
754 | doing something repeatedly for practice

answer
755 | words falling from the mouth

born
756 | a baby entering the world from the mother's womb

birthday
757 | signing *birth* + *day*

paint
758 | brushing paint on something

fall
759 | a person changing from a standing position to a reclining one

quit
760 | removing yourself from the group

rock
761 | an object being as hard as a rock

mountain
762 | rocks piled high in a heap

pass
763 | one object moving past another

include
764 | combining everything into one hand

science
765 | a scientist pouring liquid from test tube to test tube

history
767 | moving in a circular motion to indicate that history is ongoing

fat
768 | a person with a large face

thin
769 | a drawn face

thick
770 | thick as the opposite of thin

push
771 | the natural gesture of pushing something away

Vocabulary

add, addition, additional, total

number

machine, factory, plant

special, except, particular

come here, come over, come back

bridge

average, medium, mean

practice, *train, *rehearse, *drill

answer, *reply, *respond

born, birth

birthday

paint, apply, spread

fall, drop, knock over

quit, get out, drop out

rock, stone

mountain

pass, by

include, involve

science, chemistry, *biology

arithmetic, multiply, math, *calculus, *algebra

history

fat, obese

thin

thick

push, shove, knock down

honest, truthful

Additional Signs and Notes

Lesson 27

773
†notice

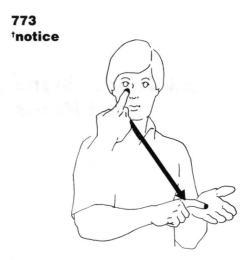

I noticed it yesterday.

774
†notice,
poster,
†put up

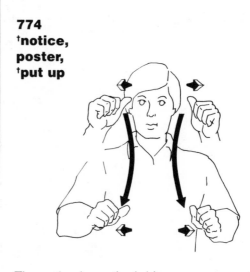

The notice is on the bridge.

775
title, quote,
theme, †subject,
topic, motto

Did you notice the title?

776
region

In which region *do* you live?

777
†strike, rebel,
disobey,
insubordinate

The workers went on strike.

778
†reduce,
diminish,
less, †cut

Why *did* you give me less money?

779
†reduce,
slim down

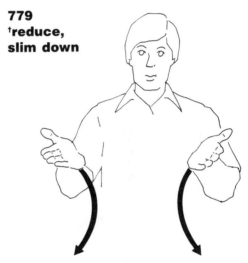

He really reduced a lot.

780
important,
worth,
significant,
***value, †count**

The notice is important.

265

781
*general (wide)

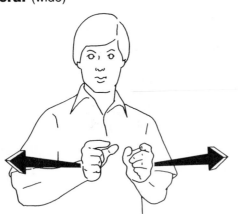

In general, he is right.

782
†fire,
blaze,
burn

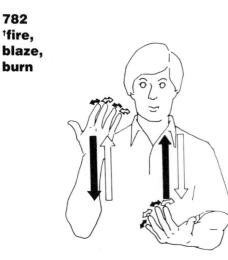

Fire hit the whole region.

783
fast, quick,
suddenly,
rapid,
†right away

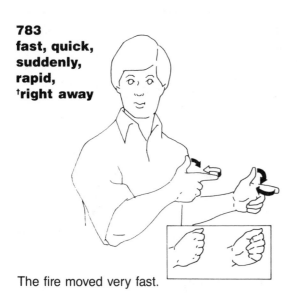

The fire moved very fast.

784
worse

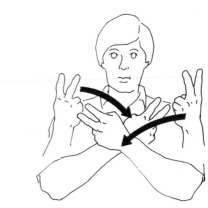

That was the worst fire.

785
excitement,
excite,
†anxious

I am excited about the trip.

786
dirty, filthy,
dirt, mud

The car was really dirty.

787
†bite

Which animal bit you?

788
mistake,
wrong,
†accident

The strike was a big mistake.

789
†accident

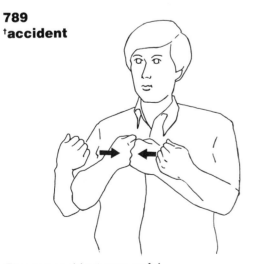

The car accident was awful.

790
attempt, *try,
***effort**

We will attempt it now.

791
park, parking

You can park here free.

792
center, *middle

Put it in the center *of* the table.

267

793
warn, †notice,
notify

We tried *to* warn them.

794
supervise,
take care of,
†watch, †house

Please supervise your child.

795
graduate

She is a college graduate.

796
from

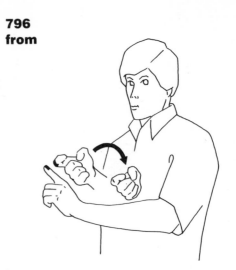

I graduated from O.S.U.

797
freeze, frozen

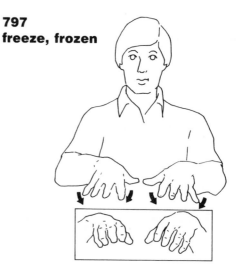

Will the water freeze tonight?

798
careful,
be careful,
†look out,
†watch out

Careful, I see an accident ahead.

268

799
also, too, as

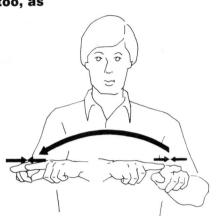

I notice she also graduated.

800
flag

What color is the flag?

Practice Sentences

		reduce 779

1. Dad is doing a good job reducing.

2. It is a mistake *to* park in the middle *of* the road.

3. The fire here was the worst one in years.

4. He was filthy from playing in the mud.

5. Dad warned you to be careful with her.

		cold 213
		accident 789
		notice 773
		notice 774

6. It was *so* cold we almost froze.

7. Was she involved in the accident too?

8. I noticed that the dog bit you again.

9. The notice was about the general strike next week.

10. It is important that you quote him exactly.

11. This region is famous for flag making.

12. My wife graduated from *Gallaudet* College in 1976.

13. How often *do* you supervise six children?

		show 525
look 562	**like** 174	**reduce** 779
	look 562	**after** 313
	subject 775	**talk** 195, 196

14. Try not *to* show your excitement today.

15. You look like you are reducing *too* quickly.

16. My brother always looks dirty after working.

17. Tell me what subject you are talking about.

18. The importance *of* history is obvious.

19. The monkey bit my hand.

20. I warned you it would be a mistake.

Mind Ticklers

Make the sign _____ | *and think about . . .*

notice 773	something that attracts your eye
notice 774	putting up a poster
quote 775	making quotation marks in the air
region 776	making the sign for *area* with *r* handshapes
strike 777	raising your fist in rebellion
reduce 778	something becoming smaller
reduce 779	outlining the body becoming slimmer
important 780	putting important things into a bag
fire 782	flames shooting upward
excitement 785	everything inside the body jumping around
dirty 786	making the sign for *pig*
bite 787	teeth biting into something
accident 789	two vehicles colliding
park 791	using the *three* handshape to represent any vehicle
center 792	the middle of the hand
warn 793	tapping a person to signal danger
supervise 794	all seeing eyes
graduate 795	putting a diploma into a student's hand
from 796	one hand moving away from a place
freeze 797	water suddenly becoming hard
also 799	repeating the sign for *same*
flag 800	a flag waving in the breeze

271

Vocabulary

notice	fire, blaze, burn	center, *middle
notice, poster	fast, quick, suddenly, rapid, right away	warn, notice, notify
title, quote, theme, subject, topic, motto	worse	supervise, take care of, watch
region	excitement, excite, anxious	graduate
strike, rebel, disobey, insubordinate	dirty, filthy, dirt, mud	from
reduce, diminish, less	bite	freeze, frozen
reduce, slim down	mistake, wrong, accident	careful, be careful
	accident	also, too, as
important, worth, *value, significant	attempt, *try, *effort	flag
*general	park, parking	

Additional Signs and Notes

Lesson 28

**801
fantasy,
make believe**

He is always fantasizing.

**802
exaggerate, drag out**

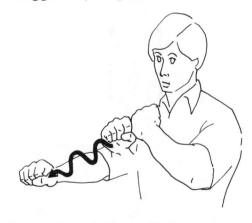

Don't exaggerate the accident.

803
advertise,
promote,
advertisement,
†word

The advertisement was funny.

804
dictionary

I also have a dictionary.

805
†advance,
promote,
high,
promotion

Her advancement came early.

806
†advance,
progress,
procedure,
process

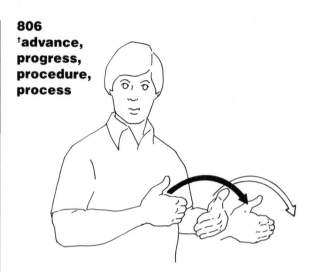

How far *did* they advance?

807
neighbor

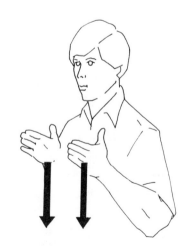

My neighbor is fantastic!

808
spoil, ruin

You spoiled my dictionary.

809
damage,
destroy,
demolish

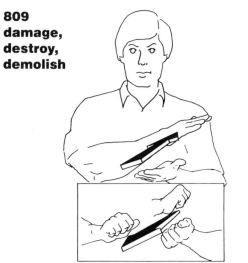

Don't damage the machine.

810
kiss

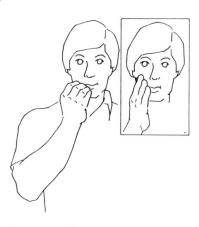

I kissed my neighbor.

811
hide, conceal

Did you hide my dictionary?

812
missing, †gone

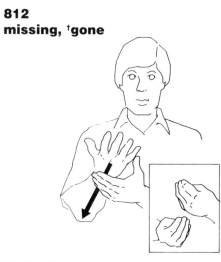

My flag is missing.

813
†gone, all gone,
†out of

The chocolate cake is gone.

814
†gone,
†left,
†out

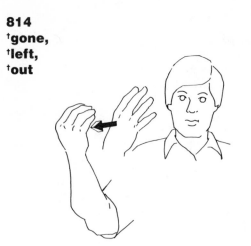

My neighbor is gone.

815
flexible

They told us to be flexible.

816
†aim, goal,
objective, †cause

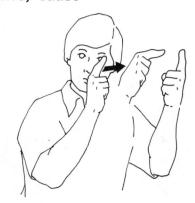

What is your aim in life?

817
†aim, †point

Don't aim that gun *at* me.

818
explain,
†*directions,
***describe,**
†tell

Please explain your goals.

819
dark

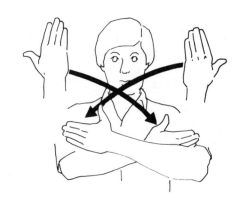

Why is it dark in here?

276

820
celebrate,
victory, anniversary

We celebrated his promotion.

821
all night,
overnight

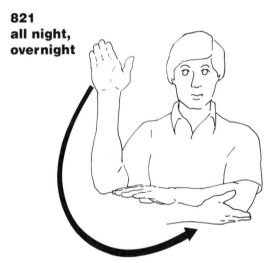

I looked for you all night.

822
†disappear, †vanish

He seems *to* disappear.

823
†disappear,
melt, dissolve,
solve, solution,
resolve, †vanish

The snow will disappear by noon.

824
cards,
playing cards,
shuffle

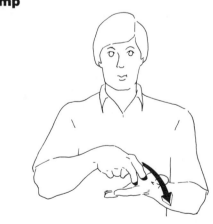

Do you have any cards?

825
†jump

Don't jump on the car.

277

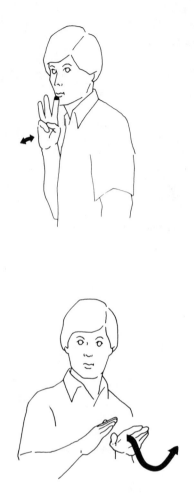

We celebrated near the ocean.

Practice Sentences

disappear
822

advance
805

advance
806

gone
814

made
290

play
329

has   **cold**
56   215

gone
813

gone
812

advance
806

present   **gone**
588   812

1. The advertisement was really exaggerated.

2. Our neighbor celebrated all night, then disappeared.

3. The awful rain and winds destroyed our farm.

4. Can you explain why you hid it?

5. The new dictionary is more advanced than the old one.

6. We will start here and advance slowly.

7. Her fantasy was *to* work in advertising.

8. I'm sorry; he is gone for the day.

9. Our goal is to be very flexible.

10. Why are you aiming that gun *at* me?

11. The oil made the ocean water dark.

12. They didn't know how *to* dissolve the oil.

13. Where are the cards? Let's start playing.

14. Don't kiss the baby; she has a cold.

15. Are the hamburgers and watermelon gone?

16. I put the cards there; now they are gone.

17. Don't jump from the bridge; it's not safe.

18. How far will the army advance tomorrow?

19. When he tells a story, you know it's *an* exaggeration.

20. The family said the presents were gone.

Mind Ticklers

Make the sign _____	*and think about . . .*
make believe 801	many thoughts coming from the mind
exaggerate 802	stretching the truth
advertise 803	how companies often stretch the truth in advertising
dictionary 804	turning pages of the dictionary to find a word
advance 805	moving up to the next level
advance 806	moving forward
neighbor 807	a person who lives near by
damage 809	tearing something apart
kiss 810	kissing the lips and then the cheek
hide 811	placing a secret object under something
gone 813	removing everything on the table
flexible 815	being able to bend something back and forth
aim 816	moving towards a goal
aim 817	the natural gesture of pointing at something
dark 819	covering the eyes to depict darkness
celebrate 820	flags waving to indicate victory
disappear 822	something dropping out of view
melt 823	something passing through your finger tips
cards 824	the natural gesture of shuffling cards
jump 825	legs jumping from one place to another
ocean 826	rolling waves

Vocabulary

make believe, fantasy	damage, destroy, demolish	dark
exaggerate, drag out	kiss	celebrate, victory, anniversary
advertise, promote, advertisement	hide, conceal	all night, overnight
dictionary	missing, gone	disappear, vanish
advance, promote, high, promotion	gone, all gone, out of	disappear, melt, dissolve, solution, resolve, vanish
advance, progress, procedure, process	gone, left	cards, playing cards, shuffle
neighbor	flexible	
	aim, goal, objective	
	aim, point	jump
spoil, ruin	explain, *directions, *describe, tell	ocean, sea

Additional Signs and Notes

Lesson 29

**827
airplane,
†flight**

I celebrated on the airplane.

**828
†fly**

We will fly over the ocean.

829
†fly

That insect cannot fly.

830
interpret,
interpreting

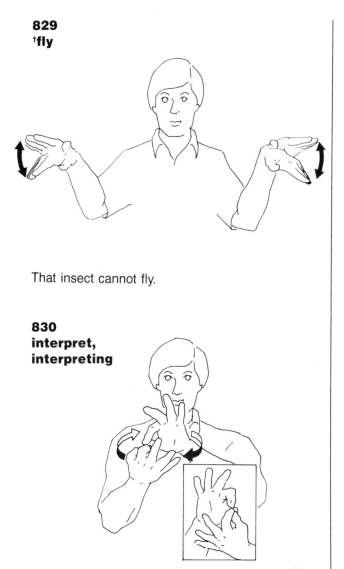

I interpret for my neighbor.

831
translate,
transliterate,
transformation

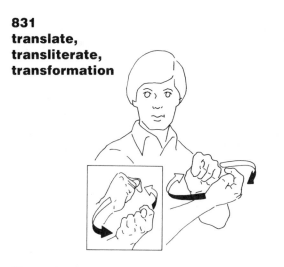

She prefers that I translate.

832
philosophy,
philosopher

Your philosophy is vague.

833
army, soldier

The army will leave tonight.

834
among

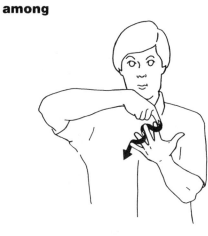

He is there among the people.

835
grass, hay

The grass is for the cows.

836
†bitter, sour

That lemon is very bitter.

837
†charge,
cost, †fine, tax

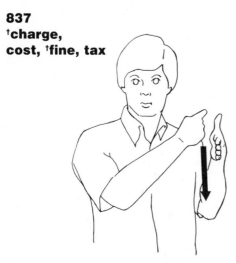

What *do* you charge for cards?

838
†charge, blame,
fault, accuse

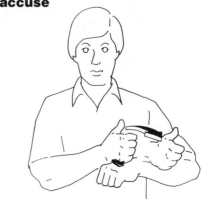

He was charged with murder.

839
†doubt

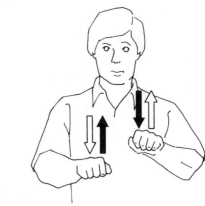

I doubt that it is bitter.

840
something,
somebody,
someone

Somebody will interpret for you.

**841
schedule**

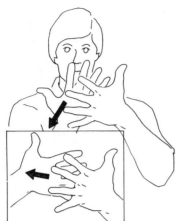

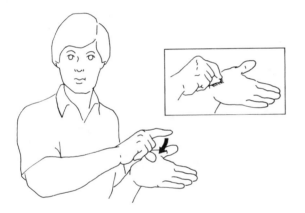

What is the flight schedule?

**842
†print, publish**

What is the printing cost?

**843
newspaper**

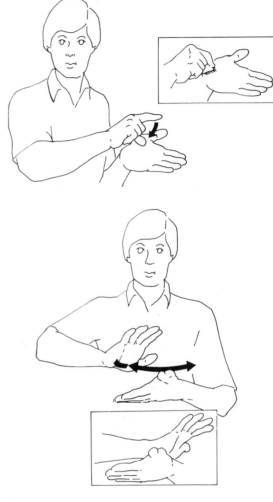

Somebody has the newspaper.

285

844
yell, call, scream

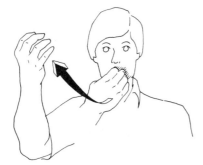

Did the soldier yell?

845
relationship
†association

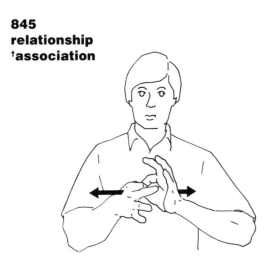

Our relationship is good.

846
regular

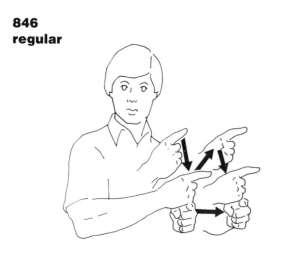

Is that the regular schedule?

847
memorize

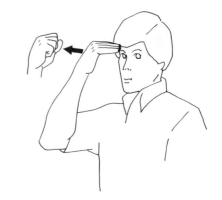

Who memorized the list?

848
***large**

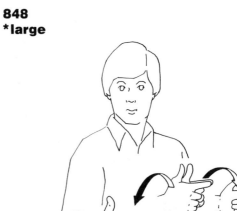

How large is your paper?

849
fight, battle

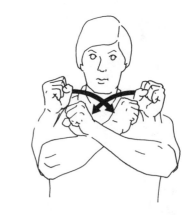

The army stopped the fight.

**850
selfish,
stingy**

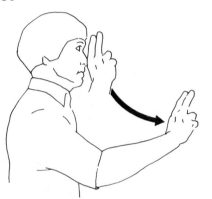

I doubt he is selfish.

**851
honor,
†*respect**

The newspaper honored them.

Practice Sentences

charge
838

charge
837

little   **fly**
426   829

flew
828

seems
560

left
181

charge
838

1. I doubt he was screaming for nothing.

2. The newspaper was printed on a regular schedule.

3. Soldiers were among those charged.

4. Somebody needs *to* interpret for the deaf man.

5. In college we always translated for the deaf people.

6. *Do* they charge for the weekly newspaper?

7. We honored the soldiers who fought.

8. Somebody told the little girl that elephants fly.

9. We flew across the country in 3½ hours.

10. It seems that their relationship is very flexible.

11. She memorized all the famous philosophies.

12. That was a bitter drink.

13. It was silly, but they were fighting again.

14. That man is not selfish anymore.

15. The large airplane left hours ago.

16. The grass was becoming brown without rain.

17. My summer schedule is all mixed up.

18. Yes, they charged him with murder.

19. A lot *of* deaf people are printers.

20. What was the cost *of* your new car?

Mind Ticklers

Make the sign _____ *and think about . . .*

airplane 827	the wings and motor of an airplane
fly 828	the natural gesture of flying through the air
fly 829	a bird flapping its wings
interpret 830	changing one thing to another
translate 831	making the sign for *interpret* with *t* handshapes
philosophy 832	making the sign for *wise* with a *p* handshape
army 833	soldiers carrying guns
among 834	your finger going in and out of several objects
grass 835	a cow chewing on grass
bitter 836	making a sour expression
charge 837	the share of the money that is deducted
schedule 841	the matrix of a planning sheet
print 842	setting the type for a printing job
newspaper 843	a newspaper as a printed paper
yell 844	the natural gesture of cupping one's hands to the mouth to yell
regular 846	repeating the sign for *right*
memorize 847	grasping something in your mind
large 848	gesturing size with the hands
fight 849	the natural gesture of boxing with someone
selfish 850	pulling everything to yourself

Vocabulary

airplane, flight	bitter, sour	yell, call, scream
fly	charge, cost, fine, tax	relationship, association
interpret, interpreting	charge, blame, fault, accuse	regular
translate, transliterate, transformation	doubt	memorize
philosophy, philosopher	somebody, something, someone	large
		fight
army, soldier	schedule	selfish, stingy
among	print, publish	honor, *respect
grass, hay	newspaper	

Additional Signs and Notes

Lesson 30

**852
hurry**

Hurry, our plane is going!

**853
invent, devise,
†make, †original**

Who invented the airplane?

**854
invention**

That is a great invention.

**855
secretary**

She is our regular secretary.

**856
blind**

He was blind to her mistakes.

**857
certification,
certified, *license,
†permit**

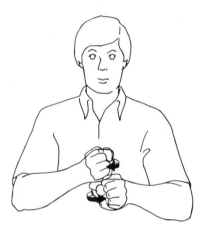

Are the certificates printed?

**858
danger,
dangerous**

That is a dangerous invention.

859
argue,
quarrel

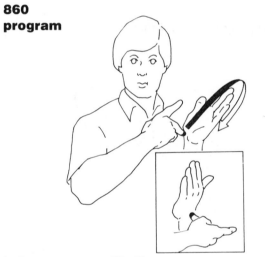

The secretary argued with me.

860
program

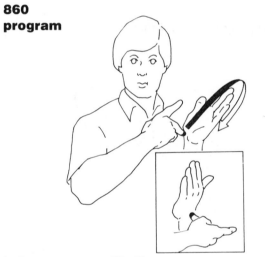

Is the program certified?

861
project

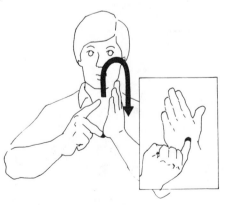

She invented another project.

862
sick, ill,
disease

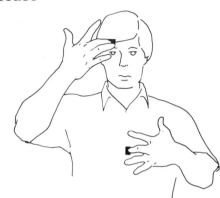

The soldier looks sick.

863
hurt, pain,
sore, painful

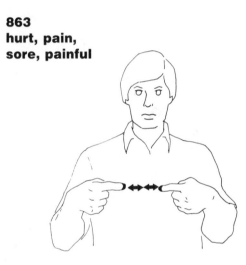

Did you hurt yourself when you fell?

864
body,
*physical

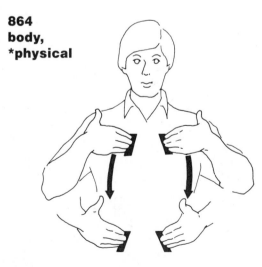

My whole body hurts.

865
mumps

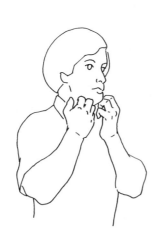

Her child has the mumps.

866
measles

She was sick with the measles.

867
cough

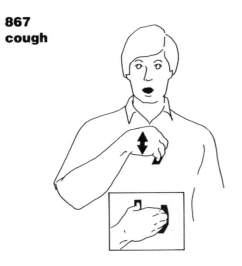

Your cough sounds awful.

868
***mental** (think)

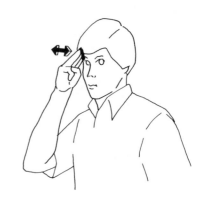

It was a mental mistake.

869
***mentally retarded** (think)

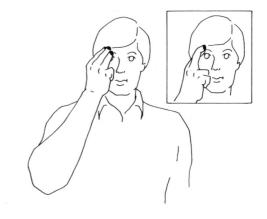

He wasn't mentally retarded.

870
psychiatry,
psychiatrist

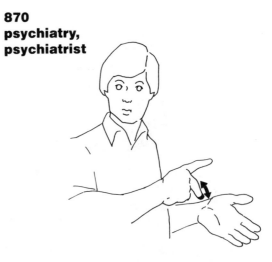

Psychiatry is *an* old field.

871
psychology,
psychologist

I enjoy my psychology class.

872
†patient

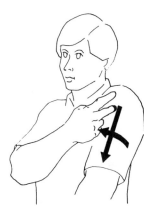

The patient was very sick.

873
dentist

The dentist has a cough.

874
hospital, *infirmary

He had to stay in the hospital.

875
operation

The operation was painful.

876
medicine,
medical

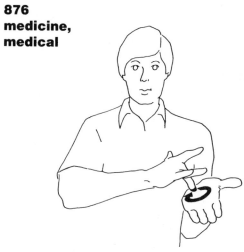

That medicine is dangerous.

877
blood

The hospital needs blood.

878
pregnant

Is your wife pregnant?

879
†well, healthy,
brave, courage

The patient is well now.

880
upset,
†disturb

Having mumps upset him.

881
***physical** (body)

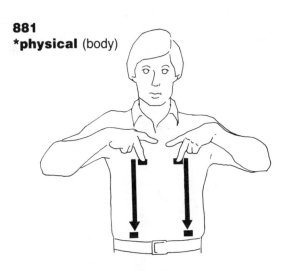

He is in good physical *shape.*

Practice Sentences

had
56

1. My daughter had measles and went to the hospital.

2. My pretty wife is pregnant now.

3. Are you upset *because* we argued?

4. Sure, he is a certified psychiatrist.

5. It was a dangerous project for the hospital.

6. The dentist's secretary became a patient.

7. His invention will help the medical profession.

8. *If* you are in pain, hurry to the hospital.

well   **look**
879   562

9. He was well yesterday; now he looks sick.

10. They invented a program for the mentally retarded.

made
290

11. It was a mental mistake that he made.

made   **have**
291   56

12. Her mother made her have the operation.

13. He was blind from birth.

14. His whole body hurt after the accident.

made   **have**
291   56

15. They made him have a complete physical.

had
56

16. Yes, I had mumps when I was 11 years old.

17. Was there blood in her *mucus* when she coughed?

18. A psychologist and psychiatrist are as different as night and day.

fine
406

19. My blood test was fine.

has
56

20. The whole family has a physical *exam* yearly.

297

Mind Ticklers

Make the sign _____	and think about . . .
hurry 852	moving ahead quickly
invent 853	ideas coming out of the head
invention 854	an idea that takes form
secretary 855	removing a pencil from behind the ear, wetting the point and then writing
blind 856	the fingers preventing the eyes from seeing
certification 857	outlining the shape of a certificate
argue 859	two people shaking their fingers at one another
program 860	a piece of paper printed on both sides
sick 862	having a headache and a stomachache
body 864	pointing to the body area with both hands
mumps 865	where mumps occur
measles 866	having small spots on the face
cough 867	miming the movement of the body while coughing
*mental (think) 868	making the sign for *think* with an *m* handshape
psychiatry 870	making the sign for *doctor* with a *p* handshape
psychology 871	the Greek letter psi
patient 872	making the sign for *hospital* with a *p* handshape
dentist 873	a dentist working on your teeth
hospital 874	the red cross patch on the shoulder
operation 875	the place where an incision was made during an operation
medicine 876	counting pills in the palm
upset 880	feeling like your stomach is turned upside down

298

Vocabulary

hurry

invent, devise

invention

secretary

blind

certification,
*license, permit

danger,
dangerous

argue, quarrel

program

project

sick, ill, disease

hurt, pain, sore,
painful

body, *physical

mumps

measles

cough

*mental

*mentally
retarded

psychiatry,
psychiatrist

psychology,
psychologist

patient

dentist

hospital,
*infirmary

operation

medicine,
medical

blood

pregnant

well, healthy,
brave, courage

upset, disturb

*physical

Additional Signs and Notes

Lesson 31

**882
thing,
†article,
†object**

Is that thing your project?

**883
*material** (thing),
***equipment**

Whose material is this?

884
column
†article

Her medical column is great.

885
key, lock

Where are the hospital keys?

886
twins

The patient had twins.

887
motorcycle

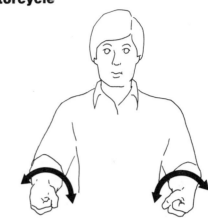

My motorcycle is dangerous.

888
share,
divide

Will you share the material?

889
†rough,
†mean

The twins play rough.

890
†rough,
crude,
not smooth

The road is *too* rough.

891
smooth,
flat,
†clean

I prefer a smooth road.

892
queen

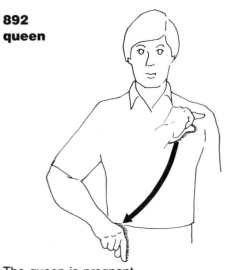

The queen is pregnant.

893
king

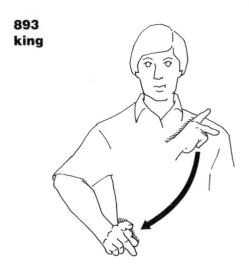

The king is not sick.

894
†join, †take part in,
participate,
get in,
†ride

The king joined in the argument.

895
†join,
put together,
connect,
connecting

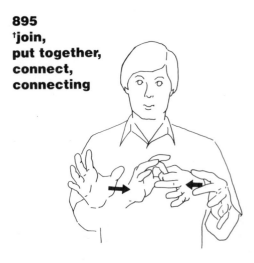

Can you connect the strings?

302

896
debt, owe, afford

I owe him for the motorcycle.

897
change, alter,
adapt, †correct,
†turn

The queen changed her dress.

898
full,
satisfied,
†fill

Are the twins both full?

899
†ground,
soil, sand

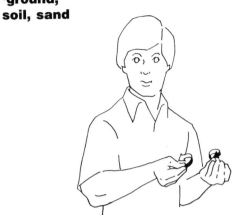

This soil is good for tomatoes.

900
†land

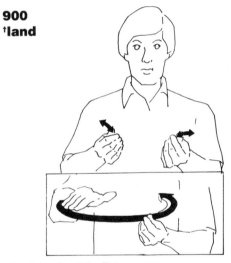

All *of* our land is flat.

901
choice, choose,
select,
†pick, †prefer

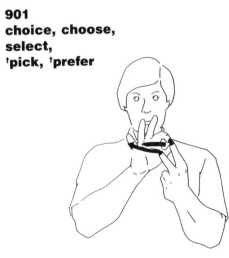

The king had no choice.

303

902
**†beat, defeat,
conquer**

Can anyone beat our team?

903
**†beat, punch,
hit, †strike**

Don't beat him again.

904
**†only,
†just,
†but**

I have only one television.

905
†just (expletive)**, †only**

That is just fine with us.

906
**†just,
recently,
awhile ago,
†a little bit ago**

The king just arrived.

907
**wet,
moist,
damp**

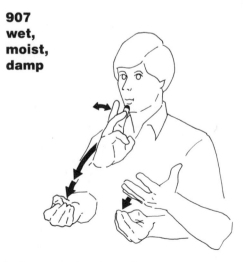

Is the ground wet now?

908
†dry,
boring,
towel

The *air* is drier in *Arizona*.

909
boil,
heat,
burn

Boil some water for tea.

Practice Sentences

1. The twins had to share their motorcycle.

2. We can't grow much on this *sandy* ground.

3. The king was the only person *to* appear.

4. The road was *too* rough for a motorcycle.

5. Who brought this thing into the house?

6. The first team was beaten *by* the second team.

7. *Do* we have a choice *of* the land we want?

8. Her brother is satisfied with your changes.

9. I don't know *if* the two cars can be joined.

10. Her article about the mentally retarded was good.

11. The queen lost her key and couldn't open the box.

12. They decided not *to* play *so* rough.

13. They changed the floors from smooth to rough.

14. When will you join the army

15. They just left, about 10 minutes ago.

16. I feel just fine after my operation.

17. The ground was wet early, then became dry.

18. Will you boil water for the eggs?

19. They doubted we could afford a new motorcycle.

20. He said just two *of* you saw it.

Mind Ticklers

Make the sign _____	*and think about . . .*
thing 882	having something in your hand
column 884	the size of a column in a newspaper
key 885	turning a key in a lock
motorcycle 887	the handlebars of a motorcycle
share 888	splitting something that is whole
rough 890	a surface that is bumpy
queen 892	the sash of a queen
king 893	the sash of a king
join 895	connecting two things together
debt 896	putting money that is owed you into your hand
full 898	a person being stuffed to the chin with food
ground 899	feeling the soil
land 900	soil spread over a broad area
choice 901	having several things to select from
beat 903	hitting something or someone
just 906	time that is almost behind you
wet 907	feeling water dripping from something
boil 909	the flames that are causing a substance to boil

Vocabulary

thing, article

*material,
*equipment

column, article

key, lock

twins

motorcycle

share, divide

rough, mean

rough, crude,
not smooth

smooth, flat

queen

king

join, get in,
participate,
take part in

join, connect,
connecting,
put together

debt, owe,
afford

change, alter,
adapt

full, satisfied

ground, soil,
sand

land

choice, choose,
select, pick

beat, defeat,
conquer

beat, punch, hit,
strike

only, just

just

just, recently,
awhile ago,
a little bit ago

wet, moist,
damp

dry, boring,
towel

boil, heat, burn

Additional Signs and Notes

Lesson 32

**910
board**

A board selected the material.

**911
member**

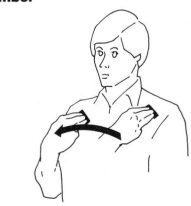

Are you a board member?

912
committee

She is a committee member.

913
president,
superintendent

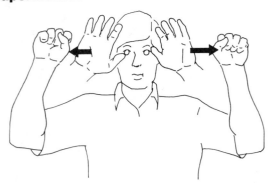

The president is on the board.

914
***politics** (government)

My committee argued politics.

915
Senate,
senator

Who is your state senator?

916
legislature,
legislator

The legislature defeated the motion.

917
Congress

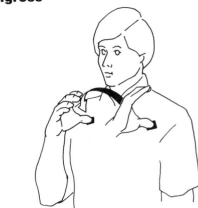

She is a member of Congress.

310

**918
legislation**

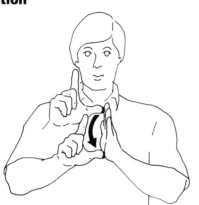

Our legislation was approved.

**919
convention,
meeting,
session**

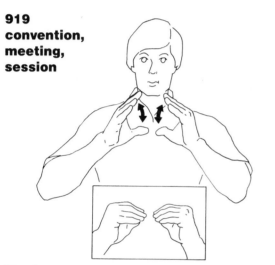

The Senate meeting is open.

**920
Democrat**

My senator is a Democrat.

**921
Republican**

It is a Republican Senate.

**922
smile**

The board member smiled.

**923
laugh**

Why is the president laughing?

**924
friendly,
pleasant,
cheerful**

My congressman is friendly.

**925
personality**

He has a friendly personality.

**926
character**

She has a lot *of* character.

**927
disagree**

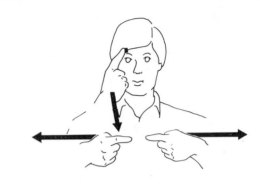

Do you disagree with us?

**928
†engagement** (wedding)

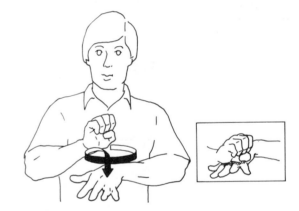

Their engagement was broken.

**929
reservation,
†engagement,
appointment**

Did you make the dinner reservation?

930
former,
previous,
†old,
†once upon a time

She is a former senator.

931
beard,
Santa Claus

The Republicans in the late 1800s had beards.

932
shave

Don't shave your beard.

933
develop,
development

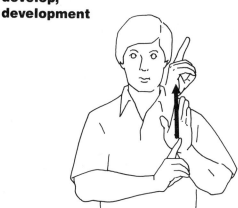

She developed character *as* she grew older.

934
attention,
pay attention,
concentrate

Smile *to* get my attention.

935
school for the deaf,
institution

We live in a school for the deaf.

936
ship

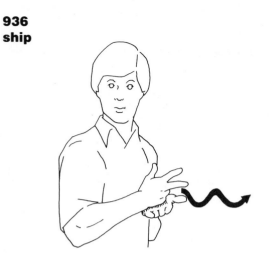

The captain never leaves the ship.

937
rubber

Why is that made *of* rubber?

Practice Sentences

engaged 928	1. They were engaged for seven years and three months.
long 275	2. How long is Congress in session?
had **no** 56 110	3. The board member had no personality.
	4. Who developed *synthetic* rubber and when?
made 290	5. When were the ship reservations made?
charge 838	6. The former senator was charged with *bribery*.
show 525	7. The Democrats showed a lot *of* character in losing.
meeting 919	8. Are you going to the committee meeting?
	9. The superintendent *of* the school for the deaf is a woman.
friendly 924	10. They disagreed about the legislation but were friendly.
	11. The president shaved his beard recently.
	12. Pay attention, and don't laugh *at* anything.
	13. The Republican legislature had 125 members.
join 894	14. The king refused *to* join the political battle.
left 181	15. The committee member smiled, then left.
friendly **made** 924 290	16. His friendly personality made us laugh.
next 302	17. Our next convention will be on a ship.
talk **next** 195, 196 303	18. When the legislator is finished talking, you are next.
	19. Why *do* Republicans and Democrats disagree?
	20. My dentist appointment is Monday *at* 11:30.

Mind Ticklers

Make the sign ————	*and think about . . .*
committee 912	committee members who wear name tags
president 913	a leader having to take the bull by the horns
politics 914	making the sign for *government* with a *p* handshape
convention 919	conventioneers sitting around talking
smile 922	how your mouth turns up at the corners when you smile
laugh 923	how your mouth repeatedly turns up when you laugh
personality 925	personality coming from the heart
character 926	character coming from the heart, too
disagree 927	thinking the opposite of someone else
engagement 928	pointing to your ring finger with an *e* handshape
engagement 929	reserving or locking up time for someone
former 930	something that was in the past
beard 931	the shape of a beard
shave 932	the natural gesture of shaving a beard
attention 934	wearing horse blinders that force you to look straight ahead
ship 936	the ship's mast going over the waves

Vocabulary

board

member

committee

president,
superintendent

*politics

Senate, senator

legislature,
legislator

Congress

legislation

convention,
meeting,
session

Democrat

Republican

smile

laugh

friendly,
pleasant,
cheerful

personality

character

disagree

engagement

reservation,
engagement,
appointment

former,
previous, old

beard,
Santa Claus

shave

develop,
development

attention,
pay attention,
concentrate

school for the
deaf, institution

ship

rubber

Additional Signs
and Notes

Lesson 33

938
†release, let go, disconnect, unfasten

Someone released the dog.

939
†release, disseminate, †give out

Who released the papers?

**940
apply, reserve,
put to use,
relevant,
assignment**

He applies his knowledge daily.

**941
apply,
spread,
put on**

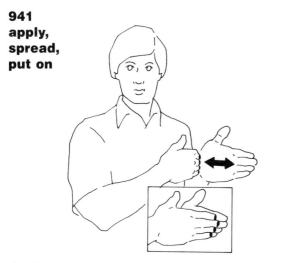

Apply the *glue* evenly.

**942
†apply,
applicant,
volunteer**

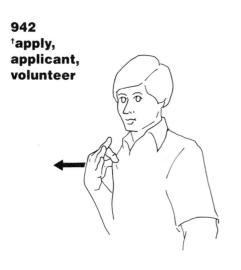

Did you apply for the job?

**943
sew, sewing**

Do you sew your own clothes?

**944
†sense**

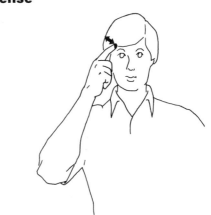

Can you make sense *of* this?

**945
music, *sing,
*song, *poem**

Who released the music?

946
discourage,
†disappoint,
depressed,
†blue, †let down

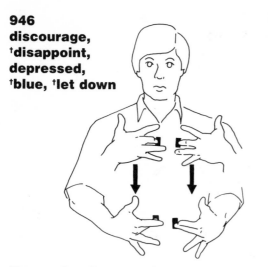

The meeting discouraged us.

947
†match, †light

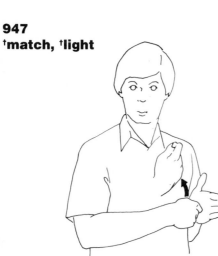

Give us a match for the fire.

948
†match, agree,
go together,
combine,
merge, †check

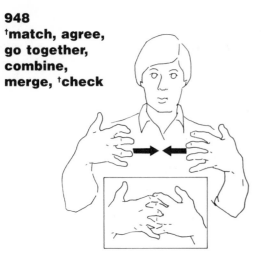

Your socks don't match.

949
lonely,
lonesome

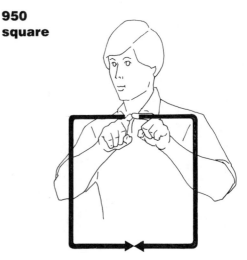

The president is lonely.

950
square

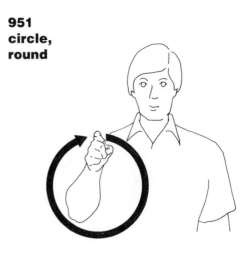

She sewed a square hat.

951
circle,
round

He made a round cake.

952
smart, †sharp

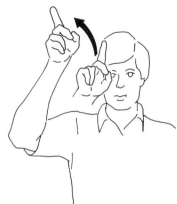

They did a smart thing.

953
ignorant,
stupid

He was ignorant *of* the law.

954
cigarette

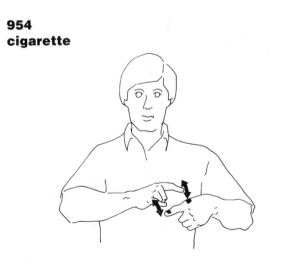

Do you have a cigarette?

955
smoke

No, I don't smoke.

956
vacation,
holiday,
***retire,**
†break,
†leave

My vacation is a month long.

957
lazy

The Democrats were not lazy.

**958
march,
parade**

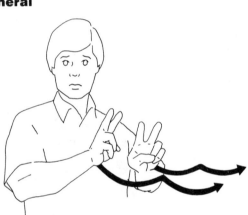

They marched in a circle.

**959
funeral**

The funeral was depressing.

**960
learn**

Where *did* you learn *to* sew?

**961
smell,
odor**

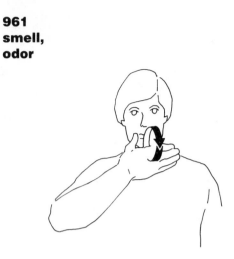

I smell something funny.

**962
habit, custom,
†used to**

Smoking is a bad habit.

**963
postpone,
delay, †put off**

The funeral was postponed.

964
evil, sin,
wicked

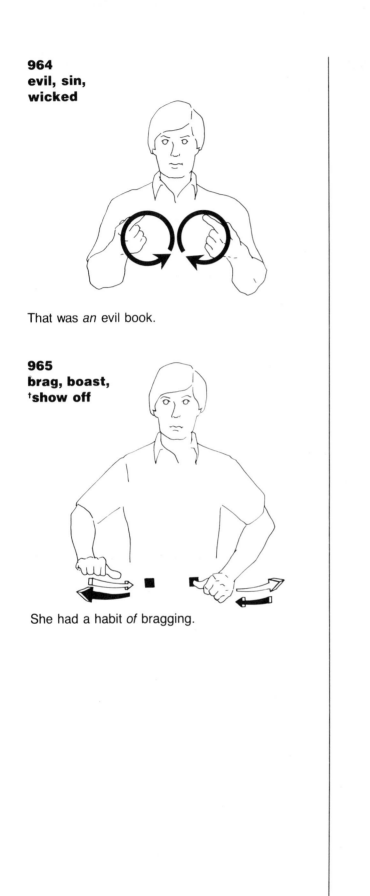

That was *an* evil book.

965
brag, boast,
†show off

She had a habit *of* bragging.

Practice Sentences

ways
539

apply
941

had   **apply**
56   940

this
44

release
939

just
904

little   **play**   **match**
426   329   947

match
948

which
54

tied
286

make   **big**
290   404

apply
940

match
948

1. The cigarette *smoke* caused the whole house to smell.

2. Your wicked ways are nothing *to* brag about.

3. They were smart *to* postpone their vacation.

4. He has a bad habit *of* applying *too* much *glue*.

5. Mom sewed 20 squares and 15 circles for her *quilt*.

6. She had enough sense to apply early.

7. There were only 121 volunteers this year.

8. Why did he release the music papers early?

9. Her sister's funeral was just last week.

10. The little boy was playing with matches.

11. She never learned *to* match her socks.

12. We were all very lonely, which made us lazy.

13. Our vacation was very disappointing.

14. We tied the string in a knot, but it later became unfastened.

15. She stopped smoking and bragged about it.

16. He learned several bad habits from her.

17. Make a big circle and then sit in its center.

18. Why *do* I always say stupid things?

19. I think we can apply for *tickets* until tomorrow.

20. The colors *of* both cars seemed *to* match.

Mind Ticklers

Make the sign _____	*and think about . . .*
release 938	two things being disconnected
release 939	giving something to everyone
apply 940	putting written information on a spindle to be acted upon
apply 941	applying something with a brush
apply 942	volunteering for something
sew 943	the natural gesture of sewing by hand
music 945	conducting music
discourage 946	having a sinking feeling
match 947	striking a match
match 948	joining things that are alike
lonely 949	a person who is silent
square 950	drawing a square in the air with two fingers
circle 951	drawing a circle in the air
ignorant 953	barring ideas from your mind
cigarette 954	the length of a cigarette
smoke 955	the natural gesture of smoking a cigarette
vacation 956	sitting back and relaxing
march 958	how the legs of marchers move in unison
funeral 959	carrying a bier
learn 960	taking knowledge from a book and placing it in your head
smell 961	bringing an odor to your nose
postpone 963	putting something off into the future

Vocabulary

release,
let go,
disconnect,
unfasten

release,
disseminate

apply, reserve,
put to use,
relevant

apply, spread,
put on

apply, applicant,
volunteer

sew, sewing

sense

music, *sing,
*song, *poem

discourage,
disappoint,
depressed

match, light

match, agree,
go together,
combine, merge

lonely,
lonesome

square

circle, round

smart, sharp

ignorant, stupid

cigarette

smoke

vacation,
holiday, *retire

lazy

march, parade

funeral

learn

smell, odor

habit, custom,
used to

postpone, delay,
put off

evil, sin, wicked

brag, boast,
show off

Additional Signs and Notes

Lesson 34

**966
cooperate,
cooperation**

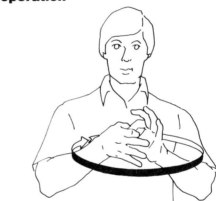

She is smart *to* cooperate.

**967
deep, detail,
in depth**

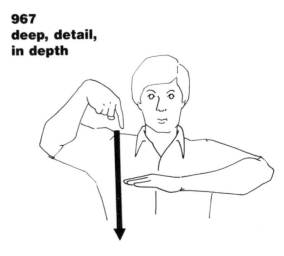

How deep is the water?

**968
drown**

The cat almost drowned.

**969
drunk**

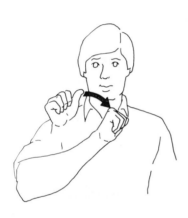

He was drunk *at* their party.

**970
everybody**

Everybody looked lonely last night.

**971
soap**

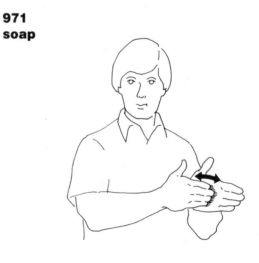

Where is the square soap?

972
bathe, bath

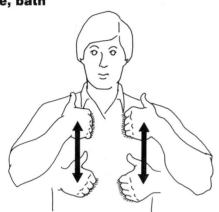

He bathes without soap.

973
shower

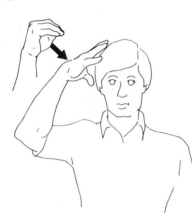

The soap is in the shower.

974
wash, laundry

They wash clothes on Monday.

975
†prefer,
preference,
rather

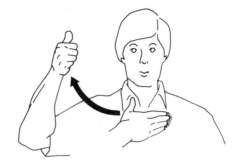

I prefer the blue soap.

976
*duty (work),
†part

She just did her duty.

977
*job (work)

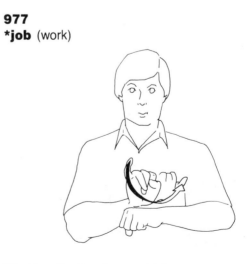

Washing the dog is a real job.

978
*industry (work),
*function

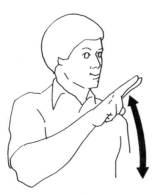

There is no industry near us.

979
†look over,
eyeing

Why *do* men look over women?

980
†look over,
observe

Did you look over my car?

981
†look up, find

Look up this word for me.

982
†look like,
look alike

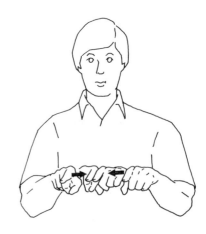

You look like you are drunk.

330

983
paragraph,
chapter

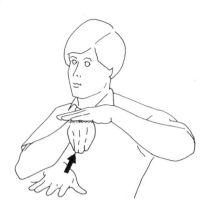

Write a short paragraph.

984
clock, †time

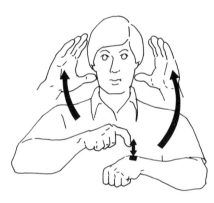

The clock is above the door.

985
†copy, imitate,
†follow

Copy what I do.

986
†copy

Make three copies of this page.

987
every so often,
every now and then

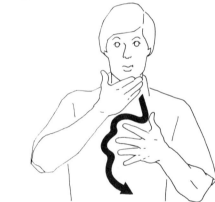

He bathes every now and then.

988
earn, collect
gather,
†make, †raise

Do you earn much on that job?

**989
city, town,
community,
village**

The city had no industry.

**990
improve,
improvement,
progress,
†advance,
†gain**

His earnings are improving.

**991
basement,
cellar**

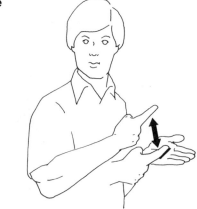

They have a shower in the basement.

**992
discuss, discussion,
debate**

We can discuss your duties.

Practice Sentences

		copy	**looks like**
		986	982

1. That copy looks like it is dirty.

2. Why *do* you prefer washing here?

3. Our town's industry is improving.

4. Everybody cooperated with the police.

5. How detailed *do* you want this chapter?

6. They put the drunk in the shower.

		take
		460
		eye
		979

7. How can you take a bath without soap?

8. Every so often a guy comes in, and the girls eye him.

		look over
		980
		copy
		985

9. He was looking over the old clock in the basement.

10. You can't copy that without a *pencil.*

get	**look up**	**this**
130	981	54, 55

11. Get the dictionary and look up this word.

12. *Do* you earn a lot on your new job?

13. We need *to* sit down and discuss your duties.

ask	**run off**	**copy**
338	454	986
		looks like
		982
	make	**progress**
	290	806
	make	**progress**
	290	990

14. She asked me *to* run off 500 copies.

15. It looks like your clock is broken.

16. Our city is making good progress.

17. Yes, your son is making better progress now.

18. Everybody is trying *to* imitate our success.

		have
		56
		did
		331

19. We have both a shower and bath*tub.*

20. They all cooperated and did the job.

Mind Ticklers

Make the sign _____ | *and think about . . .*

cooperate 966	people joining together in harmony
deep 967	gesturing how deep something is
drown 968	going under the water head first
drunk 969	not being able to hit the mouth with a drink
soap 971	lathering soap in the hand
bathe 972	the natural gesture of bathing
shower 973	water coming from an overhead spigot
wash 974	the natural gesture of washing clothes by hand
look over 979	looking someone up and down (this carries a negative connotation)
look over 980	examining something with four eyes
look up 981	thumbing through pages
paragraph 983	the length of a passage on a page
copy 985	taking something and putting it on paper
copy 986	duplicating something on a copying machine
earn 988	collecting wages in the hand
city 989	a place with many roof tops
improve 990	getting better in small steps
basement 991	the area under the house or foundation

Vocabulary

cooperate, cooperation	duty, part	copy
	*job	every so often, every now and then
deep, detail, in depth	*industry, *function	
drown		earn, collect, gather, make, raise
	look over, eyeing	
drunk		
	look over, observe	city, town, community, village
everybody		
soap	look up, find	
bathe, bath	look alike, look like	improve, improvement, progress, gain, advance
shower		
wash, laundry	paragraph, chapter	basement, cellar
prefer, preference, rather	clock	discuss, debate
	copy, imitate, follow	

Additional Signs and Notes

335

Lesson 35

993
communicate, communication

Everybody should communicate.

994
*total communication (converse)

Total communication is not new.

995
promise,
oath,
swear

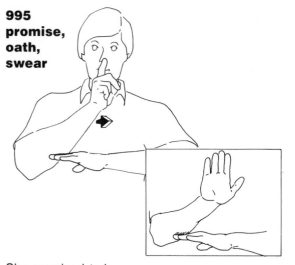

She promised *to* improve.

996
principle,
policy

My principle is *to* work well.

997
principal

The school principal is sick.

998
purpose,
intention

What is the purpose *of* this?

999
*office (box)

Go to the principal's office.

1000
misunderstand,
change of mind

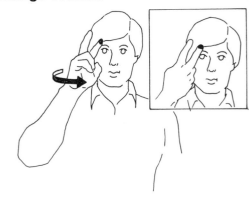

I misunderstood his purpose.

1001
feed

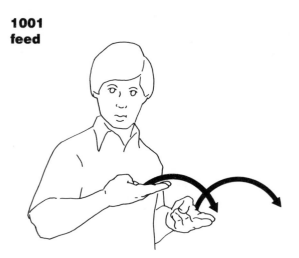

Who will feed us tonight?

1002
because,
†since

I am happy because you are here.

1003
late,
have not,
yet, not yet

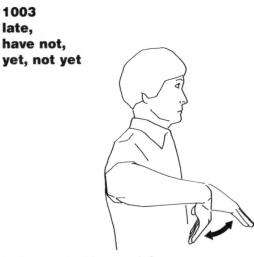

Is the principal late again?

1004
have,
own,
possess

Yes, she has the clock.

1005
have been,
all along,
†since,
ever since

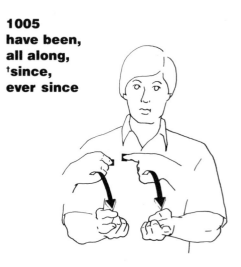

I have been sick a lot.

1006
have, finish

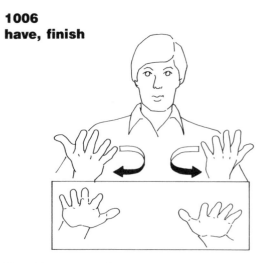

Yes, I have seen that.

1007
embarrass

The principal is embarrassed.

1008
ashamed,
shy, shame

He is ashamed *of* his past.

1009
river,
stream

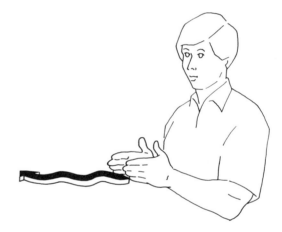

The river has been dry for several months.

1010
relieve,
content,
relief

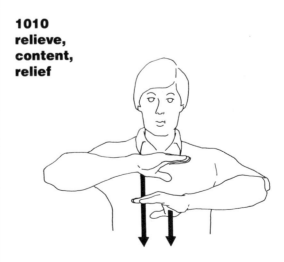

That is good; I am relieved.

1011
wrestle

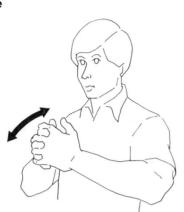

He has not wrestled before.

1012
†kick, soccer

He kicked him intentionally.

1013
volleyball

I have a volleyball.

1014
football

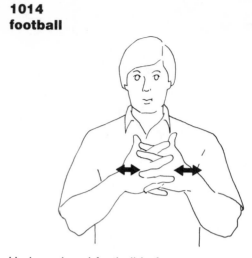

He has played football before.

1015
baseball

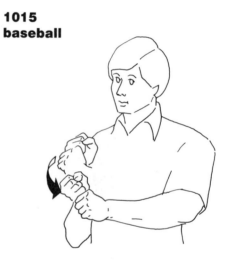

The baseball office is open.

1016
ball, †catch

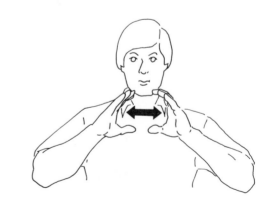

My ball is in the river.

340

**1017
game, †match,
contest**

They began the game late.

**1018
throw**

Throw the small ball to her.

**1019
punish,
penalty,
†correct**

Who punished the wrestler?

341

Practice Sentences

last
267

1. The volleyball team lost again last night.

2. We lost the ball on purpose.

3. That *restaurant* has been feeding the football team for years.

4. The principal is in the baseball coach's office.

have
1006
have
1004

5. They have wrestled here for eight months.

6. *Do* you have a new soccer ball?

7. His new policy prevented any real communication.

8. Total communication is *used* here daily.

hasn't
1003
have
1004

9. She hasn't promised *to* communicate with us.

10. I have my *own* purpose for doing this.

11. We were embarrassed because we misunderstood.

12. The child threw the ball into the river.

time
120

13. Dad was relieved *to* finish on time.

14. Her sister was afraid *to* swim in the river.

15. She misunderstood what I was trying *to* communicate.

have   **join**
1006   894

16. Have you joined the football team?

17. The principal promised not *to* change the policy.

18. Why is your sister *so* shy?

19. The principal punished eight *of* the ten boys.

time
120

20. We didn't start on time because you were late.

Mind Ticklers

Make the sign _____ | *and think about . . .*

communicate 993	two people talking back and forth
promise 995	putting your hand up to swear an oath
principle 996	a principle written on a page in a book
***office** 999	making the sign for *box* with *o* handshapes
misunderstand 1000	thoughts being turned around or confused in the mind
late 1003	time that is in the past
have 1004	possessing something or pulling it towards you
have been 1005	moving from the past to the present
finish 1006	the idea that what you had in your hands to do is already done
embarrass 1007	how blood rushes to the face when someone is embarrassed
ashamed 1008	wanting to hide behind your hand because you are ashamed
river 1009	the width and movement of the river
relieve 1010	everything inside you being relaxed
wrestle 1011	grasping the hands as in wrestling
volleyball 1013	hitting a volleyball
football 1014	scrimmage lines
baseball 1015	the natural gesture of batting a ball
ball 1016	the shape of a ball
game 1017	butting heads with someone in competition
throw 1018	the natural gesture of throwing something

Vocabulary

communicate, communication

*total communication

promise, oath, swear

principle, policy

principal

purpose, intention

*office

misunderstand, change of mind

feed

because, since

late, have not, yet, not yet

have, own, possess

have been, since, all along, ever since

have, finish

embarrass

ashamed, shy, shame

river, stream

relieve, content, relief

wrestle

kick, soccer

volleyball

football

baseball

ball, catch

game, match, contest

throw

punish, penalty, correct

Additional Signs and Notes

Lesson 36

1020
throw out,
discard

I threw out all the copies.

1021
†ride (on an animal)

Can you ride a horse?

1022
†ride (in a vehicle)

We will ride to the game.

1023
electric,
electricity

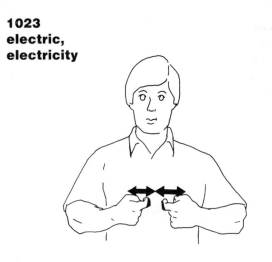

Is the electricity on now?

1024
***evaluate** (judge),
***evaluations**

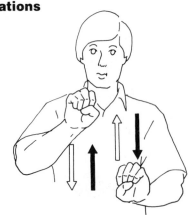

When can we evaluate you?

1025
earth,
geography

The earth is like a ball.

1026
quiet,
be quiet,
calm,
†still

The baseball team is quiet.

1027
compare,
comparison,
†match

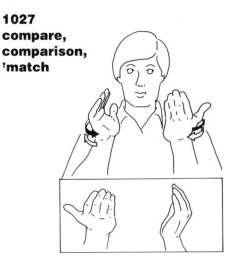

I promise *to* compare them.

**1028
enemy**

The enemy is near.

**1029
star**

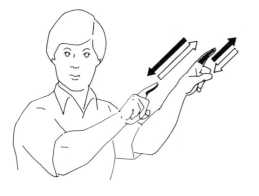

Look at all the stars.

**1030
toothbrush,
brush**

Don't throw out my toothbrush.

**1031
strong,
*energy,
*power,
*authority,
†pull**

She is a strong enemy.

**1032
*energy** (strong)

Is that electric energy?

1033
†put off, postpone, delay

He put off evaluating us.

1034
†front

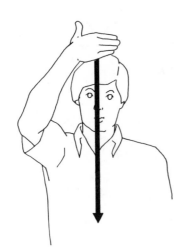

You may ride in the front.

1035
emphasize, stress, emphasis

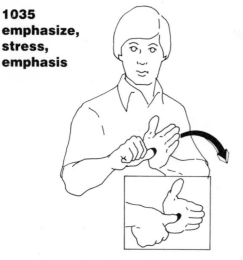

Don't emphasize that point.

1036
demand, require

They demand that you be quiet!

1037
insurance

I compared insurance policies.

1038
library

She was quiet in our library.

**1039
establish,
set up,
found,
form, set**

We established a new team.

**1040
guilty**

The strong man was guilty.

**1041
touch,
†reach**

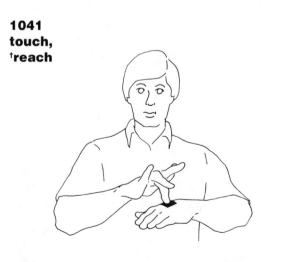

Don't touch my toothbrush.

**1042
†drop**

She dropped the ball.

**1043
†drop,
give up**

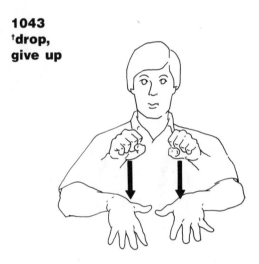

I dropped my insurance.

**1044
variety,
various**

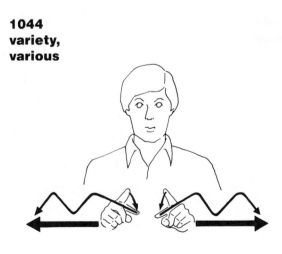

There are a variety of books.

349

1045
vote,
election,
elect

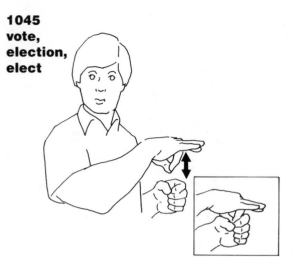

He set up the various voting places.

1046
visit

I visited the guilty man.

1047
weak

Our enemy is becoming weaker.

Practice Sentences

	made 291	1. The principal made the library discard several books.
	ride 1021	2. When we visit your aunt, you can ride her horses.
	no 110	3. No one knew how strong the enemy was.
	save 713	4. They emphasized saving electric energy.
ride 1022	**around** 531	5. He wanted *to* ride a bicycle around the earth.
	big 399	6. The sun is really a big star.
	like 259	7. I would like you *to* compare the evaluations.
		8. They established *an* insurance *company* for deaf people.
	drop 1043	9. He dropped his guilty *plea* in court.
	drop 1042	10. He dropped his toothbrush and couldn't find it.
	before 299	11. She demanded that the plane reach *Florida* before noon.
		12. Everything was quiet in front *of* the library.
had to 277	**put off** 1033	13. Mother had to put off her visit for various reasons.
		14. They voted for *an* increase in insurance prices.
		15. The teacher received a weak evaluation.
	drop 1042	16. The enemy dropped his gun and fled.
make 290	**like** 174	17. Your sister can't make demands like that!
		18. Who threw out my old geography book?
	notice 773	19. I noticed your voice is becoming weaker.
		20. Walk to the front *of* the house and tell him.

Mind Ticklers

Make the sign _____ | *and think about . . .*

throw out 1020	the natural gesture of throwing something out
ride 1021	straddling an animal
ride 1022	getting into a vehicle
electric 1023	how an electric charge jumps from one pole to another
evaluate 1024	making the sign for *justice* with *e* handshapes
earth 1025	the rotation of the earth
quiet 1026	making the *ssh* gesture with a calming motion
compare 1027	looking at two things
toothbrush 1030	the natural gesture of brushing one's teeth
strong 1031	showing the muscle
energy 1032	making the sign for *strong* with an *e* handshape
put off 1033	extending something into the future
front 1034	something that is physically in front of you
establish 1039	setting something up on the horizon
guilty 1040	how your heart beats faster if you are guilty
touch 1041	the natural gesture of touching something
drop 1042	physically dropping something
vote 1045	the act of putting your ballot in the election box
visit 1046	*v* handshapes moving from one place to another
weak 1047	not being able to stand firmly

Vocabulary

throw out, discard

ride (animal)

ride (vehicle)

electric, electricity

*evaluate, *evaluations

earth, geography

quiet, be quiet, calm, still

compare, comparison, match

enemy

star

toothbrush, brush

strong, *energy, *power, *authority, pull

*energy

put off, delay

front

emphasize, stress, emphasis

demand, require

insurance

library

establish, set up, found, form, set

guilty

touch, reach

drop

drop, give up

variety, various

vote, election, elect

visit

weak

Additional Signs and Notes

Lesson 37

**1048
restroom**

Where is the restroom?

**1049
nation**

This nation is strong.

1050
nature,
normal,
naturally,
†of course

It is not my nature *to* yell.

1051
***normal** (same)

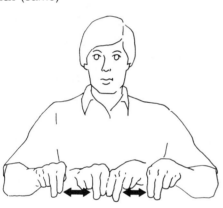

Was it a normal visit?

1052
pet

Of course, that is my pet.

1053
steal

He didn't steal your pet.

1054
jealous,
envy

I am jealous *of* you.

1055
***or** (then),
***either,**
***nor,**
***neither**

Which is it, this or that?

355

1056
*oral (lipread)

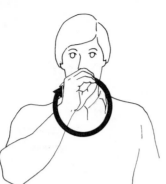

She was very oral.

1057
mainstream

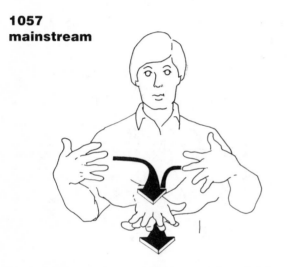

Our son was mainstreamed into public school.

1058
manners,
courteous,
polite

She demanded good manners.

1059
formal,
fancy,
sophisticated,
elaborate,
†class

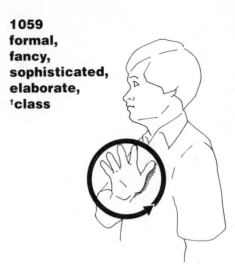

Why are you *so* formal?

1060
†back,
support,
in favor of,
*reinforce,
†stand behind

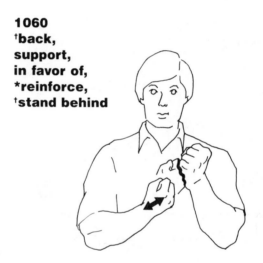

We all back our nation.

1061
†back,
return

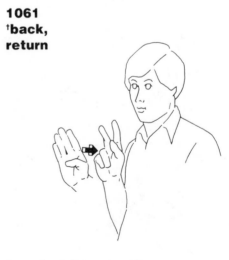

I was back home in a day.

**1062
kneel**

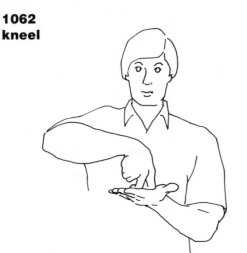

You may kneel here, beside me.

**1063
loan,
†lend**

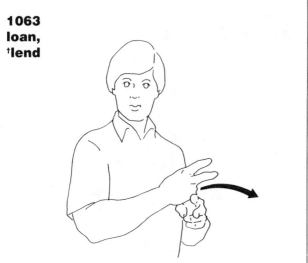

Don't loan him any money.

**1064
tired,
exhausted,
worn out**

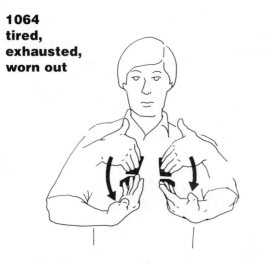

Your pet looks exhausted.

**1065
fail**

He failed the final exam.

**1066
cents**

Do you have 40 cents?

**1067
†fair,
adequate**

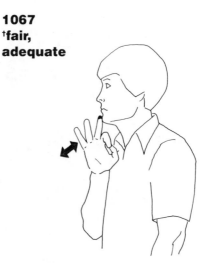

The library book was fair.

357

1068
†fair,
equal,
even,
tie,
†just

It was not a fair game.

1069
empty,
bare,
nude,
vacant,
available

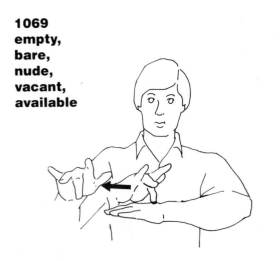

The restroom is empty now.

1070
†line,
line up

The cars are really lined up.

1071
line, string

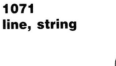

Who put that line there?

1072
†use,
utilize,
†apply

May I use that again?

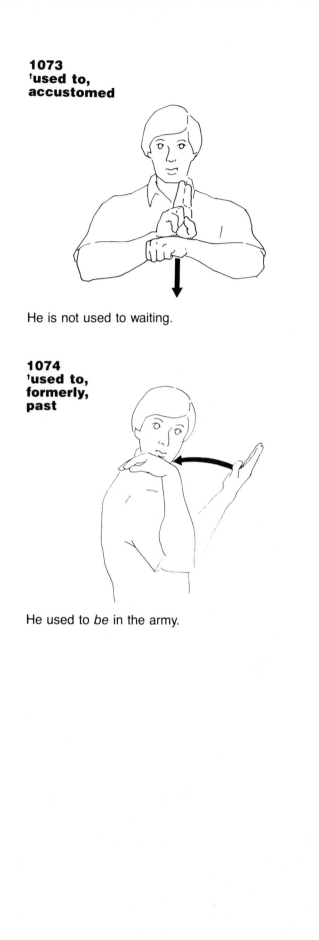

1073
†used to,
accustomed

He is not used to waiting.

1074
†used to,
formerly,
past

He used to *be* in the army.

Practice Sentences

	used to 1073	**have** 1004
long 274	**line** 1070	**back** 1061
		fair 1068
	used to 1074	**have** 1004
		fair 1067
	of course 1050	**use** 1072
	used to 1073	**around** 529
		back 1060
looks 562	**normal** 1050, 1051	

1. Is the restroom upstairs or downstairs?

2. The school is used to having mainstreamed children.

3. A long line *of* tired people walked back.

4. It was a very fair game.

5. She used to have nine pets in her house.

6. We can expect fair weather all week.

7. She was jealous *of* all our friends.

8. The nation is loaning money to everyone.

9. Of course, we can use this string.

10. She is used to *being* formal around her parents.

11. Father failed *to* find the 30¢ he lost.

12. We always kneel a lot in church.

13. Sure, we will back your dad for president.

14. Everything looks normal to me today.

15. They say it is part *of* his nature.

16. Will the oral children be mainstreamed?

17. They taught their son very good manners.

18. When the restroom is empty, you can clean it.

19. My aunt and uncle went to a formal dance.

20. I know I am dirty and tired.

Mind Ticklers

Make the sign _____	*and think about . . .*
restroom 1048	abbreviating the word *restroom* with double *r* handshapes
normal 1051	making the sign for *same* with *n* handshapes
pet 1052	the natural gesture of petting an animal
steal 1053	stealing something underhandedly
back 1060	showing physical support for something
kneel 1062	the legs being in a kneeling position
tired, exhausted 1064	the shoulders and body being bent over to indicate weariness
fair 1068	two things that are on the same level
line 1070	people standing behind one another
line, string 1071	a piece of string the size of the little fingers
use 1072	making the sign for *work* with a *u* handshape
used to 1073	making the sign for *habit* with a *u* handshape
used to 1074	time that is in the past

Vocabulary

restroom	manners, courteous, polite	cents
nation		fair, adequate
nature, normal, naturally, of course	formal, fancy, sophisticated, elaborate, class	fair, equal, even, tie, just
*normal	back, support, in favor of, *reinforce, stand behind	empty, bare, nude, vacant, available
pet		line, line up
steal	back, return	line, string
jealous, envy	kneel	use, utilize, apply
*or, *either, *nor, *neither	loan, lend	used to, accustomed
*oral	tired, exhausted, worn out	used to, formerly, past
mainstream	fail	

Additional Signs and Notes

Lesson 38

1075
taste

Let us taste it again.

1076
spoon

Your spoon is on the floor.

363

1077
fork

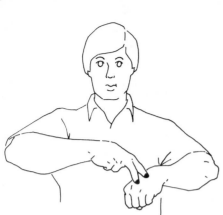

That is my fork.

1078
knife, †cut

The knife and fork are gone.

1079
napkin

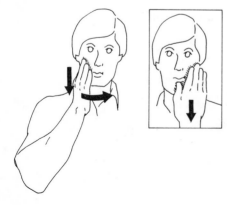

The spoon is on the napkin.

1080
restaurant

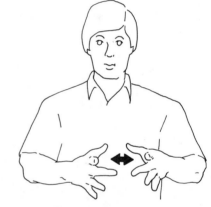

The restaurant is very formal.

1081
dish, plate

The napkin is on the plate.

1082
cup

Where is my cup?

1083
†glass

I won't use this dirty glass.

1084
†glass

The plate is made *of* glass.

1085
†glasses,
eyeglasses

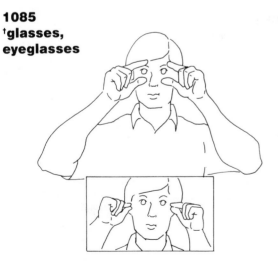

I can see with my glasses.

1086
delicious,
tasty

That pie is delicious.

1087
favorite

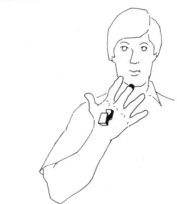

My favorite glasses are lost.

1088
encourage,
persuade

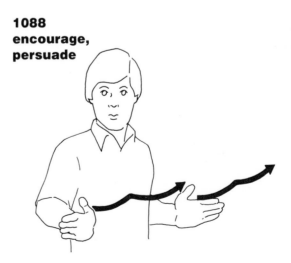

Encourage him to taste it.

**1089
limit,
*restrict,
*minimum**

They limited the *amount of* our loan.

**1090
hill**

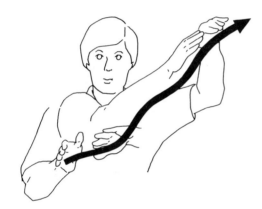

Their house is on a hill.

**1091
stranger**

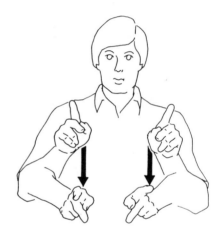

The stranger has a knife.

**1092
divide, split**

Why not divide the napkins?

366

1093
awkward, clumsy

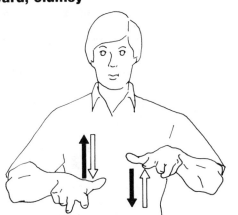

The stranger felt awkward.

1094
stubborn

The stranger looks stubborn.

1095
narrow

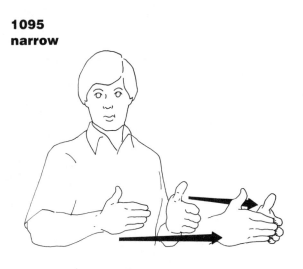

The mountain road is narrow.

1096
intelligent, clever

He has *an* intelligent pet.

1097
stupid, ignorant

He made some stupid mistakes on the exam.

1098
lucky

She is always lucky.

Practice Sentences

put
336

glass
1083

glass
1084

glasses
1085

left
182

around
531

has
1004

act
283

have
56

glass
1084

1. The stranger was lucky; the restaurant was open.

2. The knife, fork, and spoon were on the table.

3. Why *did* you put the napkin on the plate?

4. Where are the water glasses?

5. It was stupid *to* divide the food.

6. The glass on the table is *cracked*.

7. I think I lost my favorite glasses.

8. The road up the hill was narrow.

9. Why are you always *so* stubborn?

10. Did you taste your mother's cooking?

11. There is some liquor left in the cup.

12. My parents always encouraged us *to* work.

13. He is very awkward around women.

14. Is there a limit on your earnings?

15. The restaurant has very fancy *flatware*.

16. The stranger acted intelligently.

17. She prefers the blue and white dishes.

18. We are lucky *to* have good friends.

19. Their front door was almost all glass.

20. How can we divide the work equally?

Mind Ticklers

Make the sign _____	*and think about . . .*
taste 1075	putting something on the tongue
spoon 1076	the shape of a spoon
fork 1077	stabbing something with a fork
knife 1078	sharpening a knife
napkin 1079	wiping your mouth with a napkin
dish 1081	outlining the shape of a plate
cup 1082	the size and shape of a cup
glass 1083	how a glass is taller than a cup
glass 1084	the idea that window glass is like the enamel on your teeth
glasses 1085	the rims of eyeglasses
encourage 1088	pushing someone to do something
limit 1089	showing boundary lines
hill 1090	the shape of hills
divide 1092	splitting something in half
awkward 1093	walking in an awkward manner
stubborn 1094	imitating the ears of a donkey and, thus, alluding to its temperament
narrow 1095	indicating the narrowness of something
intelligent 1096	wonderful thoughts emanating from the mind
stupid 1097	the idea of nothing getting through the head

Vocabulary

taste	glass	stranger
spoon	glasses, eyeglasses	divide, split
fork	delicious, tasty	awkward, clumsy
knife, cut	favorite	stubborn
napkin	encourage, persuade	narrow
restaurant		intelligent, clever
dish, plate	limit, *restrict, *minimum	stupid, ignorant
cup	hill	lucky
glass (drink)		

Additional Signs and Notes

Lesson 39

**1099
war,
battle,
†engagement**

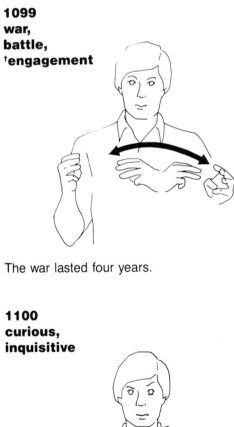

The war lasted four years.

**1100
curious,
inquisitive**

Is he curious about the war?

1101
summary,
condense,
abbreviate

He summarized the process.

1102
temperature

What is the temperature?

1103
*thermometer (temperature)

Is the thermometer broken?

1104
subtract,
deduct,
remove,
†take away,
eliminate

Will you subtract the cost?

1105
add, addition,
additional

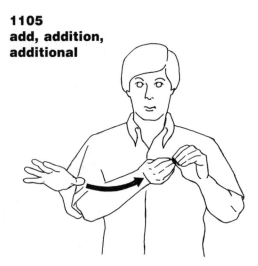

The army added soldiers.

1106
negative,
minus,
subtract

Don't feel *so* negative.

1107
positive,
advantage,
plus, add,
†cross

You need *to* feel positive.

1108
metal

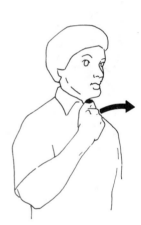

Where is the metal window?

1109
†iron, steel

Is that made *of* iron?

1110
†iron, press

Did you see mom ironing?

1111
fishing,
fish,
go fishing

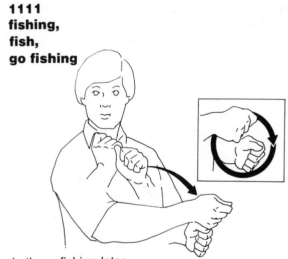

Let's go fishing later.

1112
***method** (street), ***way**

The best method is *to* add.

1113
island

The island has no trees.

1114
†lie, lie down,
recline

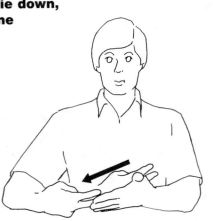

Lie here and rest *an* hour.

1115
†lie, fib,
untruth

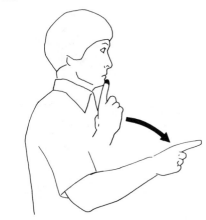

That was a lie!

1116
truth, true

Tell dad the truth.

1117
false, fake,
fiction

The army faked a battle.

374

**1118
forest,
woods,
trees**

The island is one big forest.

**1119
wood**

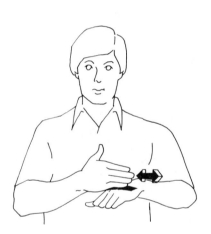

We need more wood.

**1120
*result** (happen)

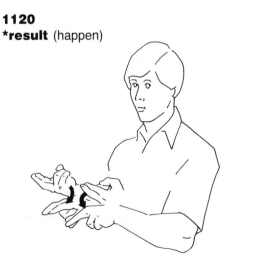

He lied about the results.

**1121
rich, wealth,
wealthy**

They are a wealthy family.

**1122
magazine,
brochure,
pamphlet**

Where is my magazine?

375

1123
audience,
group,
crowd,
†house

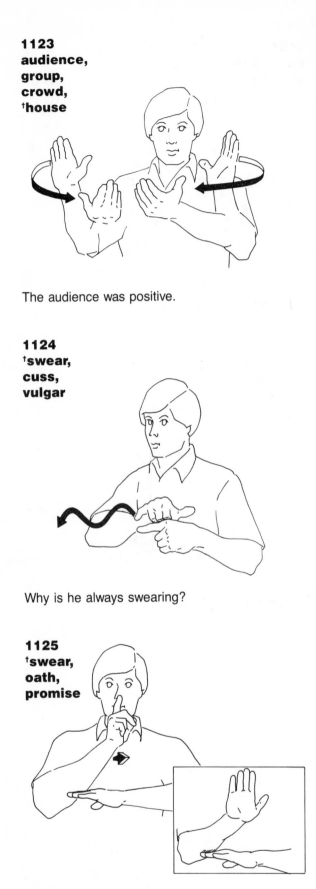

The audience was positive.

1124
†swear,
cuss,
vulgar

Why is he always swearing?

1125
†swear,
oath,
promise

Do you swear *to* tell me?

Practice Sentences

	play 329	1. The wealthy playboy went to war.
		2. What is the temperature outside?
	glass 1084	3. The thermometer is made *of* glass and metal.
make 290	**iron** 1109	4. They didn't make the bridge *of* iron.
	get 129	5. Can we find a way *to* get to the island?
		6. The whole audience sang together.
		7. Who can summarize the magazine article for us?
	swore 1125	8. In court he swore *to* tell the truth.
		9. Which is correct, addition or subtraction?
	lie 1114	10. Lie here on the wooden floor.
has 56	**swear** 1124	11. She has very negative feelings about swearing.
	lie 1115	12. Don't lie to us! Were you in the forest?
	little 387	13. Her method *of* fishing was a little *odd.*
	no 109	14. Oh no, not another true-false test!
	like 49	15. You may not like the results *of* the test.
like 49	**iron** 1110	16. I don't know anyone who likes ironing.
	positive 1107	17. Do you feel positive about the recent move?
		18. They are all curious about the baby.
glass 1084	**iron** 1109	19. The table is made *of* wood, glass, and iron.
		20. He dreams *of* becoming rich some day.

Mind Ticklers

Make the sign _____ | *and think about . . .*

war 1099	battle lines moving back and forth
curious 1100	extending your neck to see everything
summary 1101	condensing something big into something small
temperature 1102	the mercury going up and down in a thermometer
subtract 1104	taking away something from the total
add 1105	putting two or more things together
negative 1106	the minus symbol
positive 1107	the plus symbol
iron 1109	steel rails sliding out of a furnace
iron 1110	the natural gesture of ironing clothes
fishing 1111	the act of fishing with a rod and reel
island 1113	the boundaries of an island
lie 1114	the natural position of lying down
lie 1115	a statement not coming straight from the mouth
truth 1116	words coming straight from the mouth
false 1117	brushing the truth away
forest 1118	a forest being made up of many trees
wood 1119	the motion of cutting wood
rich 1121	dropping many coins into the hand
magazine 1122	the binding of a magazine
audience 1123	outlining the size of a group of people
swear 1125	raising your hand to swear an oath

Vocabulary

war, battle, engagement

curious, inquisitive

summary, condense, abbreviate

temperature

*thermometer

subtract, deduct, remove, take away, eliminate

add, addition, additional

negative, minus, subtract

positive, advantage, plus, add, cross

metal

iron, steel

iron, press

fishing, fish, go fishing

*method, *way

island

lie, lie down, recline

lie, fib, untruth

truth, true

false, fake, fiction

forest, woods, trees

wood

*result

rich, wealth, wealthy

magazine, brochure, pamphlet

audience, group, crowd, house

swear, cuss, vulgar

swear, oath, promise

Additional Signs and Notes

379

Lesson 40

1126
*tradition (habit)

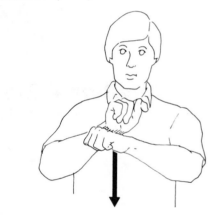

Is that *an* army tradition?

1127
unfair,
worthless

Do you think it is unfair?

1128
†tall,
†high

How tall is the mountain?

1129
take me

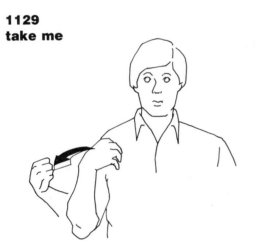

Please, take me with you.

1130
proof,
evidence

Do you have proof it is true?

1131
†suspect,
suspicious

Do you suspect him?

1132
sweetheart

My sweetheart is rich.

1133
swallow

Will you swallow it now?

1134
†high,
†tall

That looks *too* high.

1135
†high,
important,
advance

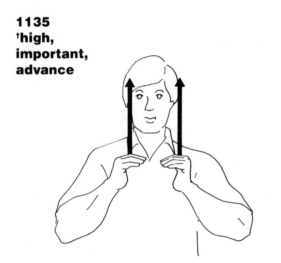

He has a high position.

1136
***low**
***lower,**
***less**

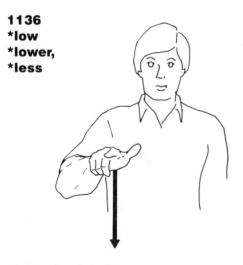

No, put it a little lower.

1137
jail,
prison
prisoner

Is your sweetheart in jail?

1138
loud, noise,
vibrate,
sound

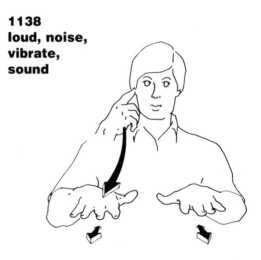

The audience was very loud.

1139
level

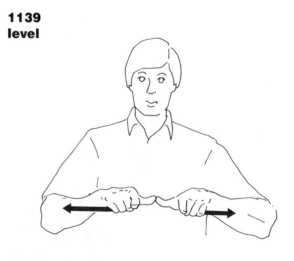

I suspect the table is not level.

1140
*foreign (country)

The foreign soldiers left.

1141
willing,
†offer

I am willing *to* help you.

1142
tendency,
inclined

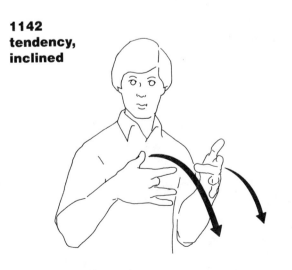

She has a tendency *to* swear.

1143
trust, faith,
confidence

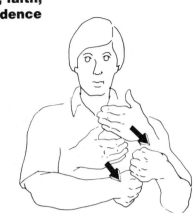

Whom can you trust here?

1144
weigh,
weight,
pounds

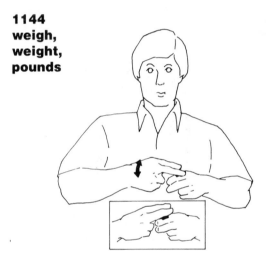
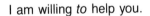

The metal weighs a lot.

1145
†cause, †move

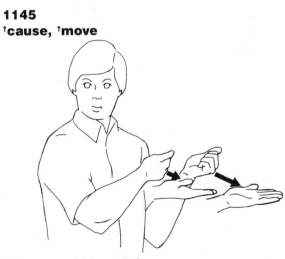

What caused him *to* lie?

1146
waves

The waves were not very high.

1147
wall

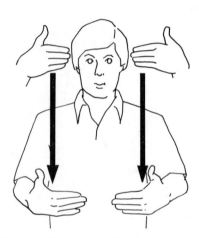

A thermometer is on the wall.

1148
opposite,
†against

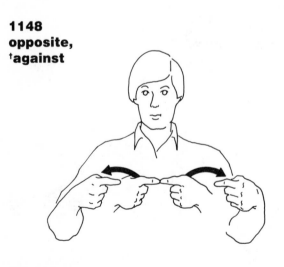

Who sits opposite you in class?

1149
workshop

The workshop was worthless.

1150
†*well (good),
†fine

How well *do* you know her?

1151
win, †carry

Our team won the game.

384

1152
traffic

The traffic caused accidents.

1153
ticket

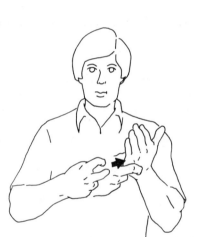

I got a parking ticket.

1154
plant

Have you planted your corn?

1155
†plant, grow

My plant looks dead.

1156
perfect

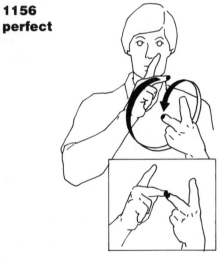

Your weight is perfect.

385

Practice Sentences

suspect		**got**
1131		130
plant	**feet**	**high**
1155	742	1134
	advance	**sign**
	805	706

high
1134

suspect
189

seem
560

plant
1154

high
1134

high
1135

have
56

big **pounding**
399   903

this
42

1. My weight is almost perfect now.

2. Take me with you to the workshop.

3. Yes, I planted my garden last week.

4. I suspect he got another traffic ticket.

5. The corn plants will be three feet high by July.

6. Are you in the advanced sign language class?

7. Father is not willing *to* go to jail.

8. She has a tendency *to* trust everyone.

9. What caused the waves *to* be *so* high?

10. The suspect sat opposite the yellow wall.

11. It was unfair; he seemed *to* win everything.

12. You should plant things on level land.

13. His sweetheart was from a foreign country.

14. Traditionally, the workers won all the prizes.

15. I don't remember that building *being so* tall.

16. First it's *too* high, then *too* low; can't you decide?

17. He tried *to* swallow the evidence, but he was *too* late.

18. How high up is she in the organization?

19. How many football tickets *do* you have?

20. My sister trusts me *to* make the decision.

21. The big waves were pounding the wall.

22. Our house is opposite the workshop.

23. Why is the traffic here always terrible?

24. Swallowing fish in college was a tradition years ago.

25. This is the perfect place *to* vacation.

Mind Ticklers

Make the sign _____ | *and think about . . .*

tradition 1126	making the sign for *used to* with a *t* handshape
tall 1128	pointing upward to indicate height
take me 1129	grabbing yourself to be pulled along
proof 1130	placing tangible evidence into your hand
suspect 1131	scratching your head as if pondering something
sweetheart 1132	sweethearts whispering to each other
swallow 1133	something going down the throat
high 1134	motioning upward to indicate height
high 1135	a level above other people
jail 1137	the bars of a jail cell
loud 1138	sound vibrations in the air
level 1139	something that is flat
willing 1141	extending your heart for someone
tendency 1142	extending your entire self for someone
trust 1143	something that you are able to hold on to or grasp
weigh 1144	balancing a set of scales
waves 1146	the shape of waves
opposite 1148	two things going in opposite directions
workshop 1149	making the sign for *group* with *w* and *s* handshapes
win 1151	grabbing the opposition's flag and waving it
traffic 1152	traffic going in both directions
ticket 1153	punching holes in a ticket
plant 1154	sowing seeds in the ground
plant 1155	plants growing up through the ground

Vocabulary

*tradition	jail, prison, prisoner	wall
unfair, worthless	loud, noise, vibrate, sound	opposite, against
tall, high		workshop
take me	level	*well, fine
proof, evidence	*foreign	win, carry
suspect, suspicious	willing, offer	traffic
sweetheart	tendency, inclined	ticket
swallow	trust, faith, confidence	plant
high, tall	weigh, weight, pounds	plant, grow
high, important, advance	cause, move	perfect
*low, *lower, *less	waves	

Additional Signs and Notes

Lesson 41

1157
†train,
railroad

Where is my train ticket?

1158
*train (practice), ***rehearsal**

I have to train tonight.

**1159
picture,
photograph**

This is a picture *of* me.

**1160
odd, strange,
peculiar,
queer**

That is *an* odd-looking train.

**1161
nervous,
†anxious**

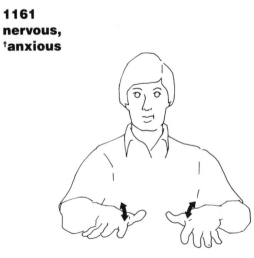

Training makes me nervous.

**1162
*busy (work), *business**

Are you busy tomorrow?

**1163
Pittsburgh**

We will take the train to Pittsburgh.

**1164
Philadelphia**

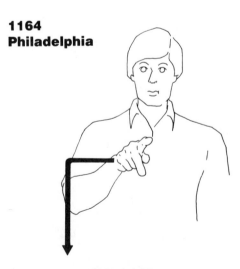

I was born in Philadelphia.

390

1165
Washington, D.C.,
Washington (state)

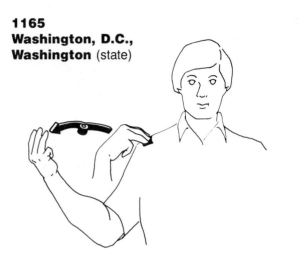

Washington, D.C. is a busy place.

1166
San Francisco

San Francisco is a hilly city.

1167
New York,
New York City

I have a picture *of* New York City.

1168
Milwaukee

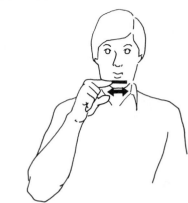

Milwaukee is a beer town.

1169
Los Angeles

Los Angeles is a huge city.

1170
California,
gold

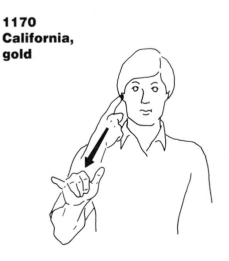

The weather in southern California is great.

391

1171
U.S., United States

The U.S. team is training for the World Games.

1172
America

See America *by* train.

1173
Europe

Have you visited Europe?

1174
Scotland

Where is Scotland?

1175
England,
English

Scotland is near England.

1176
France,
French

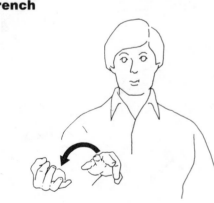

French is a good language *to* know.

**1177
Germany,
German**

German trains run on schedule.

**1178
Ireland,
Irish**

Ireland is a country *of* great beauty.

**1179
Italy,
Italian**

Italy is shaped like a boot.

**1180
India**

The food in India is very *spicy*.

**1181
Russia,
Russian**

Russia makes me nervous.

**1182
Canada,
Canadian**

Canada is a good neighbor.

393

1183
Spain,
Spanish

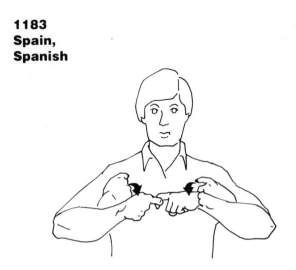

We saw a *bull*fight in Spain.

1184
Mexico,
Mexican

Mexico is south *of* the U.S.

1185
Japan,
Japanese

Japan and the U.S. have a trade agreement.

Practice Sentences

have
1006

has
1004

get
128

train **through**
1157 330

train
1158

has
56

last **time**
267 121

get along
521

called
103

take monument
460 741

train
1157

make
290

1. Yes, I have traveled in most *of* Mexico.

2. Grandfather has businesses in Pittsburgh and Washington.

3. We always get nervous walking in Philadelphia.

4. The train goes through England, Scotland, and *Wales*.

5. The deaf olympic team trained in New York.

6. She has many pictures of Europe.

7. San Francisco and Los Angeles are both in California.

8. When was the last time you were in Germany or France?

9. Was pizza invented in Italy?

10. Milwaukee is the city famous for beer.

11. It is odd how the U.S. and Russia get along.

12. My Canadian friend is in India now.

13. I want *to* vacation in Spain again.

14. How far is Japan from America?

15. Philadelphia is called "the city of brotherly love."

16. England and Ireland continue *to* battle each other.

17. Yes, my grandmother was born in Germany.

18. Don't forget *to* take a picture *of* the Washington Monument.

19. The train stops only once in New York.

20. *Did* the Russian doctor make you nervous?

Mind Ticklers

Make the sign _____ | *and think about . . .*

train 1157	the friction of the wheels on the track
train 1158	doing something over and over for practice
picture 1159	putting what is seen on paper
odd 1160	seeing something strange or twisted
nervous 1161	your hands shaking
Pittsburgh 1163	Pittsburgh as the city where steel pins are made
Philadelphia 1164	taking a quill from an inkwell to sign the Declaration of Independence
Washington 1165	General Washington's epaulets
Milwaukee 1168	wiping beer off the chin
California 1170	pointing to a golden earring
America 1172	the split rail fences that were common in the frontier days of America
Scotland 1174	the plaids worn by the Scots
England 1175	an Englishman leaning on an umbrella
France 1176	an aristocrat waving a handkerchief
Germany 1177	the eagle as a symbol of Germany
Ireland 1178	the Irish potato
Italy 1179	the cross as representing Italy's religion
India 1180	the caste mark of Hinduism
Russia 1181	the Cossacks dance
Canada 1182	shaking snow off a coat
Spain 1183	fastening a cape
Mexico 1184	a Mexican's mustache
Japan 1185	the almond shape of oriental eyes

Vocabulary

train, railroad	San Francisco	France, French
*train, *rehearsal	New York, New York City	Germany, German
picture, photograph	Milwaukee	Ireland, Irish
	Los Angeles	Italy, Italian
odd, strange, peculiar, queer	California, gold	India
nervous, anxious	U.S., United States	Russia, Russian
*busy, *business	America	Canada, Canadian
Pittsburgh	Europe	Spain, Spanish
Philadelphia	Scotland	Mexico, Mexican
Washington, D.C., Washington	England, English	Japan, Japanese

Additional Signs and Notes

Multi-sign Word Appendix

The student is encouraged to cover the far right column on the page that shows the appropriate gloss and reference number. This provides a self-checking system.

ABOUT

It is **about** time to leave.	almost	424
I saw it **about** here yesterday.	vicinity	530
What **about** your friend?	about	529

ABOVE

The airplane is **above** the mountains.	above	40
It is **above** my limit.	over	737

ACCIDENT

He **accidently** came early.	happen	261
His license was suspended after the **accident.**	vehicle	789
Forgetting his mother's birthday was an awful **accident.**	mistake	788

ACT

The first two **acts** were great!	drama	328
Don't **act** like that around my sister.	do	283

ADD

Add all these numbers for me.	add	747
Add up my bill, please.	count	740
He is always **adding to** my bill.	increase	359

ADMIT

Don't **admit** anyone under ten to the party.	permit	500
He **admitted** everything in court.	confess	733
The plan is to **admit** only the first ten people.	welcome	732

ADVANCE

The **advanced** sign class is over.	promote	805
The Indians **advanced** toward the group slowly.	progress	806
His knowledge of sign language has **advanced.**	improve	990

AFTER

See me **after** the second act.	finish	313
My arithmetic class is **after** French.	line	312
Is that dog **after** my cat again?	chase	311
I'll go first; you come **after** me.	turn	303
You can play **after** you eat.	finish	313
Don't look now, but someone is **after** you.	chase	311

AGAINST

Are you really **against** that idea?	oppose	1148
	or **against**	507
Put the TV **against** the wall.	near	530

AIM

He took careful **aim** and fired.	point	817
Her **aim** is to become a doctor.	goal	816

ANXIOUS

Before a test, she always becomes **anxious.**	worry	246
	or **nervous**	1161
Are you **anxious** to start your vacation?	eager	254
	or **excited**	785

APPEAR

You always **appear** at the wrong time.	show up	561
You **appear** a little flushed.	look	356
It **appears** that you made a small mistake.	seem	560
He will **appear** in the play.	act	284

APPLY

No one **applied** for that job.	volunteer	942
You need to **apply** what you learn.	use	1072
Apply the glue with care.	paint	758

AROUND

Dad walks **around** the block daily.	round	531
They lost their money **around** here.	vicinity	530

ARTICLE

Read this funny **article.**	column	884
He lost four of the five **articles** he bought.	thing	882

ASK

I can't **ask** for that again.	request	338
He knows; **ask** him when he arrives.	question	339

ASSOCIATION

The National **Association** of the Deaf is big.	association	222
My **association** with him is better than ever.	mingle	596
	or **contact**	1041

BACK

Will you **back** the President again?	support	1060
My **back** is aching again.	back	418
When will you come **back** home?	return	1061
That happened **back** about ten years.	past	46
Give that money **back** to me.	return	1061

BEAR

That is either a grizzly or a black **bear.**	bear	628
I cannot **bear** the thought of your leaving.	tolerate	597

BEAT

Our team **beat** theirs badly.	defeat	902
He **beat** on his dog.	hit	903
	or **hit**	516

BEFORE

I never saw that happen **before.**	past	267
	or **before**	300
He spoke **before** the group **before** lunch.	in front of	301
	before	299
Look it over **before** buying it.	**before**	299

BELOW

We put the flower seeds **below** the ground.	under	41
	or **beneath**	357
You told me it was **below** $20.00.	less than	358

BITE

Let's get a **bite** before the play.	eat	24
Careful, the cat **bites** strangers.	bite	787

BLACK

Black was the new color.	black	93
Several **Blacks** came to the party.	black	93
	+ **people**	190

BLOCK

I run about 14 **blocks** daily.	block	728
The car was **blocked** by the truck.	stuck	729
They succeeded in **blocking** the vote.	prevent	730
The baby plays with wooden **blocks.**	box	557
Don't **block** my view.	bother	595

BLUE

The **blue** car is mine.	blue	89
Mondays make me **blue.**	depressed	946

BREAK

Who will **break** the news to them?	tell	192
He meant to **break** the pencil.	break	559
We will now take a 15-minute **break.**	vacation	956
	or **break**	559
They **broke out** of jail this morning.	escape	448
No one thinks the war will **break out** soon.	begin	369

BRIGHT

Dad gave me a **bright** new penny.	shiny	382
That light is too **bright.**	bright	380
What a **bright** little girl.	clever	381

BUT

No one showed up **but** her.	except	750
I saw her, **but** she didn't see me.	but	172
He is **but** a child.	only	904
It never rains, **but** it pours.	that	54

BY

Drive **by** my old house.	pass	763
Put the broom **by** the door.	near	282
He does everything **by** the book.	follow	701
Enter **by** the front door.	through	330
He studied **by** night for his degree.	during	344
They did everything **by** force.	with	185

CALL

The teacher always **calls** on me.	summon	101
They plan to **call** the baby Jonah.	name	103
I **called** my mother in Boston yesterday.	telephone	100
Mother always **called** us for dinner at 5:00.	yell	102
The recipe **called** for chocolate chips.	required	1036

CAN

I **can** do that for you.	can	125
You think he **can** still be living?	might	197

CARRY

Carry the girls' books.	carry	375
New York will **carry** the election for him.	win	1151
Her decisions always **carry** considerable weight.	have	56
The ball **carried** over 200 yards.	went	39
The crime **carried** a stiff penalty.	require	1036

CATCH

The police cannot **catch** the robber.	apprehend	533
When I throw this, you **catch** it.	catch	534
I always **catch** a cold in the fall.	get	130
My foot was **caught** in the door.	stuck	729

CAUSE

His **cause** was to defeat the enemy.	goal	816
What do you think **caused** the accident?	caused	1145

CHARGE

They **charged** $2.00 a person.	cost	405
	or **charge**	837
He was **charged** with child neglect.	blame	838
The children were in her **charge.**	responsibility	696
	or **control**	449

CHECK

Check my paper for me, please.	correct	444
I need to **check** our food supply.	inspect	443
Write a **check** for $12.00.	check	442
He had no **checks** on his paper.	marks	441
Do the copies **check** with the originals?	agree	948

CLASS

She has no **class.**	polite	1059
Class was cancelled for the second time.	class	218

CLEAN

The car had very **clean** lines.	nice	396
Clean up the room before tomorrow.	clean	395
Make sure you get a **clean** copy.	good	183
The robbers **cleaned out** the room.	empty	1069
It was cut to make a **clean** edge.	smooth	891

CLOSE

You have to **close** the door when you leave.	close	281
My friend lives very **close** to me.	near	530
	or close	282
We are very **close**.	friend	169
She is very **closed** mouth about her family.	secret	599
It was very **close** competition.	tie	285
	or hot	211
Obviously, we have to **close** this meeting.	stop	370
	or finish	313

COLD

Is it **cold** outside?	temperature	213
I have an awful **cold**.	cold	215

COME

No one will **come** here today.	come	38
Come over and stay with me.	come over	751
I am happy nothing like that **came up**.	appear	561
The total bill **came to** $45.00.	add	747
No one believed it would **come true**.	success	517

COMMAND

The foreign student had a good **command** of English.	understand	243
The general **commands** the army.	controls	449
No one gave the **command** to leave.	order	392

COMPLETE

When can you **complete** this job?	finish	313
When will the **complete** job be done?	whole	136
The party was a **complete** surprise.	total	325

CONTENT

She was very **content** with her work.	satisfied	252
The book's **content** was interesting.	information	723

COPY

Copy what is on the board.	imitate	985
Make a **copy** for the teacher.	copy	986

CORRECT

The teacher will **correct** the papers.	check	444
What is the **correct** time?	right	178
If it is wrong, can I **correct** it later?	change	897
Father **corrected** the boy for breaking the window.	punish	1019

COUNT

You can always **count on** his help.	depend	569
Melissa can **count** to 100.	count	740
Of course, everything you say **counts**.	important	780
Count me **in**; that's probably what I need.	include	764

COURSE

My arithmetic **course** is easy.	course	440
Which **course** will take us to Mexico?	way	539
Of course, I agree with you.	naturally	1050

COVER

Be sure to put on some **covers** tonight.	blanket	535
We **covered** all the material in the book.	finished	313
The men **covered up** their mistakes.	vague	537
Today we will **cover** chapters 2 and 3.	cover	536

CROSS

We'll **cross** that bridge when we come to it.	across	736
She is **cross** with her son.	mad	307
Place the **cross** on the altar.	cross	1107

CRY

Don't **cry** when everyone leaves.	cry	28
Their **cry** was "Remember the Alamo."	motto	775
The hurt men **cried** for help.	yell	102

CUT

Three boys were **cut** from the team.	fired	432
I had to take a **cut** in pay.	reduce	778
Don't **cut** the ribbon yet.	scissors	433
How will Dad **cut** the meat?	cut	434
	or knife	1078
Sorry, I can't **cut** class again.	miss	435
You have to **cut** that **out**.	stop	370
Why do you always **cut up** in class?	silly	383

DECLINE

There has been a **decline** in the economy.	decline	739
He **declined** to say anything until tomorrow.	refuse	390

DIRECT

She **directed** each person to leave immediately.	ordered	392
Who will **direct** the play?	manage	449
I expect **direct** answers from you.	precise	714
Can you **direct** me to the bathroom?	explain	818
	or show	525

DISAPPEAR

He **disappeared** after staying only ten minutes.	disappear	822
The snow seemed to **disappear** overnight.	melt	823

DISAPPOINT

The **disappointed** people left early.	discourage	946
I was **disappointed** you didn't show up.	disappoint	697

DISTURB

He **disturbed** the papers on my desk.	mix up	527
Your father is working; don't **disturb** him.	bother	595
Seeing the accident obviously **disturbed** her.	upset	880

DOUBT

Mother **doubts** whether she will leave tomorrow.	doubt	839
Everyone **doubted** the story he told.	disbelieve	408

DRAW

After seven rounds the fight was a **draw.**	tie	285
Draw several pictures for me.	draw	35
Will you **draw** the curtain please?	close	281
The first thing to do is to **draw** trump.	pull	519
He **draws** a big salary for his job.	get	130
She **drew** several comparisons for us.	made	290

DRESS

Who volunteered to **dress** the deer?	clean	395
Mother's **dress** is an old one.	dress	497
Hurry, **dress** the baby before he becomes cold.	dress	496

DROP

I had to **drop** playing golf and tennis.	stop	370
	or give up	1043
Drop over for some coffee or tea.	come over	751
She **dropped out** of college during her second year.	quit	760
Did you **drop** this pencil?	drop	1042
My uncle **dropped** dead playing golf.	fall	759
The plane had to **drop** its speed to land.	decrease	739

DRY

The show was **dry.**	boring	334
The basement was warm and **dry.**	dry	908
I'm **dry;** can you give me some water?	thirsty	687
The first two oil wells were **dry.**	empty	1069

ENGAGEMENT

Our **engagement** is for 12:00.	appointment	929
She decided to return her **engagement** ring.	engagement	928
The army was not prepared for any **engagement.**	battle	1099

EVER

They have done that for **ever.**	always	506
Do you **ever** play football?	sometimes	427
Have you **ever** played football?	before	267

FACE

He tried to **face** his wife, but couldn't.	confront	301
The soldiers were ordered to **face** right.	look	207
She had several marks on her **face.**	face	356
Face him like a man.	meet	36
	or confront	301

FAIR

The movie was just **fair.**	fair	1067
It looks like it may be a **fair** day.	nice	396
My daughter is very **fair.**	light	380
It appeared to be a **fair** fight.	equal	285

FALL

I enjoy **fall** when the leaves change colors.	autumn	677
Don't **fall** from the porch.	fall	759
After dinner, several people **fell** sick.	become	128

FIGURE

What do you **figure** will happen now?	feel	389
I cannot **figure** my scores.	count	740
The **figure** of a woman was on the screen.	figure	741
Can you **figure** this **out** for me?	explain	818
Name a famous **figure** in American history.	person	189
I've already **figured out** the best course.	decide	602

FILL

The delicious dinner **filled** me.	satisfy	898
Please **fill** each can with milk.	fill	325

FINAL

The **final** week in December is Christmas vacation.	last	268
Finally, you graduated from college.	at last	517

FIND

Help me **find** my shoes, please.	look for	354
Did you **find** that on the bed?	find	262

FINE

He was **fined** $20.00 for speeding.	charge	405
You all look **fine** today.	fine	406
This was a very **fine** dinner.	good	183
What a **fine** day for skiing.	beautiful	288

FIRE

The **fire** lasted all night.	fire	782
He was **fired** from his fourth job.	expel	432
His team was **fired up** and ready to play.	excite	785

FLY

How often do you **fly** to Miami?	fly	828
The **flies** are terrible around here.	insect	625
The bird couldn't **fly** with a broken wing.	fly	828
The whole family took **flight** from Europe.	escape	448
Our **flight** leaves at noon today.	airplane	3

FOLLOW

Try to **follow** his example.	copy	985
Do you always **follow** her advice?	accept	695
Follow me out of this place.	follow	701

GAIN

His first year in business, he showed little **gain.**	profit	565
Faster, he is **gaining** on us.	chase	311
After the operation she showed considerable **gains.**	improvement	990
I notice you are **gaining** a little weight.	increase	359

GET

What will you **get** for your birthday?	receive	130
She **gets** mad when you leave early.	become	128
I plan to **get** home around 11:30.	arrive	129
Can you **get** her to quit work?	force	291

GIVE

Please **give** my brother his hat.	hand	377
The army **gave up** after four months.	surrender	379
Why did you have to **give up** tennis?	quit	378
	or **stop**	370

GLASS

Hand me a **glass** of water.	glass	1083
The **glass** table top is broken.	glass	1084
His **glasses** are always falling off.	eyeglasses	1085

GONE

All the fruit salad is **gone.**	out of	813
Will you be **gone** a long time?	leave	181
	or **gone**	814
He was **gone** from class again.	absent	435
All of my grandparents are **gone.**	dead	592

GRANT

Can you **grant** me several requests?	give me	377
No one can **grant** that except your father.	allow	500
I **grant** that what I did was a mistake.	admit	733
Granted, that happened before I knew it.	correct	178

GROUND

Put the boxes on the **ground.**	ground	899
His play**ground** is the world.	place	337
What **grounds** do you have for saying that?	basis	726

GROW

I have three **grown** children.	mature	512
Mother **grows** odd-looking flowers.	grows	513
He has **grown** very cautious recently.	become	128

HAND

How did you hurt your **hand**?	**hand**	414
Hand that to me, please.	**give**	377
The ranch **hand** quit working.	**person**	189
Give me a **hand** in finishing this, please.	**help**	202
That picture shows the **hand** of a master.	**skill**	690
I want you **on hand** if there is an accident.	**here**	42

HANG

Finally, he is learning to **hang** his clothes.	**hang up**	688
The judge sentenced him to **hang.**	**hang**	689
His future **hangs on** having a good year.	**depend**	569
We will **hang** around until a decision is made.	**wait**	201

HARD

It was a **hard** problem to solve.	**difficult**	296
The chair was old and **hard.**	**hard**	421
The boss was **hard** on his employees.	**mean**	233
Try your **hardest** to succeed.	**best**	273

HAVE

They **have** several new cars.	**possess**	56
I **have had** mumps before.	**finish**	313
	and **possess**	56
Dad **has been** working here 12 years.	**since**	429
Mother and I **have not** left for work.	**yet**	520
They **have to** leave before noon.	**must**	277

HEAD

My **head** hurts again.	**head**	409
Who is the **head** of the department?	**boss**	515
I plan to **head** the group into the mountains.	**lead**	514
He is **out of his head.**	**crazy**	735

HIGH

How **high** can you reach?	**high**	1134
She recently moved to a **high** position.	**important**	780
	or **advance**	805
Everything in the store is **high** today.	**expensive**	488

HIT

She never **hits** her dog.	**punch**	516
The painting made a big **hit.**	**success**	517

HOLD

Hold this for me while I'm on vacation.	**keep**	265
Hold this for a second.	**hold**	264
The beliefs some people **hold** are silly.	**have**	56
He **held** that we never landed on the moon.	**believe**	306

HOT

The contest was **hot** throughout.	**even**	285
	or **hot**	211
Hot coffee tastes good on cold nights.	**hot**	211
She was really **hot** after being fired.	**angry**	307
He only wants $50.00 for the TV so it must be **hot.**	**steal**	1053
They are really **hot** to get this finished.	**eager**	254

HOUSE

Can you visit grandmother's old **house**?	**house**	1
They expected a large **house** on opening night.	**audience**	1123
Don't worry; my parents can **house** all ten animals.	**take care of**	794

HUNT

Do you enjoy **hunting** deer?	**hunting**	518
I was **hunting** for my shoes.	**look for**	354

IN FRONT OF

Put the car **in front of** the house.	**in front of**	1034
No one could stand **in front of** that crowd.	**before**	301

IRON

Mother **irons** every Saturday morning.	**iron**	1110
I got a steam **iron** for Christmas.	**iron**	1110
Grandfather is an old **iron** worker.	**steel**	1109

JAM

Put some butter and **jam** on my toast, please.	**jelly**	651
Tell me if you are in a **jam.**	**trouble**	246
My foot was **jammed** in the door.	**stuck**	729

JOIN

Can you **join** us for lunch next week?	**participate**	894
Take each end of the pipes and **join** them.	**connect**	895

JUDGE

Where is the **judge** going now?	judge	12
	+ -er	34
Who will **judge** the horse show?	judge	12
The **judgment** was made last week.	decision	602

JUMP

Don't **jump** on the chair.	jump	825
He **jumped** bail for the second time.	escape	448
Prices seem to **jump** every day.	increase	359
Everyone **jumped on** him for what he said.	criticize	444

JUST

We **just** saw him leave.	recently	906
I want **just** one sandwich.	only	904
That was a **just** decision.	fair	285
	or **good**	183
The new car cost **just** more than I had.	little bit	387
We thought it was **just** right.	exactly	714
Just sit down and wait for me.	just	905

KEEP

Keep my watch while I swim.	hold	264
Milk will not **keep** for a long time.	last	266
Keep away while I am working.	go away	287
Will you **keep** my dog for several weeks?	keep	265

KEY

The house **key** is lost again.	key	885
He knew the **key** thing to say.	important	780
What is the **key** to your heart?	way	539

KICK

Don't **kick** the door again.	kick	1012
Why **kick** about things you cannot change?	complain	253
She always gets a **kick** out of his stories.	enjoyment	259

KIND

What a **kind** person you are!	gentle	203
What **kind** of person are you?	type	204

KNOCK

Knock on the door twice.	knock	717
Who saw him **knock down** the woman?	push	771
The fighter was **knocked down** several times.	fall	759

LAND

Dad **landed** a terrific job.	get	130
Illinois is the **land** of Lincoln.	home	223
Our **land** is full of trees.	land	900
They left the **land** of Israel.	country	568

LAST

This is the **last** apple I have.	final	268
Will this **last** a long time?	continue	266
What happened **last** night?	last	267

LEAVE

Can we **leave** here soon?	depart	181
He is on annual **leave** for two weeks.	vacation	956
Don't **leave** your pictures on the desk.	abandon	182

LEFT

Go two blocks, then turn **left**.	left	180
They **left** everything behind the store.	abandon	182
They **left** more than an hour ago.	depart	181

LEND

Lend my uncle $10.00 until next week.	loan	1063
Lend me a hand with this engine.	give me	377
Doesn't this picture **lend** beauty to the office?	add	747

LENGTH

What was the **length** of the first show?	time	120
The **length** of the rope is 23 feet long.	long	274
What **length** of time did you wish?	long	275

LET

The movie was a real **let down**.	disappoint	946
Let him **know** the second it happens.	inform	723
Let me go so I can pay you.	let	501

LIE

That was not a white **lie**.	lie	1115
Lie here and sleep for a little bit.	lie	1114

LIGHT

It is **light** in here now.	bright	380
That old box is **light** now.	weight	372
It looks like the **light** has blown.	light	373
No **light** is coming in the window.	sun	711
Do you have a **light** please?	match	947
His punishment was very **light**.	easy	556

LIKE

We all **like** the same thing.	enjoy	259
Is it **like** that all the time?	same	157
I would **like** to finish college.	like	49

LINE

What is your **line** of work?	line	551
Put a **line** on the floor.	string	553
What a long **line** of people!	line up	1070

LITTLE

The **little** girl ran away from home.	small	426
Can you lend me a **little bit** of money?	little bit	387
That happened a **little bit ago.**	little bit ago	906
That was just a **little** house, but it was comfortable.	quantity	398

LOCATE

When you leave here, where will you **locate**?	live	446
Can you **locate** your home town on the map?	find	262
The best **location** is near the restaurant.	place	337

LONG

It looks about seven inches **long**.	long	274
How **long** will you stay with us?	time	275
He always **longs for** his sweetheart.	wish	471
They will all leave **before long**.	soon	548

LOOK

Look and tell me what you see.	look	355
The brothers all **looked** healthy.	appear	356
Look at me while I do this.	look at me	208
We decided to **look for** gold.	look for	354
It **looks like** it might rain.	looks like	982
The girls **looked** him **over** when he entered.	look over	979
We better **look over** our notes again.	inspect and observe	443 980
Look up the new vocabulary right away.	look up	981
Look out! The dog is dangerous.	careful	798
Will you **look after** my pet rats?	keep	265

MAKE

You can't **make** him do that!	force	291
I will **make** coffee for us.	make	290
Please **make** the bed for tonight.	prepare	564
That **make** of car is very popular now.	kind	204
You better **make up your mind** now.	decide	602
She is very good at **making up** stories.	invent	853
They decided to **make** a horse barn.	build or make	725 290
My aunt **makes** it home in an hour.	arrive	129
Father used to **make** $10,000 a year.	earn	988
I know you will **make** a good doctor.	become	128

MATCH

I need a **match** to start the fire.	match	947
He lost all four of his tennis **matches.**	game	1017
You cannot **match** apples and oranges.	compare	1027
The little girl's shoes **match** her dress.	go together	948
The lion was no **match** for the elephant.	equal	285

MEAN

He is a **mean** person.	unkind	233
They didn't **mean** to say that.	intend	234
Add these numbers for me to get the **mean.**	average	753

MIND

Do you **mind** if I kiss you?	care or object	253 368
Children should **mind** their parents.	obey	366
Try to improve your **mind**.	mind	238
I **don't mind** what you say or do.	don't care	407

MISS

Will we **miss** the train now?	miss	699
My sister really **misses** mom.	miss	697
The children's clothes are **missing.**	gone	700
I decided to **miss** class tomorrow.	cut	435

MOTION

His **motion** was defeated.	suggestion	586
All this **motion** is making me sick.	move	376

MOVE

I **move** that this meeting be adjourned.	**motion**	586
Sit there without **moving** for a minute.	**move**	376
Something **moved** him to say that.	**cause**	1145

NAME

I won't change my **name.**	**name**	145
He **named** all of his dogs the same.	**name**	103
I want that; **name** your price.	**tell me**	193
The minister wants us to **name** the day.	**decide**	602

NEED

She has several **needs** which must be fulfilled.	**wish**	471
What do you **need** now?	**want**	342
Mother **needs** to lose weight.	**need**	276

NEXT

Do you want to go **next**?	**turn**	303
What do you think will happen **next**?	**next**	302
A young girl sat **next to** my brother.	**next to**	305
Uncle John can't go until **next week.**	**next year**	317
Next year will be a very good year.	**next year**	322

NO

No, she is not here any more.	**exclamation**	109
There are **no** more apples.	**quantity**	110
He refused to take **no** for an answer.	**exclamation**	109
No more people are expected to come.	**quantity**	110

NOTICE

They never **noticed** my new shoes.	**notice**	773
Put the **notices** on trees and buildings.	**poster**	774
The army moved suddenly without any **notice.**	**warn**	793

NUMBER

Write several **numbers** for me.	**number**	748
His days left in the office are **numbered.**	**limit**	1089
A large number of people did not show up.	**many**	292
I have **a number of** things to say.	**several**	293

NUTS

My aunt is a little **nuts.**	**crazy**	735
He always eats **nuts** and drinks beer.	**nuts**	674

OBJECT

Place all the **objects** on the table.	**thing**	882
Why must you always **object** to everything?	**complain**	253

OFFER

I **offered** to postpone it for several weeks.	**willing**	1141
I **offered** to give money.	**promise**	995
What do you plan to **offer** the church?	**give**	377
He **offered** several alternatives.	**proposal**	586

OLD

He was an **old** boyfriend.	**former**	930
How **old** are you now?	**old**	278
He is an **old** hand at that.	**experience**	715

ON

Who **turned on** the television?	**turn on**	304
Place the food **on** the table.	**on**	176
My apartment is **on** the beach.	**near**	530
Go on; I will stop you occasionally.	**proceed**	521
He refused to **take on** any more responsibility.	**accept**	695

ONCE

They come only **once in a while.**	**occasionally**	427
Mother said things only **once.**	**once**	428
Once upon a time, the good king had a son.	**former**	930
Father told him to come home **at once.**	**now**	113
Once I see him, I will know for sure.	**when**	139

ONLY

He knocked **only** once.	**just**	904
We have **only** three more weeks of school!	**just**	905

ORDER

The boss **ordered** two hamburgers.	**order**	392
The family is now in the **Order** of Georges.	**group**	220
His life is in good **order.**	**plan**	564

ORIGINAL

That looks like an **original** picture.	true	106
The **original** plan was changed again.	~~first~~ first	116
He always brings something **original.**	new	332
She is considered a very **original** thinker.	invent	853

OUT

They were **out of** onions.	out of	813
Leave the dog **outside** tonight.	out	133
Which way do we go **out?**	out	133
The teacher decided not to **give out** the notes.	release	939
They are **out** shopping tonight.	gone	814
It took several hours for the fire to **go out.**	go out	823
They cried **out of** hunger.	because	1002

OVER

They were fighting **over** money again.	about	529
Run **over** the bridge and wait for us.	across	736
Are the signs **over** the door yet?	above	40
Everyone is glad the work is **over.**	finish	313
My aunt **fell over** when she saw me.	fall	759
The play went **over** the alloted time.	past	763
You made a mistake, so do it **over.**	again	294
His work has improved **over** the past ten years.	during	344

PART

We want you to **take part** in family matters.	join	894
No **part** of the pie is to be cut.	part	335
They argued all night but **parted** as friends.	left or **separated**	181 37
You have to do your **part** to finish this.	duty	976
Can we **part** this in the middle?	separate	37

PAST

Forget about the **past** and move on.	past	46
They walked **past** the fire station this morning.	pass	763
Now that you are home, my worries are **past.**	finish	313

PATIENT

The **patient** was crying for help.	patient	872
Be **patient** for just a little longer.	patient	597

PERFECT

She always knows the **perfect** thing to say!	perfect	714
To be promoted, you must **perfect** your skills.	improve	990

PERMIT

I can **permit** you to leave early.	permit	500
She just got her driver's **permit.**	license	857

PICK

That dog is the **pick** of the litter.	best	273
Pick the paper that looks the best.	choose	901
Father **picked up** the dinner bill.	pay	484

PLACE

No one wanted to go back to that **place.**	place	337
Place the picture on the mantel.	put	336
Your **place** is at the head of the table.	sit	401
What is your **place** in the organization?	position	337
Be quiet! It's not your **place** to comment.	responsible	696
She lives in a high income **place.**	area	746

PLANT

My neighbor **plants** corn every summer.	plant	513
All my **plants** seem to die overnight.	plant	1155
He **planted** the seeds of doubt in her mind.	put	336
The deaf man has worked at that **plant** for 12 years.	factory	749

PLAY

You can **play** with your toys now.	play	329
The **play** was really fantastic.	performance	328
She **played** on his sympathy.	work	271

POINT

He made several good **points.**	point	391
Don't **point.** It's not polite.	you	63
What is the **point** of saying that?	purpose	998
Walk to the **point** which I described.	place	337
I wish that you would **point** that **out** for me.	show	525
Don't **point** that gun at me.	aim	817

POOR

The **poor** house is on Main Street.	poor	256
That was a **poor** choice of words.	bad	184
Poor father, the news really depressed him.	pity	255

409

PREFER

I **prefer** cake to pie anytime.	**prefer**	386
Do you **prefer** to leave now or later?	**want**	342
Let me think about which one I **prefer.**	**choose**	901

PRESENT

The best **present** was the antique clock.	**gift**	588
You must be **present** tomorrow at 9:00.	**here**	42
The **present** time is good enough to begin.	**now**	113
I want to **present** my sister to you.	**introduce**	587
Do you wish to **present** your grievances?	**propose**	586

PRINT

Print your name on the line.	**write**	34
Printing was a good occupation for deaf people.	**print**	842
The animal's foot**prints** were everywhere.	**figure** or **steps**	741 580

PROBLEM

Try to finish ten **problems** before lunch.	**problem**	295
His **problem** was complicated.	**difficulty**	296

PULL

She had a lot of **pull** with the company.	**power** or **influence**	1031 692
Pull the wagon closer to the barn.	**pull**	519
Who are you **pulling for** to win?	**support**	1060

PUT

Put the oranges in the refrigerator.	**place**	336
Put off leaving until tomorrow	**delay**	963
We **put up** several interesting signs.	**put up**	774
I can't **put up with** noisy children.	**tolerate**	597
How can I **put** it so you will understand?	**talk**	196

QUIZ

Can we **quiz** him about the accident?	**question**	339
The **quiz** was not difficult.	**test**	523

RAISE

I **raised** an adopted child.	**raise**	512
What kind of crops do you **raise**?	**grow**	513
The church is trying to **raise** the funds.	**collect**	988
Will they **raise** the rent this year?	**increase**	359
He **raised** an interesting question.	**present**	586

REACH

Can you **reach** the clock above the door?	**touch**	1041
We will **reach** home about midnight.	**arrive**	129

REDUCE

They had to **reduce** their energy bill.	**reduce**	778
Mother needs to **reduce** so she can wear her old clothes.	**slim down**	779
We need to **reduce** this picture.	**small**	547

RELEASE

After 18 years at the same store, they **released** her.	**laid off**	393
You have to **release** your end of the wire.	**disconnect**	938
Release the news bulletin now.	**disseminate**	939
Everyone was excited when the hostages were **released.**	**free**	712

RESPECT

Always **respect** what your parents tell you.	**respect**	851
Respect the government; it has a difficult task.	**support**	1060
Dad was wrong in many **respects.**	**way**	539

REST

Rest here for a few minutes.	**relax**	464
Sure, I ate the **rest** of it!	**whole**	136
Rest the gun against the fence.	**put**	336

RETURN

Will you **return** from your trip soon?	**come back**	751
Please **return** my picture and ring.	**give me**	377
They had to **return** all the money immediately.	**give**	377
Mom **returned** the hat for a larger size.	**exchange**	716

REVEAL

When will you **reveal** your invention?	**show**	525
The newspaper will **reveal** his identity.	**tell**	192

RIDE

He can **ride** a variety of animals.	**ride**	1021
You can **ride** with me tomorrow.	**vehicle**	1022
They are always **riding** him for his mistakes.	**tease**	298
I refuse to **ride** the bandwagon.	**join**	894
The neighbors took a **ride** to Disney World.	**trip**	719

RIGHT

His **right** to an interpreter was denied.	privilege	177
Turn to the **right** after the second traffic light.	direction	179
The **right** decision was to leave now.	correct	178
Everything is **right** where you left it.	exact	714
Do it for me **right away.**	quick	783

ROUGH

He is a **rough** person to please.	difficult	296
It was a **rough** road to travel.	crude	890
The dog plays too **rough** with the baby.	mean	233

RULE

I need a **rule** to get this exactly.	measure	742
What **rule** did you break this time?	principle	745
The queen **ruled** with an iron hand.	govern	449

RUN

Who **runs** the government when the President is away?	control	449
You will **run** against the country's best athletes.	compete	453
Run around the block with me.	jog	450
His nose **runs** all the time.	nose	451
I think I hear the water **running.**	water	452
Will you **run off** 200 copies for me?	run off	454
She **ran away from** home four times.	escape	448

SAFE/SAVE

I will **save** you from that gang of boys.	protect	600
Save some of that for me please.	keep	264
Save your money for college.	save	713
He **saved** the soldiers from jail.	free	712
Is your purse **safe** on the desk?	all right	177
It is a **safe** bet to make.	good	183

SAME

All the horses look the **same.**	standard	175
She does the **same** thing everyday.	same	174

SECOND

He is the **second** from the right.	numerical	117
Wait a **second** for me to finish.	time	122

SEE

See that man in the blue coat?	see	137
I **see!** You do it without adding.	understand	243
Can you **see** if it is right every hour?	check	443
I want you to **see** how this is done.	watch	207
Please **see** all the girls home.	take	459

SENSE

He had no **sense** of remorse.	feeling	389
You look like you have more **sense.**	thought	238

SENTENCE

He was **sentenced** to jail for two years.	send	436
The first **sentence** of the paragraph is not clear.	sentence	461

SHARP

Be careful! That knife is **sharp.**	bright	382
She has a **sharp** car.	beautiful	288
She is really **sharp** in arithmetic.	smart	952

SHORT

My brother is very **short.**	short	549
I only need a **short** piece of string.	small	547
The lecture was very **short.**	short	548

SHOW

Let me **show** you what to do.	show	525
Shogun was an excellent **show.**	film	524
The first **show** of the season was *Oklahoma.*	performance	284
Try not to **show off** for company.	brag	965
Will she **show up** for her appointment?	appear	561

SIGN

The circus **sign** is an old one.	poster	707
Sign language class starts at 8:00 a.m.	sign	706
Can you **sign** my card for me?	signature	708

SPEECH

The teacher's **speech** was really good.	lecture	195
His **speech** is much more intelligible.	talk	348

STAND

Stand closer to me for the picture.	**stand**	400
The deer **stand** he uses is gone.	**place**	337
My sister can't **stand** her cousin.	**tolerate**	597
Will you **stand behind** me on this issue?	**support**	1060
Stand up when she comes in here.	**stand up**	402

STEP

Take two **steps** and then turn around.	**walk**	505
The porch **step** is broken again.	**flight**	581

STILL

Why is it so **still** in the nursery?	**quiet**	1026
I **still** think you are right.	**continue**	266
The book is not perfect; **still** it is very good.	**but**	172

STRIKE

The iron workers' **strike** lasted four months.	**rebel**	777
He promised never to **strike** his dog again.	**hit**	903
The singer wanted to **strike** the first paragraph of her contract.	**cancel**	444

SUBJECT

My **subject** for tonight is "The History of Deafness."	**topic**	775
My best **subject** is English.	**course**	440
Several **subjects** were required for the experiment.	**people**	190

SUSPECT

The **suspect** escaped during the evening.	**person**	189
Do you **suspect** anything has changed?	**suspect**	1131
I know that he is honest, and I **suspect** that he is right.	**imagine**	242
	or **suspect**	1131

SWEAR

Do you **swear** to tell the whole truth?	**oath**	995
I heard you **swearing** at the cat last night.	**cuss**	1124

TAKE

Take this suitcase with you.	**take**	459
I can't **take** this anymore.	**tolerate**	597
Take this road to Philadelphia.	**follow**	701
How did your aunt **take** the news?	**accept**	695
Take away all the wrong words.	**take away**	1104
He is **taking** 18 credits this semester.	**take up**	460

TALK

We **talked** almost all night.	**conversation**	194
I think you need to **talk** more often.	**say**	196
All three **talks** were excellent.	**speech**	195

TALL

How **tall** is that building?	**height**	1128
My oldest daughter is very **tall**.	**tall**	425

TELL

She was **telling** him how to go.	**explain**	818
Tell me what you are thinking.	**tell me**	193
Tell everyone who is the boss here.	**tell**	192

THROUGH

Run through that again for me.	**say**	196
I'm finally **through** with my book.	**finish**	313
Go through the book from front to back.	**read**	502
Through this door walk great people.	**through**	330

TIE

The first match ended in a **tie** score.	**even**	285
Tie a blue string around the box.	**knot**	286
He got five **ties** for Christmas.	**necktie**	495

TIME

What **time** is it now?	**time**	120
We have only a short **time** to complete this.	**period**	121

TO

Come with me **to** the farm.	**to**	127
They sang and drank **to** the music.	**with**	185
What will Mother say **to** this mistake?	**about**	529
He wants **to** sing, **to** play, and **to** dance.	fingerspell **to**	
Father made a toast **to** mother's health.	**for**	171

TOTAL

No one mentioned the **total** number to expect.	**all**	136
	or **complete**	325
Please **total** these numbers for me.	**add**	747
Our vacation was a **total** failure.	**complete**	325

TRADE

My uncle is **trading** cars again.	**exchange**	716
The tinker **trade** is almost extinct.	**work**	271
	or **profession**	551

TRAIL

The hunters **trailed** the animal for almost a mile.	follow	701
Which **trail** takes us to the forest?	street	538
The dogs followed the **trail** of the lost boy.	smell	961

TRAIN

The **train** came into town empty.	train	1157
How long did he **train** for the team?	practice	754

TURN

Turn the bolt with your hand.	turn	304
When is it my **turn** to watch?	time	120
Can you **turn this crank** for me?	run off	454
They **turned** all the animals **loose.**	release	712
They **turned** the defeat into a victory.	change	897
He **turned** a quick profit and left the country.	made	290

UGLY

He is in an **ugly** mood.	awful	558
Why is your dog so **ugly?**	ugly	289
That is an **ugly** thing to say.	bad	184
	or awful	558

USE

Let me **use** your new sewing machine.	use	1072
We are **used to** going to work early.	habit	962
I **used to** play football in college.	past	46

VANISH

He just **vanished** from sight.	disappear	822
Don't worry; by morning the ice will have **vanished.**	melt	823

VISION

My grandmother's **vision** is improving.	see	137
Last night she had a **vision.**	dream	260

WAIT

She didn't like **waiting** tables all day.	serve	727
Wait a minute for dad to get here.	minute	122
I will **wait** until you return.	wait	201

WATCH

Your new **watch** looks expensive.	watch	209
Watch your baby brother for an hour.	supervise	794
Watch me while I change this light.	watch me	208
Watch out! That dog will bite.	careful	798
We can **watch** TV tonight.	watch	207

WELL

After a long illness, he is now **well.**	healthy	879
How **well** do you know him?	good	1150

WHICH

Which man is she planning to marry?	which	143
No one was arrested, **which** was only fair.	that	54

WORD

What does the **word** mean?	word	340
When you are through, I need a **word** with you.	talk	194
We'll be back after this **word** from our sponsor.	advertise	803
	or announcement	720

WORK

You begin **work** next week on Monday.	work	271
If this doesn't **work,** I'll give up.	succeed	517
Grandfather can **work** any puzzle.	solve	823

Index

In this Index, the numbers refer to the illustration numbers of signs, not to page numbers. Some of the glosses found in the Index do not appear with the numbered illustrations to which they refer. Although several glosses may be listed with each illustration, space did not permit the inclusion of all possible glosses. For this reason, glosses for specific signs have been added to the Index.

You will notice that some items in the Index have more than one number, such as "absent, 435, 698." That means that more than one sign can be translated by the same English word, so you should consult the Multi-sign Word Appendix to determine precisely which sign best conveys your idea. Also you will see that some items are referenced by two numbers and a plus sign, such as "actress, 8 + 284." This means that two signs are needed to represent that concept.

Some items are followed by a word written in parentheses, such as "act (do)" or "act (drama)." The word inside the parentheses is meant to help you locate the sign that best conveys the right idea in the right context. Again, you should probably consult the Multi-sign Word Appendix to clarify the conventional use of such a sign. An asterisk next to the number, such as "elementary, *726," means that Manual English has adapted the initial letter of the English word and modified the traditional sign referenced by that number in order to represent the English word manually.

415

a, 53

a little bit ago, 906

a large number, 292

a lot, 397

a number of, 293

abandon, 182

abbreviate, 1101

ability, 690

able, 125

about, 529, 530, 424

above, 40, 737

absent, 435, 698, 1005

accept, 695

accident (mistake), 788

accident (vehicle), 789

accidently, 261

accuse, 838

accustom, 1073

achievement, 517

acquire, 130

across, 736

act (do), 283

act (drama), 284, 328

action, 283

activity, 283

actor, 8 + 284

actress, 9 + 284

adapt, 897

add, 359, 740, 747, 1105, 1107

addition, 747, 1105, 1107

additional, 747, 1105, 1107

address, *446

adequate, 252, 898

admit (confess), 733

admit (permit), 500

admit (welcome), 732

adopt, 695

advance (improve), 990

advance (progress), 806

advance (promote), 805, 1135

advantage, 565, 1107

advertise, 803

advice, 692

advise, 692

afford, 896

afraid, 704

after (chase), 311

after (finish), 313

after (succession), 312

after (turn), 303

afternoon, 17

after a while, 124

again, 294

against (near), 530

against (oppose), 507, 1148

age, 278

ago, 267, 300

agree, 948

ahead, 509

aid, 351

aim (goal), 816

aim (point), 817

airplane, 3, 827

algebra, *766

alike, 174

all, 136

all along, 429

all gone, 813

all night, 821

all right, 177

allow, 500

almost, 424

alone, 702

along, 521

already, 326

also, 799

alter, 897

altitude, 1134

always, 506

am, *81

amazed, 469

America, 1172

among, 834

amount, 397

and, 51

anger, 307

angry, 307

anguish, 598

animal, 603

anniversary, 820

announce, 720

announcement, 720

annoy, 595

another, 510

answer, 755

anticipate, 245

anxious (eager), 254, 785

anxious (worry), 246, 1161

any, 198

anyhow, 362

anymore, 198 + 361

anything, 269

anyway, 362

apologize, 250

apparently, 560

appear (act), 284

appear (look), 356, 562

appear (seem), 560

appear (show up), 561

appearance, 356

apple, 630

applicant, 942

apply (put to use), 941, 1072

apply (spread), 758, 941

apply (volunteer), 942

appointment, 929

appreciate, 259

apprehend, 533

approach, 522

appropriate, 178, 846

approximate, 529

are, *82

area, *746

argue, 859

arithmetic, 766

arm, 411

army, 833

around (about), 529

around (round), 531

around (vicinity), 530

arrange, 564

arrest, 533

arrive, 129

art, 35

article (news), 884

article (thing), 882

artist, 35

concentrate, 934

concept, *249

condense, 1101

confess, 733

confident, 1143

confront, 301

confuse, 527

confusion, 527

Congress, 917

connect, 895

connection, 895

conquer, 902

consider, 239

construct, *725

construction, *725

contact, 1041

content (adjective), 252

content (noun), 723

contest, 453, 1017

continue, 266

control, 449

convention, 919

conversation, 194

cook, 681

cookie, 663

cooperate, 966

cop, 6

copy (imitate), 985

copy (xerox), 986

corn, 658

corn-on-the-cob, 644

corner, 731

correct (change), 897

correct (reprimand), 1019

correct (right), 178, 444

cost, 405

costly, 488

cough, 867

could, 125

counsel, 692

count (figure), 740

count (importance), 780

count in, 764

count on, 569

count to, 740

country, 568

county, 568

courage, 879

course (class), 440

course (way), 539

court, 12

courteous, 1058

cousin, 168

cover (blanket), 535

cover (finish), 313

cover (go over), 536

cover up, 537

cow, 606

cracker, 650

crank, 454

crave, 471

crazy, 735

create, 290

critic, 444

criticize, 444

cross (across), 736

cross (mad), 307

cross (religion), 1107

crowd, 1123

crude, 890

cry (motto), 775

cry (tears), 28

cry (yell), 102

culture, *591

cup, 1082

curious, 1100

cuss, 1124

custom, 962

cut (fired), 432

cut (knife), 434

cut (miss), 435

cut (reduce), 778

cut (scissors), 433

cut it out (stop), 370

cut up (silly), 383

cute, 673

dad, 149

daily, 345

damage, 809

damp, 907

dance, 503

danger, 558, 858

dangerous, 558, 858

dark, 819

daughter, 156

day, 16

dead, 592

deaf, 353

death, 592

debate, 992

debt, 896

decide, 602

decision, 602

declare, 720

decline (reduce), 739

decline (refuse), 390

decrease, 739

deduct, 1104

deep, 967

deer, 605

defeat, 902

defend, 600

delay, 963, 1033

delicious, 1086

demand, 1036

Democrat, 920

demolish, 809

demonstrate, *525

dentist, 873

depart, 181

department, *218

depend, 569

depressed, 946

depth, 967

describe, 818

desire, 471

dessert, 639

destitute, 296

destroy, 809

detail, 967

detective, *6

determined, 602

develop, 933

development, 933

devil, 18

devise, 853

dictionary, 804

did, 283, 331

didn't, 107

didn't get, 699

die, 592

differ, 173

different, 173

difficult, 296

diminish, 778

dinner, *685, 686

direct (control), 449

direct (explain), 525, 818

direct (order), 392

direct (precise), 714

direction, 818

dirt, 786

dirty, 786

disagree, 927

disappear (dissolve), 823

disappear (vanish), 822

disappoint (discourage), 946

disappoint (miss), 697

disbelieve, 408

discard, 1020

disconnect, 938

discourage, 946

discover, 262

discuss, 992

discussion, 992

disease, 862

dishes, 1081

dislike, 554

dismiss, 393

disobey, 777

dissatisfied, 946

disseminate, 939

dissolve, 823

disturb (bother), 595

disturb (mix up), 527

disturb (upset), 880

divide, 888, 1092

divorce, 170

do, 283

doctor, 31

does, 283

doesn't, 107

doesn't matter, 362

dog, 48

dollar, 485

done, 326, 738

donkey, 607

don't, 107

don't believe, 408

don't care, 407

don't know, 236

don't like, 50

don't want, 343

door, 229

doubt, 408, 839

down, 206

downstairs, 206

drag out, 802

drama, 328

draw (close), 281

draw (get), 130, 519

draw (pictures), 35

draw (tie), 285

dream, 260

dress (clean), 395

dress (verb), 496

dress (noun), 497

drill, *754

drink, 25

drive, 314

drop (fall), 759

drop (physically), 1042

drop (reduce), 739

drop (stop), 370, 378, 1043

drop out (quit), 760, 1043

drop over, 751, 759

drown, 968

drunk, 969

dry (boring), 334

dry (empty), 1069

dry (not wet), 908

dry (thirsty), 687

duck, 612

due, 896

dull, 908, 334

duplicate, 454

during, 344

duty, *976

dying, 592

each, 363

each other, 596

eager, 254

early, 422

earn, 988

earth, 1025

east, 543

eastern, 543

easy, 556

eat, 24

educate, 722

effort, 790

egg, 646

either, *1055

elaborate, 1059

elect, 1045

election, 1045

electric, 1023

electricity, 1023

elementary, *726

elephant, 616

eliminate, 1104

else, *510

embarrass, 1007

emotion, 389

emphasis, 1035

emphasize, 1035

empty, 1069

encourage, 1088

end, *439

endure, 597

enemy, 1028

energy, *1032

engagement (appointment), *929

engagement (marital), 928

engagement (war battle), 1099

England, 1175

English, 1175

enjoy, 259

enjoyable, 259

enjoyment, 259

enough, 327

enter, 132

enthusiastic, 254

entrance, 132

envious, 1054

environment, *591

envy, 1054

equal, 285, 1068

equipment, *883

error, 788

escape, 448

establish, 1039

Europe, 1173

evaluate, 1024

evaluation, 1024

even, 285, 1068

evenly, 285

ever (always), *506

ever (past), 267

ever (sometimes), 427

ever since, 429

every, 363

every day, 345

every so often, 427

everybody, 365

everyday, 345

everyone, 365

everything, 364

evidence, 1130

evil, 964

exact, 714

exaggerate, 802

exam, 523

examination, 523

example, *526

except, 172, 750

exception, 750

exceptional, 750

exchange, 716

excite, 785

excitement, 785

excuse, 393, 394

exhausted, 1064

expand, 546

expect, 245

expel, 423

expensive, 488

experience, 715

expert, 690

expertise, 690

explain, 818

expression, 555, 775

eye, 416

eyeglasses, 1085

eyeing, 979

face, 356

face (in front of), 301, 1034

face (look), 207

face (meet), 36, 301

facial, 356

factory, 749

fail, 1065

fair (adequate), 1067

fair (equal), 285, 1068

fair (nice), 396

fair (pretty), 288

faith, 1143

fake, 1117

fall (autumn), 677

fall (become), 128

fall (verb), 759

fall down, 759

fall over, 759

false, 1117

familiar, 240

family, 219

famous, 721

fancy, 1059

fantasize, 801

fantastic, *403

fantasy, 801

far, 508

farm, 568, 705

farmer, 705

fast, 783

fat, 768

father, 149

fault, 838

favorite, 1087

fear, 704

federal, *743

feed, 1001

feel, 389

female, 147

few, 293

fib, 1115

fiction, 1117

field, *552

fight, 849

figure (count), 740

figure (feel), 389

figure (person), 189

figure (shape), 741

figure out, 602, 818

fill (complete), 325

fill (satisfy), 252, 898

film, 524

filthy, 786

final, 268

finally, 268, 517

find, 262, 981

find (look for), 354

find out, 262

fine (beautiful), 288

fine (charge), 405, 837

fine (good), 183

fine (well), 406, 1150

fingerspell, 709

finish, 313, 331, 326, 1006

fire (dismiss), 432

fire (flames), 782

fire up (excite), 785

first, 116

fish, 627

fishing, 1111

flag, 800

flat, 891

flee, 448

flexible, 815

flight, 827

floor, 226

flower, 19

fly (airplane), 3, 827

fly (escape), 448

fly (insect), 625

fly (verb), 828

follow, 701

follow (accept), 695

follow (copy), 985

food, *24

fool, 383

football, 1014

for, 171

force, 291

forecast, 247

foreign, *1140

forest, 1118

foretell, 247

forget, 237

forgive, 394

fork, 1077

form, 290, 1039

formal, 1059

former, 930, 1074

formerly, 930, 1074

founded, 1039

fox, 615

hearing (person), 352

hearing aid, 351

hearing impaired, 350

heart, 417

heat, 909, 211

heaven, 476

heavy, 371

height, 1128, 1134

help, 202

her, 63, *70

here, 42

herself, 75

hide, 811

high (altitude), 1134

high (expensive), 488

high (important), 805, 1135

hill, 1090

him, 63, *69

himself, 75

hinder, 595

hire, 732

his, 65, *71

history, 767

hit (punch), 516, 903

hit (success), 517

hog, 614

hold (believe), 306

hold (have), 56

hold (keep), 264, 265

holiday, 956

home, 223

honest, 772

honor, 851

hooray, 820

hope, 245

horrible, 558

horse, 608

hospital, 874

hot (angry), 307

hot (competitive), 211, 285

hot (eager), 254

hot (stolen), 1053

hot (temperature), 211

hot dog, 642

hour, 11, 123

house (audience), 1123

house (building), 1

house (take care of), 794

how, 138

however, 172

huge, 399

human, 189

humorous, 384

hungry, 470

hunt (look for), 354

hunting, 518

hurry, 852

hurt, 863

husband, 154

I, 57

I love you, 309

ice, 455 + 797

ice cream, 21

idea, 241

identify, *773

ignorant, 953, 1097

ignore, 528

ill, 862

illness, 862

illustrate, *525

image, 741

imagination, 242

imagine, 242

imitate, 985

immediately, 783, 113

impact, 516

important, 780

impoverished, 256

impress, 1035

improve, 990

improvement, 990

in, 131

in a minute, 122

in a second, 122

in addition to, 1105

in charge of, 696, 449

in common, 175

in depth, 967

in favor of, 1060

in front of (before), 301

in front of, 1034

in order, 564

inadequate, 256

inch, 742

inclined, 1142

include, 764

increase, 359

independent, 712

India, 1180

Indian, 7

individual, 191

industrious, 254

industry, 978

infant, 22

inferior, *726

infirmary, 874

influence, 692

inform, 723

information, 723

initiate, 369

inquisitive, 1100

insect, 604

inside, 131

inspect, 443

instead, 716

institution, 935

instruct, *722

insubordinate, 777

insurance, 1037

integrate, 948

intelligent, 1096

intend, 234

intention, 998

interest, 333

interesting, 333

interfere, 595

international, *324

interpret, 830

into, 132

introduce, 587

invent, 853

invention, 854

investigate, 443

invite, *732

involve, 764

Ireland, 1178

Irish, 1178

iron (clothes), 1110

iron (steel), 1109

is, *80

island, 1113

isn't, 107

it, 54, *72

Italian, 1179

Italy, 1179

itemize, 691

itself, 75

jail, 1137

jam (jelly), 651

jam (trouble), 246, 729

Japan, 1185

Japanese, 1185

jealous, 1054

jelly, 651

Jesus, 474

Jewish, 480

job, 271, *977

join (connect), 895

join (participate), 894

joy, 259

judge, 12

judgment, 602

jump, 825

jump (increase), 359

jump on (criticize), 444

just (awhile ago), 906

just (exact), 714

just (fair), 285, 1068

just (only), 904

just (reasonable), 905

justice, 12

keep (hold), 264, 265, 794

keep (last), 266

keep away, 287

key, 885

key (important), 780

key (way), 539

kick, 1012

kick (complain), 253

kid, 297

kidding, 298

kill, 388

kind (gentle), 203

kind (type), 204

king, 893

kiss, 810

kitchen, *681

kneel, 1062

knife, 1078

knock, 717

knock down, 759, 771

knot, 286

know, 235

knowledge, 240

lady, 147

laid off, 393

lamb, 626

land (country), 568

land (get), 130

land (ground), 900

land (home), 223

language, *463

large, 848

last (continue) 266

last (final), 268

last (past), 46, 267

last week, 318

last year, 323

lasting, 266

late, 520, 1003

lately, 906

later, 124

laugh, 923

laundry, 974

law, 744

lawyer, 744

lay, 336, 1114

lazy, 957

lead, 514

league, *218

learn, 960

least, *360

leave (abandon), 182

leave (depart), 181

leave (vacation), 956

lecture, 195

led, 514

left (abandon), 182

left (direction), 180

legislation, 918

legislature, 916

lemon, 632

lend (add), 747

lend (give me), 377

lend (loan), 1063

length (long), 274, 275

length (time), 120

less, *360, 739, 1136

less than, 358

lesson, 440

let, *501

let down, 946

let go, 938

let know, 723

letter, 584

level, 1139

liberty, 712

library, 1038

license, 857

lie (fib), 1115

lie (recline), 1114

lie down, 1114

life, 446

light (bright), 380

light (bulb), 373

light (color), 380

light (easy), 556

light (match), 947

light (sun), 711

light (weight), 372

like (enjoy), 259

like (same), 174

like (want), 49

likely, 197, 560

limit, 1089

line (profession), 551

line (string), 553

line up, 1070

lion, 619

lipread, 348

liquor, 458

list, 691

listen, 346

little, 398

little (comparative), 426

little bit, 387

little bit ago, 906

live, 446

loan, 1063

locate (find), 262

locate (live), 446

location, 337

lock, 885

lonely, 949

lonesome, 949

long (measure), 274

long (time), 275

long for, 471

look (appear), 356, 562

look (watch), 207, 355

look after, 265

look at, 207, 355

look at me, 208

look for, 354

look like, 982

look out, 798

look over (eye), 979

look over (inspect), 443, 980

look up, 981

Los Angeles, 1169

lose, 694

lost, 694

lots, 397

loud, 1138

love, 310

lovely, 288

low, 1136

lower, 739, 1136

lucky, 1098

lunch, *682, 683

machine, 749

mad, 307

magazine, 1122

mail, 585

mainstream, 1057

major, 551

make, 290, 725

make (become), 128

make (earn), 988

make (force), 291

make (kind), 204

make (prepare), 564

make believe, 801

make faces, 555

make up (invent), 801, 853

make up one's mind, 602

male, 146

man, 146

manage, 449

manners, 1058

many, 292

march, 958

mark, 441

marriage, 151

marry, 151

marvelous, 403

match (combine), 948

match (equal), 285

match (fire), 947

match (game), 1017

material, *883

math, 766

mature, 512

may, 125, 197

maybe, 197

me, 58

mean (average), 753

mean (intend), 234

mean (unkind), 233, 889

measles, 866

measure, 742

meat, 656

medical, 876

medicine, 876

medium, 753

meet, 36, 919

meeting, 919

melon, 636

melt, 823

member, 911

memorize, 847

mental, *868

mentally retarded, 869

mercy, 255

merge, 948

metal, 1108

method, 539, *1112

Mexican, 1184

Mexico, 1184

middle, 792

might, 197

mighty, 1031

milk, 647

Milwaukee, 1168

mind (care), 253, 368

mind (obey), 366

mind (think), 238, 367

mine, 61

mingle, 596

minimum, 1089

minister, 472

minus, 1106

minute, 122

mirror, 231

miserly, 566

miss (absent), 435, 698

miss (action), 699

miss (feeling), 697

missing (gone), 700, 812

mistake, 788

misunderstand, 244, 1000

mix, 527

mixed up, 527

moist, 907

mom, 148

moment, 122

Monday, 570

money, 98, 486

monkey, 618

month, 319

monthly, 320

monument, 741

moon, 710

more, 361

morning, 13

morose, 308

most, 438

mother, 148

motion (move), 376

motion (suggestion), 586

motivate, 254, 1088

motivation, 254, 1088

motorcycle, 887

mountains, 762

mouth, 412

move (action), 376

move (cause), 1145

move (suggest), 586

movie, 524

much, 397

mud, 786

mule, 607

multiply, 766

mumps, 865

murder, 388

music, 945

must, 277

my, 61

myself, 77

naked, 1069

name, 145

name (decide), 602

name (tell me), 193

named, 103

napkin, 1079

narrow, 1095

nation, 1049

national, 1049

natural, 1050

naturally, 1050

nature, 1050

near, 530

nearly, 424

necessary, 276

necktie, 495

need (want), 342

needs, 471

need to, 276

negative, 1106

neglect, 528

neighbor, 807

neither, *1055

nephew, 167

nervous, 1161

never, 199

nevertheless, 362

new, 332

news, 723

newspaper, 843

New York, 1167

next (line), 302

next (turn), 303

next to, 305

next week, 317

next year, 322

nice, 396

niece, 166

night, 15

no (exclamation), 109

no (quantitative), 110

noise, 1138

noisy, 1138

none, 110

noon, 14

nor, 1055

normal, *1051, 1050

north, 544

northern, 544

not, 111

not clear, 537

not smooth, 890

not yet, 520, 1003

nothing, 112

notice, 773

notice (poster), 774

notice (warning), 793

notify, 723, 793

now, 44, 113, 589

nude, 1069

number (limit), 1089

number (math), 748

number (several), 293

nurse, 32

nuts (crazy), 735

nuts (food), 674

oath, 995, 1125

obey, 366

object (complain), 253, 368

object (thing), 882

objection, 253

objective, 816

obligate, 696

obscure, 537

observe, 207, 355, 980

obtain, 130

obvious, 380

occasionally, 427

occur, 261

ocean, 826

o'clock, 120

odd, 1160

odor, 961

of course, 1050

offer (give), 377

offer (promise), 995

offer (propose), 586

offer (willing), 1141

office, *999

officer, 6, 515

often, 563

oil, 657

old (age), 278

old (experienced), 715

old (former), 930

on, 176

on hand, 42

once (one time), 428

once (when), 139

once in a while, 427

once upon a time, 930

one, 189

onion, 670

only, 904, 905

onto, 176

onward, 521

open, 280

operation, 875

opinion, *241

oppose, 507, 1148

opposite, 1148

or, *1055

oral, *1056

orange (color), 91

orange (fruit), 91

order (group), 220

order (order), 392

order (plan), 564

organization, *218

organize, 564

original (first), 116

original (inventive), 853

original (new), 332

original (true), 106

other, 510

our, 62

ourselves, 78

out (gone), 814

out (outside), 133

out of (all gone), 813

out of (because), 1002

out of one's head, 735

outside, 133

outstanding, 721

over (about), 529

over (above), 40, 737

over (across), 736

over (again), 294

over (during), 344

over (finish), 313, 738

over (past), 763

overcome, 902

overnight, 821

owe, 896

own, 1004

pain, 863

painful, 863

paint, 758

pamphlet, 1122

pants, 494

paper, 437

parade, 958

paragraph, 983

pardon, 394

parents, *150

park, 791

parking, 791

part (duty), 976

part (left), 181

part (section), *335

part (separate), 37

participate, 894

particular, 750

party, 504

pass, 763

passage, 330

past (ago), 46, 267, 300

past (by), 763

past (finish), 313

pastor, 472

path, 538

patient (person), 872

patient (tolerant), 597

pay, 484

pay attention, 934

peach, 631

peanut, 674

pear, 635

peculiar, 1160

penalty, 1019

people, 190

pepper, 669

perfect (correct), 714, *1156

perfect (improve), 990

perform, 284

performance, 284

perhaps, 197

period, 121

periodically, 427

permanent, 266

permission, *500

permit (allow), *500, 501

permit (license), *857

person, 189

personality, 925

persuade, 1088

pet, 1052

Philadelphia, 1164

philosophy, 832

photograph, 1159

physical, 864, *881

pick (best), 273

pick (choose), 901

pick up (pay), 484

picture, 1159

pie, 26

piece, 335

pig, 614

pink, 96

Pittsburgh, 1163

pity, 255

pizza, 666

place (location), 337, 746

place (position), 337, 401, 746

place (put), 336

place (responsibility), 696

plan, 564

plane, 3

plant (factory), 749

plant (noun), 513, 1155

plant (put), 336

plant (sow), 1154

plate, 1081

play (action), 271, 329

play (drama), 328

playground, 337

playing cards, 824

pleasant, 924

please, 251

pleasure, 259

plenty, 327

plus, 1107

pocketbook, 499

poem, 945

poetry, 945

point (aim), 817

point (gesture), 63

point (place), 337

point (purpose), 998

point (statement), 391

point out, 525

police, 6

police officer, 6

policy, 996

polite, 1058

political, 743, *914

politics, 743, *914

ponder, 239

poor (bad), 184

poor (impoverished), 256

poor (pity), 255

poorly, 256

pop, 667

popcorn, 648

portion, 335, 216

position, 337

positive, 1107

possess, 56

possible, 125

poster, 707, 774

postpone, 1033

potato, 653

pounds, 1144

power, 1031

powerful, 1031

practice, 754

pray, 473

preach, 472

preacher, 472

precious, 780

precise, 714

predict, 247

prefer, 386, 975

prefer (choose), 901

prefer (want), 342

sharp (pointed), 382

sharp (smart), 952

shave, 932

she, 63, *68

sheep, 626

shiny, 382

ship, 936

shoes, 491

shoot, 518

shopping, 490

short (comparative), 549

short (small), 547

short (time), 548

shortly, 548

should, 276

shout, 102

shove, 771

show (demonstrate), 525

show (film), 524

show (performance), 284

show off, 965

show up, 561

shower, 973

shuffle, 824

shut, 281

shy, 1008

sick, 862

sickness, 862

sight, 137, 773

sign (language), 706

sign (poster), 707

sign (signature), 708

signature, 708

significant, 780

silly, 383

silver, 382

similar, 174, 175

simple, 556

sin, 964

since (because), 1002

since (time), 429, 1005

sing, 945

sister, 158

sit, 401

sit down, 401

situation, 591

size, 742

skill, 690

skin, 410

skinny, 769

skirt, 492

sleep, 467

slim down, 779

slow, 684

slowly, 684

small, 398, 426, 547

smart, 952

smell, 961

smile, 922

smoke, 955

smooth, 891

snake, 610

snow, 430

soap, 971

soccer, 1012

socialize, 596

society, *218

socks, 493

soda, 667

soft, 550

soil, 899

soldier, 833

solution, 823

solve, 823

some, 216

some thing, 217

somebody, 840

someone, 840

something, 840

sometime, 427

son, 155

song, 945

soon, 548

sophistication, 1059

sore, 863

sorry, 250

sound, 347, 1138

soup, 661

sour, 836

south, 545

southern, 545

spaghetti, 645

Spain, 1183

Spanish, 1183

special, 750

specific, 714, 750

speak, 30, 196

speech (lecture), 195

speech (talk), 30, 348

speechreading, 348

spell, 709

spend, 489

spider, 622

spoil, 808

spoon, 1076

spread, 758, 941

spring, 675

square, 950

squirrel, 623

stamp, 583

stand, 400

stand (place), 337

stand (tolerate), 597

stand behind (support), 1060

stand up, 402

standard, 175

star, 1029

start, 369

starve, 470

statue, 741

stay, 541

steal, 1053

steel, 1109

step (flight of), 581

step (walk), 505, 580

still (but), 172

still (continue), 266

still (quiet), 1026

stingy, 566, 850

stone, 761

stop, 370

store, 482

story, 462

straight, 551

strange, 1160

stranger, 1091

strawberry, 633

stream, 1009

street, 538

stress, 1035

strike (cancel), 444

strike (hit), 516, 903

strike (rebel), 777

string, 553, 1071

strong, 1031

structure, *725

stubborn, 1094

stuck, 729

student, 960

study, 703

stupid, 953, 1097

subject (course), 440

subject (people), 190

subject (topic), 775

substitute, 716

subtract, 1104, 1106

succeed, 517

success, 517

sudden, 783

suddenly, 783

sue, 507

suffer, 598

sufficient, 327

sugar, 671

suggest, 586

suitcase, 499

summary, 1101

summer, 676

summon, 101

sun, 711

Sunday, 576

sunshine, 711

superintendent, 913

supervise, 794

supervisor, 794

supper, 686

support, 1060

surprise, 469

sure, 106

surrender, 379

suspect, 1131

suspect (person), 189

suspicious, 242, 1131

swallow, 1133

swear (cuss), 1124

swear (oath), 995,
  1125

sweet, 671

sweetheart, 1132

swim, 23

symbol, 526

sympathy, 255

system, 593

table, 224

take (accept), 695

take (follow), 701

take (participate), 460

take (remove), 459

take (tolerate), 597

take away, 1104

take care of, 265, 794

take me, 1129

take on, 695

take part in, 894

take up, 460

talent, 690

talk (conversation),
  194

talk (say), 30, 196

talk (speech), 195

tall (comparative), 425

tall (height), 1128,
  1134

taste, 1075

tasty, 1086

tax, 405, 837

tea, 655

teach, 722

teacher, 722

team, *221

tears, 28

tease, 298

teeth, 413

telephone, 100

television, 230

tell, 192, 818

tell me, 193

temperature, 1102

temple, 478

tend, 1142

tendency, 1142

terrible, 558

test, 523

than, 200

thank, 263

thank you, 263

Thanksgiving, 617

that, 54

the, *52

theatre, 524, 284

their, 66

them, 64, *74

theme, 775

themselves, 76

then, 119

there, 43

thermometer, 1103

these, 64

they, 64, *73

thick, 770

thin, 769

thing, 882

think, 238, 367

think about, 239

think over, 239

third, 118

thirsty, 687

this, 44, 54, *55, 589

those, 64

thought, 238

through (finished),
  313, 331

through (passage),
  330

throw, 1018

throw out, 1020

Thursday, 573

ticket, 1153

tie (even), 285, 1068

tie (knot), 286

tie (necktie), 495

time (clock), 120, 984

time (period), 121

time (turn), 120, 303

tired, 1064

tissue, 437, 215

title, 775

to, 127

to (about), 529

to (for), 171

to (with), 185

to be, 79

toast, 654

today, 114

together, 447

toilet, 582

tolerate, 597

tomato, 660

weight, 1144

welcome, *732

well (good), 183, *1150

well (healthy), 406, 879

went, 39

were, 79, *84

west, 542

western, 542

wet, 907

what, 144

when, 139

where, 140

which, 143

which (that), 54

while, 344

whiskey, 458

white, 92

who, 142

whole, 136

whose, 142

why, 141

wicked, 964

wide, 546

width, 546

wife, 153

will, 45

willing, 1141

win, 1151

wind, 210

window, 228

windy, 210

wine, 456

winter, 213, *678

wisdom, 248

wise, 248

wish, 342, 471

with, 185

withdraw, 761

without, 186

wolf, 609

woman, 147

wonder, *367

wonderful, 403

won't, 107, 390

wood, 1119

woods, 1118

word (advertisement), 803

word (announcement), 720

word (language), 340

word (talk), 194

work (job), 271, 940

work (solve), 823

work (succeed), 517

workshop, 1149

world, *324

worm, 620

worn out, 1064

worry, *246

worse, 784

worth, 780

worthless, 1127

would, 45

wrestle, 1011

write, 34

writer, 34

wrong, 788

year, 321

yell, 102, 844

yellow, 90

yes, 108

yesterday, 104

yet, 520, 1003

you, 63

young, 279

your, 65

yours, 66

yourself, 75

This book was typeset by Mid-Atlantic Photo Composition, Baltimore, Md. It was printed by Kingsport Press (Arcata Graphics Group) of Kingsport, Tennessee. The cover was designed by Lisa Ann Feldman.